EVERYMAN,

I WILL GO WITH THEE,

AND BE THY GUIDE,

IN THY MOST NEED

TO GO BY THY SIDE

EVERYMAN'S LIBRARY

SØREN KIERKEGAARD

FEAR AND TREMBLING

THE BOOK ON ADLER

TRANSLATED BY WALTER LOWRIE

WITH AN INTRODUCTION BY GEORGE STEINER

EVERYMAN'S LIBRARY
Alfred A. Knopf New York London Toronto
178

26-29
30-37
38-64
64-77

THIS IS A BORZOI BOOK
PUBLISHED BY ALFRED A. KNOPF

First included in Everyman's Library, 1994

Typography by Peter B. Willberg
Fourth printing (US)

 Published in the United States by Alfred A. Knopf, a division of Random House, Inc., New York, and simultaneously in Canada by Random House of Canada Limited, Toronto. Distributed by Random House, Inc., New York. Published in the United Kingdom by Everyman's Library, Northburgh House, 10 Northburgh Street, London EC1V 0AT, and distributed by Random House (UK) Ltd.

US website: www.randomhouse.com/everymans

ISBN: 0-679-43130-6 (US)
LC 94-75208
1-85715-178-X (UK)

A CIP catalogue reference for this book is available from the British Library

Book design by Barbara de Wilde and Carol Devine Carson

Typeset in the UK by AccComputing, North Barrow, Somerset

Printed and bound in Germany by GGP Media GmbH, Pössneck

FEAR AND TREMBLING

THE BOOK ON ADLER

CONTENTS

INTRODUCTION

It is difficult to write about Søren Kierkegaard (1813–55). He has written about himself with a mixture of immediacy and indirection, of confessional urgency and ironizing distance so vivid, so diverse as to beggar commentary from outside. Famously, Kierkegaard's pseudonyms, the *dramatis personae* he alleges to be the begetters of some of his exemplary works (while assuming that the reader will detect the figure beneath the mask), enact a system of self-mirroring. But the aim is in no straightforward sense autobiographical. Sharp-edged as are the assumed guises of S.K., they also achieve effects of dispersal, of dissemination. (At key points, current deconstructive notions of 'dissemination' and of the 'abolition of the author' go back to Kierkegaard.) Kierkegaard purposes to remain elusive also to himself, to be opaque and in motion as he traverses successive 'stages on life's way'. Pseudonyms, the division of the self into contradictory voices (the 'dialectic'), the brusque pendulum swing between prayer and sophistry, gravity and play, keep open (in Kierkegaard's memorable phrase) 'the wounds of possibility'. They prevent the frozen certitudes of the dogmatic, the inertia of the canonic. If music, notably that of Mozart, was to Søren Kierkegaard a touchstone of the pulse of meaning, the reason is clear: he sought in his reflexes of argument and sensibility, in his prose, to translate out of music its capacities for counterpoint, for plurality of simultaneous moods and movements, for self-subversion. Like no other major thinker, perhaps, Kierkegaard is polyphonic.

We must, in consequence, respond with a provisional, questioning lightness matching his own to even those fundamental aids to understanding to be found in his writings. The Kierkegaardian 'triad' is well known. It proceeds from an aesthetic stance to one of ethics; from ethics to religion. The aesthetic modulates into the ethical; from the ethical a 'leap of faith', the quantum jump 'into absurdity' (which twentieth-century existentialism took from Kierkegaard), conveys a chosen or afflicted few into the transcendent adventure of God. Kierkegaard often insists on the tripartite construct of his life and labours. The early *Either/Or* dramatizes the conflictual temptations of the aesthetic and the ethical conditions of spirit. The leap across the abyss of mundanity and of reason – ethics is still a worldly, a calculable strategy – which makes accessible the religious sphere, is carefully prepared for and plotted in successive meditations and pseudonymous tracts. Yet Kierkegaard lays traps both for himself and for us. In such texts as the *Edifying Discourses*, as the enigmatic but probably decisive treatise on *Repetition*, as the teasing reflections on Kierkegaard's own 'authorship', the inwoven triplicity of voices and points of view is manifest. There is, from the outset, a moralistic malaise in the paradoxes and avowals of the aesthete, of the romantic dandy and seducer. Kierkegaard's ethical 'scenarios' and self-scrutiny are charged with poetic, rhetorical display and the disinterested exuberance in stylistic experiment of a literary master. The 'transgression' into sacrificial, uncompromising faith, the tormented acceptance of the demands of the absolute in 'imitation of Christ' is latent throughout Kierkegaard. As I read and re-read this exsensive, kaleidoscopic body of work, the 'decision for God' in the image of Jesus seems to me discernible, like the flash of a distant lighthouse, as early as Kierkegaard's doctoral dissertation on Socratic irony, with its subtle but unmistakable critique of even the loftiest of pre-Christian souls. The three strands are interwoven almost to the very end. The 'credal' totality prevails only near that very end, in those polemic indictments of the imperfection of the established church which so clearly spell out Kierkegaard's own imminent death.

Furthermore, an external factor obtrudes. In mid-October 1843, Kierkegaard, at one simultaneous stroke, published three books: *Fear and Trembling*, signed Johannes de Silentio; *The Repetition*, under the name of Constantine Constantius; and *Three Edifying Discourses* by Søren Kierkegaard. In one sense, we are confronted by a single 'speech-act'. In another, these three texts qualify, scrutinize and even ironize each other. But all three arise immediately from a crisis at once intimate and strangely public (Copenhagen was a small city addicted to censorious gossip). They enact Kierkegaard's torment and analytic apologia in respect of his broken engagement to Regine Olsen. The drama of self-alleged infidelity and philosophic licentiousness had already been played out, all too transparently, in *Either/Or*. Now two occurrences precipitated Kierkegaard's anguish: Regine had nodded to him in church, suggesting forgiveness and a true understanding of her 'betrayer's' motives (the root incompatibility of the philosophic and the married state). Then he learnt of her betrothal to another. The psychological effect was both ruinous and liberating. Wild energies of argumentative, allegoric self-dramatization and social satire erupted in Kierkegaard. His henceforth aloneness turned to strategy. He took his stance at the frontiers of his community and of his own psyche. Each of the three treatises published in that *mirabilis* month bore on Regine Olsen's conventional retreat from what might have been a solitude, a symbolic apartness concordant with S.K.'s. Allusions to intimate episodes and storms of sensibility are encased in the psychological, metaphysical and theological motions of argument even where these appear to be most abstract and general. Kierkegaard, in manoeuvres of rhetoric not always attractive, strips himself naked while advocating uttermost reticence and the burial of the heart. The very pen-names advertise: 'the constant one' and the 'apostle of silence', itself a reference to a fairy-tale by the brothers Grimm in which a lover turns to stone rather than betray his secret despair.

As a rule, I find current modes of 'psycho-biography' fatuous. The fibres which relate a man to his work are, where anyone of Kierkegaard's dimensions and refinement go, of a tautness and complication which rebuke our indiscretions. But in the case of *Fear and Trembling* (and the two masterpieces which closely accompany it), the private domain compels notice were it only because Nietzsche, indirectly, and Wittgenstein, in plain awareness, were attentive to Kierkegaard's precedent when they conducted their own spiky lives and when they failed at or rejected certain 'normal' human relations (such as marriage).

Regine Olsen's is not the only biographical presence in *Fear and Trembling*. The black persona of Kierkegaard's dead father looms. The vacant, sombre heath invoked at the outset of chapter one is not that of biblical Canaan, but of Jutland. It was there that Søren's father, in starved and despairing childhood, had cursed God. This distant malediction became a life-long obsession. It was revealed by the father to his son. In moods of 'Lamarckian Calvinism', Kierkegaard persuaded himself that he had inherited this scar of anathema and was, ineluctably, an object of God's retribution. Again, a certain willed cultivation of terror and of a psycho-doctrinal tragic drama is palpable. But the ensuing *Angst* was none the less graphic, nor the trembling any less feverish. In the double shadow of his 'infidelity' and pariahdom on the one hand, and of the sin inherited from his father's blasphemy on the other, Kierkegaard was able, as has been no other imaginer or exegete, to make his own Genesis 22.

The sub-title is exactly challenging. 'A dialectical lyric'. The tensed interplay between philosophic propositions and poetic-dramatic means of expression dates back to the pre-Socratics and, supremely, to Plato's dialogues. It is instrumental in Wittgenstein's *Tractatus*, itself heir to the rhetorical genius of Lichtenberg and of Nietzsche. A great philosophy is always 'stylish': this is to say that its impact on the listener or reader, the force of coherence which it generates, its music of persuasion, are necessarily cognate with its performative means (those of language). Søren Kierkegaard was a craftsman of prose of the very first order. We can locate his tonality, the darting, intensely personalized dynamics of his presentations, within the more general context of European romanticism. He comes after Rousseau, after the early Goethe no less than does, say, Carlyle. It was in Schiller, in Novalis, that Kierkegaard could find full justification for the co-existence, in the same work, of philosophic and poetic components, of technical meditation and fictive-dramatic genres. Kierkegaard's fascination with the theatre and the ambiguous authenticity of the actor's trade never ceased. He writes incomparably of Mozart. His critical reviews of contemporary drama or novels are maliciously informed. He observed a rival in Hans Christian Andersen. Only towards the end are his philosophical and theological books, essays, sermons, unmarked by quotations from, by analogies with, literary examples. *Fear and Trembling* draws, among others, on Plato, Euripides, Shakespeare, Cervantes and Goethe as well as on the brothers Grimm and Andersen. *Don Quixote* is the subtext to the Bible.

Hence the concept of a 'dialectical lyric', of a narration of thought. The logical contradictions posited, the psychological and philosophic-religious endeavours to resolve them – the 'dialectic' in the Platonic sense, as this sense is taken up and modified by Hegel – are set out in what appears, at moments, to be an arbitrary, fictive manner. But the play of possibilities and of voices has its own severe logic, as do the successions of myths and of seeming digressions in a Platonic dialogue. *Fear and Trembling* is, above all, a fable of insight.

*

In a technique which anticipates the semiotic games of Umberto Eco and of today's deconstructionists, S.K. sketches a set of variants on the parable of Abraham and Isaac. Each variation on the given theme of the scriptural narration raises further psychological, moral and credal dilemmas. Immanuel Kant had opined that God, so far as we can attach to that concept and presence within us any intelligible meaning, *could not* order a father to slaughter his own beloved, miraculously conceived son. For Kant, the commandment heard by Abraham is daemonic. It stems from the voice of absolute evil. Abraham is the victim of infernal deceit. A degree of culpability attaches to his confusion. (How could he possibly have taken this to be a message from God ?). Kierkegaard's reading is rigorously antithetical to Kant's. *Only* the true God can demand of Abraham the sacrifice of Isaac. It is in the (sickening) unreason, in the incomprehensible enormity of precisely such an injunction that the believer will recognize God's authentic summons. It is the profound error of Kant and of Hegel to seek to identify the God of Abraham, Isaac and Jacob, the God who ordains the hideous death of His Son on the cross, with categories of human understanding and reasoned ethics. In intimate echo to Pascal, Søren Kierkegaard would have us discriminate unflinchingly between the *dieu des philosophes* and the living God, into whose hands it is indeed 'terrible to fall'.

There follows the harsh yet exultant eulogy of Abraham. Kierkegaard spirals characteristically around one pivot, probing now from one angle of incidence, now from another. No aesthetic of tragic heroism, no rational morality, however high they are pitched, will bring us in reach of Abraham's journey to Mount Moriah. When men of war or guardians of civic virtue such as Jephthah and Brutus sacrifice their children to the Lord of Hosts or to the laws of the state, they do so with intelligible, albeit mistaken or fanatical, motivations. The barbaric sacrifice of Iphigenia ensures the departure to Troy of the Greek fleet. Creon the despot sacrifices his son so as to ensure the salvation of Thebes from murderous and blaspheming foes. Such exemplary acts and the devastating consequences which they have on their agents are the very stuff of heroic chronicles, sagas and tragic dramas. (S.K. had toyed with the project of composing his own version of *Antigone*.) But they throw no genuine light on the matter of Abraham and Isaac.

Nor does ethics. It is here that Kierkegaard's analysis is most arduous. Ethically considered, Abraham's acquiescence in God's commandment or indeed that of any man enjoined to carry out human sacrifice, is indefensible. Obedience may arise from fear of supernatural retribution, from superstition, from atavistic usages (the history of blood-offerings is immemorial and has its unsettling survival into periods which we associate with mature civilization). None of these categories is moral. Where morality is at its most elevated, in a Socrates, in a Kant, inhumanity and irrational absurdity have no place. Confronted with God's demand, the response of the ethical must be one of counter-challenge. How can God justify the order to slay Isaac? Is such a behest not *prima facie* a trap, a means of testing human courage and compassion (i.e. God waits for man's refusal)? Should divine coercion be so imperious as to make any such refusal finally impossible, morality and reason have a further resource. There are those who have chosen suicide rather than injustice, self-destruction rather than manifest criminality.

Kierkegaard is acutely cognizant of these arguments. He dwells with loving irony on their dialectical strengths. They are, he rules, wholly irrelevant to the *Akedah*, to the overwhelming enigma and interpretation of Abraham's obedience. The sole pertinent rubric is that of absolute faith, of a faith which transgresses against and thus transcends all conceivable claims of intellectual accountability and of ethical criteria. Abraham's readiness to sacrifice Isaac, his son, to enact God's prescription unquestioningly, lies beyond good and evil. From any point of view other than that of total faith, of total trust in the Almighty, Abraham's conduct is appalling. There can be no intellectual or ethical excuse for it. If we are to grasp Genesis 22, we must apprehend 'enormity' (a term whose etymology points, precisely, towards transgression, towards a sphere of meaning outside any reasoned legality). The cardinal notion is that of *the absurd*. Fixing on this crux, S.K. looks back to certain legacies of mystical illumination, of self-abolition in God, and forward to modern 'surrealism' and existentialism. Abraham's actions are radiantly absurd. He becomes the 'Knight of Faith' riding forth like Don Quixote as God's champion in the face of humanist revulsion and ridicule. He dwells in paradox. His quantum leap of and into blinding faith isolates him completely. The heroic and the ethical can be generalized. They belong to arguable systems of values and representations. Faith is radically singular. The encounter with God as experienced by Abraham is, eternally, that of an individual, of a private being in the grip of infinity. Only to a 'Knight of Faith', in his unbearable solitude and silence, is the living God simultaneously unfathomable and so close as to eradicate, to burn away, the limits of the self. No synagogue, no *ecclesia* can house Abraham as he strides, in mute torment, towards his appointment with the Everlasting.

*

Do such appointments come to pass in modern times ? This question is, theologically envisaged, vexatious. Judaism, in its orthodox vein, holds Elijah to have been the last mortal man sanctified by a direct meeting with God. In non-mystical Christianity, the divine epiphany does disclose itself, miraculously, to certain men, women or children; but does so via the figure of the Son or of the Blessed Virgin. Islam, if I interpret its position correctly, does not look to any face-to-face encounter with Allah after the time of the Prophet. In December 1842, in Copenhagen, Adolph Peter Adler, clergyman and *Magister* in theology (Kierkegaard had attended his academic *viva* in June 1840), experienced a direct visitation and revelation from Christ. The Son of God had bidden Adler to burn all the manuscripts of his Hegelian writings and had dictated to him, in complete immediacy, the true doctrine concerning the origins of evil. On 12 June 1846, *Magister* Adler published simultaneously no less than four books. One consisted of sacred verse; the other three set out Adler's revealed insights as granted to him by Jesus. S.K. seems to have been among the very first buyers of these four titles.

The result was *The Book on Adler*. Whereas *Fear and Trembling* is among the best-known and influential works in nineteenth- and twentieth-century philosophic theology and literature, the treatise on Adler has remained almost unknown to the general reader. This obscurity inheres in its genesis. Kierkegaard began composition in the summer of 1846, immediately after perusing the *Magister*'s revelations. The polemicist in Kierkegaard aimed at rapid publication. Dissatisfied with his first version, S.K. withdrew the manuscript in 1847, completing a third and more or less definitive version late that same year. Again, he chose not to publish. Having extracted from *The Book on Adler* two major essays on the relations between 'genius' and the apostolic and on the dilemma of whether or not a Christian has a right to solicit martyrdom, to offer his life for his faith, S.K. left the book itself among his *Papierer* (the diaries, the fragments, the voluminous notes). It appeared after his death.

Why this withholding ? Plainly, Kierkegaard found himself in an exceedingly awkward personal situation in regard to Adler. They were acquainted. Adler had called on S.K., informing him that he, Kierkegaard, was in some sense the John the Baptist to the *Magister* whom the Lord had chosen as

His special messenger. Kierkegaard pondered the probability that Adler (whom the ecclesiastical authorities had suspended from his ministry in 1844) was quite simply mentally deranged. Why, moreover, draw further public attention (and derision) to a wretched business soon forgot? But substantive as they may have been, these inhibitions do not touch on the heart of the problem. Adler's conviction that mundane, rationalistic, officious Christianity in Denmark must be electrified into authentic crisis, was exactly Kierkegaard's. The *Magister*'s readiness to suffer ridicule and ostracism on behalf of his 'absurd', existentially enforced certitudes, must have struck a deep, unsettling chord in S.K. himself. As we will see, Adler's claims, however suspect and, indeed, pathological, embroiled Kierkegaard in psychological-theological dilemmas which even his acutest dialectical means failed to unravel convincingly. The Adler 'case' might well prove trivial and wholly ephemeral. The issues which it raised would not go away. Thus there is a perspective in which the wretched Adler defeated his grand inquisitor.

As so often in Kierkegaard's speculations and dialogues, the 'third presence' is that of Hegel. S.K.'s ironies sparkle: the *Magister* no doubt committed his Hegelian lucubrations to the fire, but he remains arch-Hegelian in his confusions. Incapable of discriminating between subjective phenomena and objective truths, Adler, like so many of Hegel's uncritical adepts, makes naive use of the Hegelian concept of synthesis between the self and the external world. As it were, he 'hallucinates reality'.

But S.K. is after bigger game. The crux of the Adler affair is that of 'calling', in the very strongest sense of the term. How does a human being *know* that he/she is being summoned by God? How can human sensibility and intellect differentiate between an ecstatic, deeply felt intimation of divine solicitation, whose actual sources are those of personal need or emotion, and the authentic voice of God? The enigma is not one of possible psychic disorder (as it may have been in *Magister* Adler's instance); nor is it one of calculated self-deception or public falsehood (as in the case of innumerable gurus and market-place mystics). What, asks Kierkegaard, could be the conceivable criteria by which to determine the roots and verity of God's summons to any individual human person? Even visible excellence of moral conduct, even sacrificial suffering, such as is endured by martyrs, provides no *proof* for the spiritual validity of a vocation from God. As T.S. Eliot has it in his meditation on the possibly opportunistic martyrdom of Becket, 'doing the right thing for the wrong reason' may, especially in respect of the religious, be 'the subtlest form of treason'.

Nothing is more fascinating to note than Søren Kierkegaard's almost despairing attempts to clarify, to unravel a conundrum whose intricacies, whose scandalous implications, seem to ebb from his ardent grasp. The focus is not, of course, poor Adler: it becomes Kierkegaard himself and his most deep-buried anguish and hopes.

The dialectical motions of proposal and qualification, of imaginative thrust and self-deconstruction, are of a complexity, indeed of a fragility, which make any outline crass. Neither intellectual lucidity and analytic rigour ('genius') nor ethical, sacrificial engagement, necessarily lead towards the 'hand-to-hand' encounter with God. Here the image burning between the lines is that of Jacob wrestling with the Stranger. It may well be that genius and reasoned morality of even the loftiest order – say in Kant – inhibit the mystery of a veritable calling. There is, and S.K. touches at this point on an elusive paradox, a self-sufficiency in moral excellence, a harmonic finitude at the heart of goodness, which in some manner excludes or renders marginal the dread, the devastating nearness of God. Only the Apostle is *called*. He alone embodies, literally, the act of possession by God and is authorized to enunciate, to translate into mortal speech, the message which he has – there is no other way of putting it – become. Does this election glorify the Apostle? On the contrary, argues Kierkegaard. The authenticating mark of the apostolic is an existential humility of the most radical kind. The true Apostle is humbled beyond all other humilities known to man. Hence the rebellious terror, the surge of refusal, with which Old Testament prophets respond to the charge which God puts upon them. An Apostle is, at any given moment – be it in a street in nineteenth-century Copenhagen – in a synchronic correspondence with the *humilitas* of Jesus, of the mocked, scourged, spat-upon and done to death Jesus of the Passion. (Adler's evident satisfaction in consequence of his 'visions', the vanity in his resolve to make them public, disqualify him at once from any claim to being an instrument of God's purpose.) Only the man or woman contemporaneous with, 'synchronized with', the suffering Christ and compelled to speak, to exemplify the meaning of that suffering, can be held to reveal God, to be – McLuhan knew his Kierkegaard – the medium made message.

Yet, at once, perplexities bristle. Whence, then, the power and the glory of the apostolic, its imperative hold on human acquiescence and imitation? How, moreover, can we reconcile Kierkegaard's insistence on the kerygmatic obligations of the apostolic, on the necessity of the declared revelation, with an emphasis on secrecy, on an ultimate inwardness? Kierkegaard grapples subtly, tenaciously, with these formidable questions. He sets himself nakedly at stake. Once again, the logic of contradiction, of the paradox (so Hegelian in essence, whatever S.K.'s protestations), is instrumental. Where it attains the requisite pitch of lived intensity, where it is fully analogous to that of Jesus, humility is total powerlessness, a finality of impotence. But it is precisely this impotence which constitutes, exactly in the sense of Jesus' revaluation of values, a greater power, very nearly an omnipotence of the absurd. Kierkegaard's thesis remains opaque. It helps, I suggest, to remember the 'powerless force' of such literary personae as Don Quixote or of Prince Muishkin, Dostoevsky's 'holy idiot'. Something of this sort is in Kierkegaard's mind when he wrestles with the contrarieties of the apostolic. Nor does he resolve the irreconcilable demands for silence, for humble self-effacement in the carrier of God's calling with the ministry entailed by that very calling. No thinker, no writer, is more illuminating than Kierkegaard on the motif of moral-metaphysical discretion, on the sacrament of secrecy which makes efficacious the love, the suffering of an Antigone or a Cordelia. S.K. is a celebrant of inward withdrawal, of absolute silence. He is, at the same time, a publicist of rare vehemence, one who bears witness loudly, self-revealingly, in public places.

The satiric journal, *The Corsaire*, had lampooned him cruelly. Kierkegaard had been made an object of open derision in his native city. This condition was the very demonstration of the burden borne by a witness ('a martyr', in Greek, signifies 'witness'). To shuffle off this burden, to leave God's discourse unproclaimed, would be nothing less than apostasy. In the pseudonym, 'Petrus minor', under which Kierkegaard planned to issue *The Book on Adler*, these unresolved contradictions are inherent.

*

From any systematic point of view – philosophical systems being S.K.'s bugbear – the demolition of Adler is flawed. We have seen that Kierkegaard hammers out neither a clear delineation of the nature of the apostolic in a modern context, nor can he harmonize the antithetical demands on the chosen spirit of self-concealment and of public witness. But even in direct reference to Adler's pretences, Kierkegaard's indictment remains, finally, dogmatic. The *Magister*'s account of divine encounter, the 'revelations' he alleges, are indeed shown to be wholly implausible and even risible. The inference of deranged vanity and mental confusion lies to hand. But nothing in S.K.'s pitiless diagnosis elucidates any formal and substantively definitive criteria whereby we may discriminate between hysterical or hallucinatory illusion and a 'God-experience' in any verifiable sense. The leap into the absurd, the abolitions of pragmatic causality and of logic which would characterize such an experience, remain, by Kierkegaard's own criteria of 'necessary impossibility', issues of trust. Ineluctably, the possibility that Adolph Peter Adler has received direct communication from Christ (however garbled, however unworthy his modulation of the message into his own words and person) survives Kierkegaard's negation. How could it be otherwise if, in S.K.'s own phrase, those 'wounds of possibility are to be kept open'?

It is precisely these flaws, these knots in the argument, which generate the fascination of our text. The mercurial *finesse* of Kierkegaard's psychological probing, its adumbration (literal 'foreshadowing') of Freudian theories of the subconscious, where Freud, however, flinches from any serious analysis of religious convictions, make of *The Book on Adler* one of the dark jewels in the history of philosophic psychology. As an examiner of the lives of the mind, of the associative pulses of the imagination at those points at which the anarchic yet somehow ordered energies of the unspoken are brought to bear on rational proposals, Kierkegaard has only two peers. His inquisition into Adler stands beside those descents into the deeps of the human psyche performed by Dostoevsky and by Nietzsche. In these three cases, we are dealing with dramatists of the abstract, with analysts of surpassing penetration, capable of circumscribing frontier zones of unreason, of ecstatic and mystical flashes, even of madness. Modern psychoanalytic and psychotherapeutic knowingness has sometimes deepened, but often flattened, the geology of consciousness explored by *The Possessed*, by Nietzsche's *Genealogy of Morals* and by *The Book on Adler*. But here already lies the essence of our psychological modernity.

There is as well a direct link. Throughout his tracking of Adler, S.K. is spiralling around himself. The *Magister* threatens to be his faithful though parodistic shadow. In short, he turns out to be Kierkegaard's double. The *Doppelgänger* theme obsesses western interest from E.T.A. Hoffmann, Poe and Gogol all the way to Kafka. It enacts an urgent intimation as to the schizophrenic potential in the ego, as to the dangers of self-splitting inherent in a certain vivacity of thought and of fantastication. Dostoevsky's novel, *The Double*, marks only one among numerous invocations of this theme in his fictions. Nietzsche and his Zarathustra circle around each other in a complex figure of rival mirrorings. On almost every page of the Adler book, we observe Kierkegaard labouring, sometimes with satiric confidence, but more often in barely muffled *Angst*, to shake off the intimacy of his scandalous familiar, of the 'house-demon' who is also his twin. A particular terror emanates from these pages.

May this edition introduce the English-language reader to an imperfect masterpiece, all but lost.

George Steiner

SELECT BIBLIOGRAPHY

BIOGRAPHY

All Kierkegaard's work is of course autobiographical, and all commentary on it is therefore in a certain sense biographical, but the autobiography is usually oblique. For the facts readers may consult Walter Lowrie's *Kierkegaard*, Oxford University Press, 1938. Patrick Gardiner's volume on Kierkegaard in the OUP Past Masters series also provides a brief biographical sketch.

JOURNALS

Selections from the *Journals* are easily available in paperback editions, including one edited and translated by Alexander Dru, Oxford University Press, 1938, reprinted and amended in Fontana Books, 1958.

WORKS

Most of Kierkegaard's major works have been translated at least twice. The complete writings are currently being published by Princeton in new translations. Texts especially relevant to this volume are *The Sickness Unto Death*, *The Concept of Dread* and *Crisis in the Life of an Actress*.

CRITICISM

Among many commentators on Kierkegaard the following are all of interest:

ADORNO, T. W., *Kierkegaard: Construction of the Aesthetic*, tr. R. Hullot-Kentor, University of Minnesota Press, 1989.

BRANDT, FR., *Søren Kierkegaard*, tr. A. R. Born, Det danske Selskab, Copenhagen, 1963.

MALANTSCHUK, G., *Kierkegaard's Thought*, tr. H. V. and E. H. Hong, Princeton University Press, 1974.

PATTISON, G., *Kierkegaard*, Macmillan, 1992.

STACK, G. J., *Kierkegaard's Existential Ethics*, University of Alabama Press, 1974.

THOMPSON, J., *Kierkegaard*, Gollancz, 1974.

CHRONOLOGY

DATE	AUTHOR'S LIFE	LITERARY CONTEXT
1813	Birth of Søren Kierkegaard, the youngest of seven, to Michael Pedersen and Ane Sørensdatter. Michael's family had worked the land of their local priest in Jutland in a feudal arrangement which gave them their name (Graveyard). Released from this arrangement at the age of twenty-one, Michael moved to Copenhagen where he worked in his uncle's hosiery business and later became a wealthy wholesaler of imported goods. In 1794 he married Kirstine Røyen who died, childless, two years later.	Madame de Staël: *De l'Allemagne* translated into English. Shelley: *Queen Mab.* The brothers Grimm: *Kinder- und Hausmärchen* (1812–15).
1814		Hoffmann: *Phantasiestücke.* Wordsworth: *The Excursion.* Oehlenschläger: *Helge.* Grundtvig: *Roskilde-riim.*
1815		A. W. Schlegel: *Lectures on Dramatic Art and Literature.* Hoffmann: *The Devil's Elixir.*
1816		Goethe: *Italian Journey* (to 1817). Hegel: *Logic.* Coleridge: *Christabel* and *Kubla Khan.* Constant: *Adolphe.* Grundtvig: *Bibelske praedikener.*
1817		Heiberg: *Christmas Fun and New Year's Jesting.* Coleridge: *Biographia Literaria.* Keats: *Poems.*
1818		F. Schlegel: *Lectures on the History of Literature.*

HISTORICAL EVENTS

Frederik VI declares the kingdom of Denmark bankrupt. The nation's bank, the Kurantbank, is replaced by the Rigsbank; all paper money is called in and exchanged for new money one-tenth the value.
Opening of first university in Oslo.
Denmark concludes new treaty with France.
War of Liberation begins; Napoleon defeated at Leipzig.

Introduction of school reforms in Denmark which provides for the compulsory education of every child from seven to fourteen. Allied forces invade Jutland and compel the Danes to conclude peace at Kiel. Congress of Vienna: democratic constitution establishes Norway (formerly under Danish control) as a free and independent state under King of Sweden. First Treaty of Paris. Abdication of Napoleon following invasion of Paris by English, Austrian, Russian and Prussian troops.
British Corn Laws hit Danish exports badly. Treaty of Vienna restores pre-Napoleonic status quo in Europe, but secures independence and neutrality of twenty-two Swiss cantons. Battle of Waterloo. Formation of German Confederation.
Agricultural riots in England. Diet of German Confederation meets in Frankfurt.

Habeas Corpus Act suspended in England. Wartburg demonstrations in favour of German unity.

Rigsbank replaced by the Nationalbank which is granted an independent status. Agricultural crisis in Denmark which lasts for roughly ten years.

DATE	AUTHOR'S LIFE	LITERARY CONTEXT
1818 *cont.*		Shelley: *The Revolt of Islam.* Keats: *Endymion.*
1819		Schopenhauer: *The World as Will and Representation.* Byron: *Don Juan* (to 1824). Hoffmann: *The Serapion Brethren* (to 1821).
1820		Hegel: *Philosophy of Right.* Shelley: *Prometheus Unbound.* Lamartine: *Méditations.* Keats: *Hyperion, Lamia, Odes.* Hoffmann: 'Princess Brambilla'.
1821	S.K. enrols in Copenhagen's Borgerdydskole (School of Civic Virtue).	Shelley: *A Defence of Poetry.* Kleist: *The Prince of Homburg.*
1822		Goethe: *Wilhelm Meister's Travels.* Heine: *Poems.*
1823	Birth of Regine Olsen.	Stendhal: *Racine and Shakespeare.* Blicher: *The Journal of a Parish Clerk.* Pushkin begins work on *Evgeny Onegin* (to 1830). Møller: *The Adventures of a Danish Undergraduate.*
1825		
1826		Sibbern: *The Posthumous Letters of Gabrieli.* Heiberg: 'On the Musical Comedy as a dramatic genre'. Hölderlin: *Poems.*
1827		Heiberg founds literary journal, the *Flying Mail*, which publishes, among others, Hans Christian Andersen and Christian Winther as well as S.K. himself. Blicher: *The Robber's Den.* Grundtvig: *Christelige praedikener* (3 vols. to 1830).

CHRONOLOGY

HISTORICAL EVENTS

Congress of Aix-la-Chapelle.
Accession of Bernadotte, former Napoleonic Marshal, to Swedish throne as Charles XIV.
Peterloo Massacre in England. German Confederation is persuaded of a conspiracy to overthrow established order in Central Europe, and a series of repressive measures – the Carlsbad Decrees – is adopted by the Federal Diet.

Federal Diet accepts 'Final Act of Vienna' which destroys all but three of the liberal constitutions granted in German states. Death of George III in England. Danish scientist Hans Christian Ørsted produces definite experimental evidence of the relationship between electricity and magnetism.
The four gates of Copenhagen cease to be closed each night. Nobility abolished in Norway. Netherlands government meat and corn taxes hit Belgian peasantry. Greek War of Independence.
Opening of Royal Art Gallery in Copenhagen. Greek War of Liberation against the Turks.

Frederick William III establishes provincial Diets in Prussia.
Würtemberg forced to accept Carlsbad Decrees by Austria; Decrees made permanent.

Grundtvig's *Kierkens Gienmaele*, a protest against 'rationalism' in the Church, provokes controversy in Denmark. Decembrist revolt in Russia. Beginning of great Czech cultural revival, inspired by German thinkers, notably Herder, up to 1848.
Russo–Swedish amicable settlement of Finmark frontiers.

Election riots in Paris. Liberalization of the British Corn Laws gives Denmark access to an important foreign market once more.

DATE	AUTHOR'S LIFE	LITERARY CONTEXT
1828	S.K. confirmed by Pastor (later Bishop) J. P. Mynster.	Heiberg: *Elfinhill.* Ingemann: *The Childhood of Erik Menved.*
1829		Blicher: *The Hosier.* Andersen: *A Walking Tour* and *Love on St Nicholas Church Tower.* Balzac: *Les Chouans.*
1830	S.K. graduates from the Borgerdydskole, and before entering university he enrols in the Royal Life Guards but is discharged as physically unfit.	Andersen: *Poems.* Stendhal: *Scarlet and Black.* Comte: *Cours de philosophie positive* (to 1842). Hertz: *Letters of a Ghost.*
1831		Andersen: *Shadow Pictures of a Journey to the Harz Mountains and Saxony.* Goethe: *Poetry and Truth.*
1832		Goethe completes second part of *Faust.* Grundtvig: *Nordens mythologi.* Lenau: *Poems.*
1833	Takes his examinations (April).	Molbech: *Danish Glossary.* Andersen: *Collected Poems.* Balzac: *Eugénie Grandet.* Müller: *The Dancing Girl.*
1834	S.K. makes his journalistic debut with a piece in the *Flying Post* entitled 'Also a Defence of Woman's Superior Capacity'. Death of his mother.	
1835	S.K. spends a summer holiday at Gilleleje in northern Sjælland. Writes in his journal of needing an idea to 'live and die' for. Until 1838 he lives the life of a man about town but the above from his journal testifies to a deepening despair and lack of direction.	Andersen: *The Improvisatore.* Loennrot: *Kalevala.* Gautier: *Mademoiselle de Maupin.* Balzac: *Le Père Goriot.*
1836	S.K. publishes two additional articles in the *Flying Post.* Begins to attend Poul Møller's lectures on the general concepts of metaphysics.	Hertz: *The Savings Bank.* Andersen: *O.T.* Coleridge: *Table Talk.* Gogol: *The Government Inspector.* Eckermann publishes his 'Conversations with Goethe'.

HISTORICAL EVENTS

Russia declares war on Turkey.

Catholic Emancipation Act passed in England.

Revolutions in France and Belgium. Abdication of Charles X of France. Revolts in Saxony, Hesse and Brunswick. Representative democracy demanded in Sweden.

Start of German Nationalistic movement in Schleswig and Holstein: Frederik VI agrees to consultative assemblies in Holstein, Schleswig, Jutland and the islands which will include representatives of the universities and the clergy. Polish Declaration of Independence. Belgian Independence from the Netherlands recognized by allied powers in Treaty of 24 Articles. Swiss cantons form two separate groups.

Armistice between Dutch and Belgians. Swiss Federal Diet meets to amend 1815 Federal Pact. Customs Union established in Germany. Abolition of Slavery Act in Britain.

First Liberal newspaper appears in Denmark – *Faedrelandet* (The Fatherland). Elections held for councils in Holstein, Schleswig, Jutland and the islands. Articles of Baden; some Swiss cantons assert rights against Roman Catholic Church. Tolpuddle Martyrs in England.

Pope Gregory XVI rejects compromise with Prussia over mixed marriages.

Establishment of Ecclesiastical Commissioners in Church of England. Louis Napoleon fails to stir up Bonapartist rising in Strasbourg.

DATE	AUTHOR'S LIFE	LITERARY CONTEXT
1837	S.K. meets Regine Olsen for the first time while visiting the Rørdams in Frederiksberg. In September he begins teaching Latin at the Borgerdydskole and moves to his own apartment on Løvstræde.	Carlyle: *The French Revolution.* Hertz: *Sven Dyring's House.* Andersen: *Only a Fiddler.* Balzac: *Les Illusions perdues.* Dickens: *Pickwick Papers.* Møller: *The Artist among the Rebels.*
1838	S.K.'s father dies (9 August). S.K.'s first book, *From the Papers of One Still Living*, is published in September.	Dickens: *Oliver Twist.* Mörike: *Poems.* Hugo: *Ruy Blas.*
1839		Hauch: *A Polish Family.* Stendhal: *La Chartreuse de Parme.* Dickens: *Nicholas Nickleby.*
1840	S.K. completes his examination for the theological degree, tours Jutland where he visits his ancestral home, and on 10 September becomes engaged to Regine Olsen. In November he enters the pastoral seminary for practical training in the ministry.	Foundation of *The Corsair*, a liberal periodical, which runs till 1846. Andersen: *Picture Book without Pictures* and *The Mulatto.* Lermontov: *A Hero of Our Time.*
1841	Preaches a sermon in Holmen's church. Defends and publishes his dissertation for the MA degree, *The Concept of Irony.* In October he breaks his engagement to Regine and flees to Berlin.	Heiberg: 'A Soul After Death'. Müller: *Adam Homo* (to 1841). Feuerbach: *The Essence of Christianity.* Dickens: *The Old Curiosity Shop.*
1842	Attends Schelling's lectures in Berlin but returns to Copenhagen in March. Writes *Either/Or.*	Andersen: *A Poet's Bazaar.* Gogol: *Dead Souls.* Hebbel: *Poems.*
1843	*Either/Or* published in February. S.K. makes a short visit to Berlin in May. *Two Edifying Discourses* (May), *Four Edifying Discourses* (December). *Fear and Trembling, Repetition* and *Three Edifying Discourses* (October).	Hertz: *King Rene's Daughter.* Dickens: *A Christmas Carol.* Mill: *System of Logic.*
1844	*Three Edifying Discourses, Philosophical Fragments, The Concept of Dread* and *Prefaces* (June). In October S.K. moves back to the family home at Nytorv 2.	Dumas: *The Three Musketeers.* Heine: *Poems.* Hebbel: *Maria Magdalena.*

CHRONOLOGY

HISTORICAL EVENTS

Seven liberal professors dismissed at University of Göttingen (including the brothers Grimm). Danish government agree to the introduction of regularly elected town councils (extended to counties and parishes in 1841). Archbishops of Cologne and Posen expelled for opposition to Prussian religious policies. Chartist movement founded in England. Queen Victoria comes to the throne.

Foundation of Anti-Corn-Law League in Britain. Austrian and French troops withdraw from Bologna and Ancona respectively.

Death of Frederik VI followed by Christian VIII until 1848. Revision in constitution of the Swiss cantons leads to Catholic–Protestant strife. Armed rising of Parisian artisans against monarchy and middle-class rule. Abdication of William I of Holland. Louis Napoleon fails to stir up rising in Boulogne.
1840s. With the opening of Kehlet's Café, cafés gradually become a recognized part of Copenhagen life.

Swiss cantons suppress Catholic monasteries; latter protected by Federal Pact of 1815.

Chartist riots in Birmingham. French occupy Tahiti.

Formation of Sonderbund in Switzerland.
Nicholas I of Russia formally recognizes Leopold I as King of Belgium.

First railway in Denmark. First Folk High School in Vienna. Swiss Sonderbund demands restoration of monasteries in Aargau; latter demand expulsion of Jesuits from Switzerland.

DATE	AUTHOR'S LIFE	LITERARY CONTEXT
1845	*Three Discourses on Imagined Occasions* and *Stages on Life's Way* (April). S.K. spends two weeks in Berlin during May.	Engels: *Condition of the Working Class in England.* Goldschmidt: *A Jew.* Andersen decorated by King of Prussia at Potsdam. First volume of Andersen published in England. Marx: *Theses on Feuerbach.* Dumas: *La Tulipe noire.*
1846	*The Corsair*, a satirical journal, attacks S.K. in January after S.K. had criticized its editor for sparing him from abuse. *Concluding Unscientific Postscript* (February) is followed by *A Literary Review* (March). In May S.K. once again visits Berlin.	Goldschmidt: *Tales.* Balzac: *Cousine Bette.* Dostoevsky: *Poor Folk.*
1847	*Edifying Discourses in Various Spirits* (March) and *Works of Love* (September). Regine marries Friedrich Schlegel (November). S.K. sells the family house (December).	Andersen meets Charles Dickens in England. Heine: *Atta Troll.*
1848	S.K. leases an apartment. Has certain spiritual and psychological experiences followed by talks with his doctor. *Christian Discourses* (April), 'The Crisis and a Crisis in an Actress's Life' (July). Completes *The Point of View for My Work as an Author* which remains unpublished until after his death.	Goldschmidt, previously editor of *The Corsair*, begins a new journal: *North and South.* Andersen: *The Two Baronesses.* Marx: *Communist Manifesto.* Mill: *Political Economy.*
1849	*The Lilies of the Field and the Birds of the Air* and *Two Minor Ethico-Religious Treatises* (May). *The Sickness Unto Death* (July) and *Three Discourses at Communion on Fridays* (November).	
1850	S.K. moves to a new apartment (April). *Training in Christianity* (September), *An Edifying Discourse* (December).	Turgenev: *A Month in the Country.* Dickens: *David Copperfield.* Wordsworth: *Prelude.*
1851	S.K. publishes, in *Fatherland*, 'An Open Letter' (January). Moves outside the city walls (April). *Two Discourses at Communion on*	Andersen: *In Sweden.* Fontane: *Poems.* Schopenhauer: *Parerga and Paralipomena.*

HISTORICAL EVENTS

Failure of potato crop in Belgium and Holland; famine. Norwegian religious dissenters granted freedom of worship.

Danish farmers form Society of Friends after the King refuses out of hand a petition requesting that conscription, limited to agricultural workers, should be widened to include others. Repeal of Corn Laws in England means that conditions for Danish economy improve.

Famine in Holland leads to riots. United Prussian Diet meets in Berlin but fails to secure constitutional government.

Outbreak of the Dano–Prussian Three Years War. Death of Christian VIII followed by rule of Frederik VII until 1863. Holstein in revolt against Denmark. Danish radicals demand constitution. Revolutions throughout Europe. Swiss Federal Diet approves new constitution.

First constitution of Denmark which guarantees religious freedom, freedom of speech and the general liberty of the individual. Legislative power is to go to a Rigsdag elected by popular vote. The King is no longer absolute monarch.

London protocol drawn up by non-German powers guaranteeing the indivisibility of the Danish monarchy. Beginning of railway-building era in Scandinavia. Foundation of Copenhagen Music Society.

Income tax, first introduced in 1848 as a temporary measure, is made permanent by Finance Minister Sponneck. Religious freedom granted to Jews in Norway.

DATE	AUTHOR'S LIFE	LITERARY CONTEXT
1851 *cont.*	*Fridays* and *On My Work as an Author* (August). *For Self Examination* (September).	Comte: *Système de politique positive* (to 1854).
1852	Moves back inside the city walls. Completes *Judge for Yourself* which is not published till 1876.	Tolstoy: *Childhood.* Turgenev: *A Sportsman's Sketches.* Dumas: *La Dame aux Camélias.*
1853	Ceases to write in his journal.	Hauch: *Robert Fulton.* Dickens: *Bleak House.*
1854	Bishop Mynster dies in January. Hans Martensen is named Bishop in April. S.K. writes an article attacking the established Church (December).	George Eliot translates Feuerbach's *The Essence of Christianity.* Keller: *Der grüne Heinrich.*
1855	From January through to May, S.K. attacks the Church in various articles published in *Fatherland.* Begins publishing his own broadside, *The Instant,* which runs for nine issues (May). Collapses in the street and is admitted to hospital where he later dies (11 November), probably of a lung infection. A week later his funeral ends in a near riot when the Church insists on officiating over the proceedings contrary to S.K.'s wishes. *This Must Be Said, So Let It Now Be Said* (May), *Christ's Judgement on Official Christianity* (June) and *The Unchangeableness of God* (September).	Winther: *The Flight of the Stag.* Andersen: *The Fairy Tale of My Life.* George Eliot begins work on an English translation of Spinoza's *Ethics.*

HISTORICAL EVENTS

Regulation of Antwerp: religious teaching in Belgian secondary schools to be in accordance with religious views of majority of pupils. Roman Catholic bishops permitted in Holland.
Swedish government gains control of brandy manufacture in an effort to control drunkenness.

Sweden makes treaty with Britain and France to avoid Russian attack.
Death of Tsar Nicholas I; accession of Alexander II.

JOHANNES DE SILENTIO

FEAR AND TREMBLING

A DIALECTICAL LYRIC

COPENHAGEN 1843
[OCTOBER 16]

Was Tarquinius Superbus in seinem Garten mit den Mohnköpfen sprach, verstand der Sohn, aber nicht der Bote. (*What Tarquinius Superbus spoke in his garden with the poppies was understood by his son, but not by the messenger.*)[1]

Hamann.

PREFACE[2]

Not merely in the realm of commerce but in the world of ideas as well our age is organizing a regular clearance sale. Everything is to be had at such a bargain that it is questionable whether in the end there is anybody who will want to bid. Every speculative price-fixer who conscientiously directs attention to the significant march of modern philosophy, every *Privatdocent*, tutor, and student, every crofter and cottar in philosophy, is not content with doubting everything but goes further. Perhaps it would be untimely and ill-timed to ask them where they are going, but surely it is courteous and unobtrusive to regard it as certain that they have doubted everything, since otherwise it would be a queer thing for them to be going further. This preliminary movement they have therefore all of them made, and presumably with such ease that they do not find it necessary to let drop a word about the how; for not even he who anxiously and with deep concern sought a little enlightenment was able to find any such thing, any guiding sign, any little dietetic prescription, as to how one was to comport oneself in supporting this prodigious task. "But Descartes[3] did it." Descartes, a venerable, humble and honest thinker, whose writings surely no one can read without the deepest emotion, did what he said and said what he did. Alas, alack, that is a great rarity in our times! Descartes, as he repeatedly affirmed, did not doubt in matters of faith. "*Memores tamen, ut jam dictum est, huic lumini naturali tamdiu tantum esse credendum, quamdiu nihil contrarium a Deo ipso revelatur. . . . Praeter caetera autem, memoriae nostrae pro summa regula est infigendum, ea quae nobis a Deo revelata sunt, ut omnium certissima esse credenda; et quamvis forte lumen rationis, quam maxime clarum et evidens, aliud quid nobis suggerere videretur, soli tamen auctoritati divinae potius quam proprio nostro judicio fidem esse adhibendam.*"[4] He did not cry, "Fire!" nor did he make it a duty for everyone to doubt; for Descartes was a quiet and solitary thinker, not a bellowing night-watchman; he modestly admitted that his method had importance for him alone and was justified in part by the bungled knowledge of his earlier years. "*Ne quis igitur putet me hic traditurum aliquam methodum quam unusquisque sequi debeat ad recte regendum rationem; illam enim tantum, quam ipsemet secutus sum exponere decrevi. . . . Sed simul ac illud studiorum curriculum absolvi (sc. juventutis), quo decurso mos est in eruditorum numerum cooptari, plane aliud coepi cogitare. Tot enim me dubiis totque erroribus implicatum esse animadverti, ut omnes discendi conatus nihil aliud mihi profuisse judicarem, quam quod ignorantiam meam magis magisque detexissem.*"[5]

What those ancient Greeks (who also had some understanding of philosophy) regarded as a task for a whole lifetime, seeing that dexterity in doubting is not acquired in a few days or weeks, what the veteran combatant attained when he had preserved the equilibrium of doubt through all the pitfalls he encountered, who intrepidly denied the certainty of sense-perception and the certainty of the processes of thought, incorruptibly defied the apprehensions of self-love and the insinuations of sympathy – that is where everybody begins in our time.

In our time nobody is content to stop with faith but wants to go further. It would perhaps be rash to ask where these people are going, but it is surely a sign of breeding and culture for me to assume that everybody has faith, for otherwise it would be queer for them to be . . . going further. In those old days it was different, then faith was a task for a whole lifetime, because it was assumed that dexterity in faith is not acquired in a few days or weeks. When the tried oldster drew near to his last hour, having fought the good fight and kept the faith, his heart was still young enough not to have forgotten that fear and trembling which chastened the youth, which the man indeed held in check, but which no man quite outgrows . . . except as he might succeed at the earliest opportunity in going further. Where these revered figures arrived, that is the point where everybody in our day begins to go further.

The present writer is nothing of a philosopher, he has not understood the System, does not know whether it actually exists, whether it is completed; already he has enough for his weak head in the thought of what a prodigious head everybody in our day must have, since everybody has such a prodigious thought. Even though one were capable of converting the whole content of faith into the form of a concept, it does not follow that one has adequately conceived faith and understands how one got into it, or how it got into one. The present writer is nothing of a philosopher; he is, *poetice et eleganter*, an amateur writer who neither writes the System nor *promises*[6] of the System, who neither subscribes to the System nor ascribes anything to it. He writes because for him it is a luxury which becomes the more agreeable and more evident, the fewer there are who buy and read what he writes. He can easily foresee his fate in an age when passion has been obliterated in favor of learning, in an age when an author who wants to have readers must take care to write in such a way that the book can easily be perused during the afternoon nap, and take care to fashion his outward deportment in likeness to the picture of that polite young gardener in the advertisement sheet,[7] who with hat in hand, and with a good certificate from the place where he last served, recommends himself to the esteemed public. He foresees his fate – that he will be entirely ignored. He has a presentiment of the dreadful event, that a jealous criticism will many a time let him feel the birch; he trembles at the still more dreadful thought that one or another enterprising scribe, a gulper of paragraphs, who to rescue learning is always willing to do with other people's writings what Trop[8] "to preserve good taste" magnanimously resolved to do with a book called *The Destruction of the Human Race* – that is, he will slice the author into paragraphs, and will do it with the same inflexibility as the man who in the interest of the science of punctuation divided his discourse by counting the words, so that there were fifty words for a period and thirty-five for a semicolon.

I prostrate myself with the profoundest deference before every systematic "bag-peerer" at the custom house, protesting, "This is not the System, it has nothing whatever to do with the System." I call down every blessing upon the System and upon the Danish shareholders in this omnibus[9] – for a tower it is hardly likely to become. I wish them all and sundry good luck and all prosperity.

Respectfully,

Johannes DE SILENTIO

PRELUDE[10]

Once upon a time there was a man who as a child had heard the beautiful story[11] about how God tempted Abraham, and how he endured temptation, kept the faith, and a second time received again a son contrary to expectation. When the child became older he read the same story with even greater admiration, for life had separated what was united in the pious simplicity of the child. The older he became, the more frequently his mind reverted to that story, his enthusiasm became greater and greater, and yet he was less and less able to understand the story. At last in his interest for that he forgot everything else; his soul had only one wish, to see Abraham, one longing, to have been witness to that event. His desire was not to behold the beautiful countries of the Orient, or the earthly glory of the Promised Land, or that godfearing couple whose old age God had blessed, or the venerable figure of the aged patriarch, or the vigorous young manhood of Isaac whom God had bestowed upon Abraham – he saw no reason why the same thing might not have taken place on a barren heath in Denmark. His yearning was to accompany them on the three days' journey when Abraham rode with sorrow before him and with Isaac by his side. His only wish was to be present at the time when Abraham lifted up his eyes and saw Mount Moriah afar off, at the time when he left the asses behind and went alone with Isaac up unto the mountain; for what his mind was intent upon was not the ingenious web of imagination but the shudder of thought.

That man was not a thinker, he felt no need of getting beyond faith; he deemed it the most glorious thing to be remembered as the father of it, an enviable lot to possess it, even though no one else were to know it.

That man was not a learned exegete, he didn't know Hebrew, if he had known Hebrew, he perhaps would easily have understood the story and Abraham.

I

"*And God tempted Abraham and said unto him, Take Isaac, thine only son, whom thou lovest, and get thee into the land of Moriah, and offer him there for a burnt offering upon the mountain which I will show thee.*"

It was early in the morning, Abraham arose betimes, he had the asses saddled, left his tent, and Isaac with him, but Sarah looked out of the window after them until they had passed down the valley and she could see them no more.[12] They rode in silence for three days. On the morning of the fourth day Abraham said never a word, but he lifted up his eyes and saw Mount Moriah afar off. He left the young men behind and went on alone with Isaac beside him up to the mountain. But Abraham said to himself, "I will not conceal from Isaac whither this course leads him." He stood still, he laid his hand upon the head of Isaac in benediction, and Isaac bowed to receive the blessing. And Abraham's face was fatherliness, his look was mild, his speech encouraging. But Isaac was unable to understand him, his soul could not be exalted; he embraced Abraham's knees, he fell at his feet imploringly, he begged for his young life, for the fair hope of his future, he called to mind the joy in Abraham's house, he called to mind the sorrow and loneliness. Then Abraham lifted up the boy, he walked with him by his side, and his talk was full of comfort and exhortation. But Isaac could not understand him. He climbed Mount Moriah, but Isaac understood him not. Then for an instant he turned away from him, and when Isaac again saw Abraham's face it was changed, his glance was wild, his form was horror. He seized Isaac by the throat, threw him to the ground, and said, "Stupid boy, dost thou then suppose that I am thy father? I am an idolater. Dost thou suppose that this is God's bidding? No, it is my desire." Then Isaac trembled and cried out in his terror, "O God in heaven, have compassion upon me. God of Abraham, have compassion upon me. If I have no father upon earth, be Thou my father!" But Abraham in a low voice said to himself, "O Lord in heaven, I thank Thee. After all it is better for him to believe that I am a monster, rather than that he should lose faith in Thee."

When the child must be weaned, the mother blackens her breast, it would indeed be a shame that the breast should look delicious when the child must not have it. So the child believes that the breast has changed, but the mother is the same, her glance is as loving and tender as ever. Happy the person who had no need of more dreadful expedients for weaning the child!

II

It was early in the morning, Abraham arose betimes, he embraced Sarah, the bride of his old age, and Sarah kissed Isaac, who had taken away her reproach, who was her pride, her hope for all time. So they rode on in silence along the way, and Abraham's glance was fixed upon the ground until the fourth day when he lifted up his eyes and saw afar off Mount Moriah, but his glance turned again to the ground. Silently he laid the wood in order, he bound Isaac, in silence he drew the knife – then he saw the ram which God had prepared. Then he offered that and returned home.... From that time on Abraham became old, he could not forget that God had required this of him. Isaac throve as before, but Abraham's eyes were darkened, and he knew joy no more.

When the child has grown big and must be weaned, the mother virginally hides her breast, so the child has no more a mother. Happy the child which did not in another way lose its mother.

III

It was early in the morning, Abraham arose betimes, he kissed Sarah, the young mother, and Sarah kissed Isaac, her delight, her joy at all times. And Abraham rode pensively along the way, he thought of Hagar and of the son whom he drove out into the wilderness, he climbed Mount Moriah, he drew the knife.

It was a quiet evening when Abraham rode out alone, and he rode to Mount Moriah; he threw himself upon his face, he prayed God to forgive him his sin, that he had been willing to offer Isaac, that the father had forgotten his duty toward the son. Often he rode his lonely way, but he found no rest. He could not comprehend that it was a sin to be willing to offer to God the best thing he possessed, that for which he would many times have given his life; and if it was a sin, if he had not loved Isaac as he did, then he could not understand that it might be forgiven. For what sin could be more dreadful?

When the child must be weaned, the mother too is not without sorrow at the thought that she and the child are separated more and more, that the child which first lay under her heart and later reposed upon her breast will be so near to her no more. So they mourn together for the brief period of mourning. Happy the person who has kept the child as near and needed not to sorrow any more!

IV

It was early in the morning, everything was prepared for the journey in Abraham's house. He bade Sarah farewell, and Eleazar, the faithful servant, followed him along the way, until he turned back. They rode together in harmony, Abraham and Isaac, until they came to Mount Moriah. But Abraham prepared everything for the sacrifice, calmly and quietly; but when he turned and drew the knife, Isaac saw that his left hand was clenched in despair, that a tremor passed through his body – but Abraham drew the knife.

Then they returned again home, and Sarah hastened to meet them, but Isaac had lost his faith. No word of this had ever been spoken in the world, and Isaac never talked to anyone about what he had seen, and Abraham did not suspect that anyone had seen it.

When the child must be weaned, the mother has stronger food in readiness, lest the child should perish. Happy the person who has stronger food in readiness!

Thus and in many like ways that man of whom we are speaking thought concerning this event. Every time he returned home after wandering to Mount Moriah, he sank down with weariness, he folded his hands and said, "No one is so great as Abraham! Who is capable of understanding him?"

A PANEGYRIC UPON ABRAHAM

If there were no eternal consciousness in a man, if at the foundation of all there lay only a wildly seething power which writhing with obscure passions produced everything that is great and everything that is insignificant, if a bottomless void never satiated lay hidden beneath all – what then would life be but despair? If such were the case, if there were no sacred bond which united mankind, if one generation arose after another like the leafage in the forest, if the one generation replaced the other like the song of birds in the forest, if the human race passed through the world as the ship goes through the sea, like the wind through the desert, a thoughtless and fruitless activity, if an eternal oblivion were always lurking hungrily for its prey and there was no power strong enough to wrest it from its maw – how empty then and comfortless life would be! But therefore it is not thus, but as God created man and woman, so too He fashioned the hero and the poet or orator. The poet cannot do what that other does, he can only admire, love and rejoice in the hero. Yet he too is happy, and not less so, for the hero is as it were his better nature, with which he is in love, rejoicing in the fact that this after all is not himself, that his love can be admiration. He is the genius of recollection, can do nothing except call to mind what has been done, do nothing but admire what has been done; he contributes nothing of his own, but is jealous of the intrusted treasure. He follows the option of his heart, but when he has found what he sought, he wanders before every man's door with his song and with his oration, that all may admire the hero as he does, be proud of the hero as he is. This is his achievement, his humble work, this is his faithful service in the house of the hero. If he thus remains true to his love, he strives day and night against the cunning of oblivion which would trick him out of his hero, then he has completed his work, then he is gathered to the hero, who has loved him just as faithfully, for the poet is as it were the hero's better nature, powerless it may be as a memory is, but also transfigured as a memory is. Hence no one shall be forgotten who was great, and though time tarries long, though a cloud[13] of misunderstanding takes the hero away, his lover comes nevertheless, and the longer the time that has passed, the more faithfully will he cling to him.

No, not one shall be forgotten who was great in the world. But each was great in his own way, and each in proportion to the greatness of that which he *loved*. For he who loved himself became great by himself, and he who loved other men became great by his selfless devotion, but he who loved God became greater than all. Everyone shall be remembered, but each became great in proportion to his *expectation*. One became great by expecting the possible, another by expecting the eternal, but he who expected the impossible became greater than all. Everyone shall be remembered, but each was great in proportion to the greatness of that with which he *strove*. For he who strove with the world became great by overcoming the world, and he who strove with himself became great by overcoming himself, but he who strove with God became greater than all. So there was strife in the world, man against man, one against a thousand, but he who strove with God was greater than all. So there was strife upon earth: there was one who overcame all by his power, and there was one who overcame God by his impotence. There was one who relied upon himself and gained all, there was one who secure in his strength sacrificed all, but he who believed God was greater than all. There was one who was great by reason of his power, and one who was great by reason of his wisdom, and one who was great by reason of his hope, and one who was great by reason of his love; but Abraham was greater than all, great by reason of his power whose strength is impotence, great by reason of his wisdom whose secret is foolishness, great by reason of his hope whose form is madness, great by reason of the love which is hatred of oneself.

By faith Abraham went out from the land of his fathers and became a sojourner in the land of promise. He left one thing behind, took one thing with him: he left his earthly understanding behind and took faith with him – otherwise he would not have wandered forth but would have thought this unreasonable. By faith he was a stranger in the land of promise, and there was nothing to recall what was dear to him, but by its novelty everything tempted his soul to melancholy yearning – and yet he was God's elect, in whom the Lord was well pleased! Yea, if he had been disowned, cast off from God's grace, he could have comprehended it better; but now it was like a mockery of him and of his faith. There was in the world one too who lived in banishment[14] from the fatherland he loved. He is not forgotten, nor his Lamentations when he sorrowfully sought and found what he had lost. There is no song of Lamentations by Abraham. It is human to lament, human to weep with them that weep, but it is greater to believe, more blessed to contemplate the believer.

By faith Abraham received the promise that in his seed all races of the world would be blessed. Time passed, the possibility was there, Abraham believed; time passed, it became unreasonable, Abraham believed. There was in the world one who had an expectation, time passed, the evening drew nigh, he was not paltry enough to have forgotten his expectation, therefore he too shall not be forgotten. Then he sorrowed, and sorrow did not deceive him as life had done, it did for him all it could, in the sweetness of sorrow he possessed his delusive expectation. It is human to sorrow, human to sorrow with them that sorrow, but it is greater to believe, more blessed to contemplate the believer. There is no song of Lamentations by Abraham. He did not mournfully count the days while time passed, he did not look at Sarah with a suspicious glance, wondering whether she were growing old, he did not arrest the course of the sun, that Sarah might not grow old, and his expectation with her. He did not sing lullingly before Sarah his mournful lay. Abraham became old, Sarah became a laughing-stock in the land, and yet he was God's elect and inheritor of the promise that in his seed all the races of the world would be blessed. So were it not better if he had not been God's elect? What is it to be God's elect? It is to be denied in youth the wishes of youth, so as with great pains to get them fulfilled in old age. But Abraham believed and held fast the expectation. If Abraham had wavered, he would have given it up. If he had said to God, "Then perhaps it is not after all Thy will that it should come to pass, so I will give up the wish. It was my only wish, it was my bliss. My soul is sincere, I hide no secret malice because Thou didst deny it to me" – he would not have been forgotten, he would have saved many by his example, yet he would not be the father of faith. For it is great to give up one's wish, but it is greater to hold it fast after having given it up, it is great to grasp the eternal, but it is greater to hold fast to the temporal after having given it up.[15]

Then came the fulness of time. If Abraham had not believed, Sarah surely would have been dead of sorrow, and Abraham, dulled by grief, would not have understood the fulfilment but would have smiled at it as at a dream of youth. But Abraham believed, therefore he was young; for he who always hopes for the best becomes old, and he who is always prepared for the worst grows old early, but he who believes preserves an eternal youth. Praise therefore to that story! For Sarah, though stricken in years, was young enough to desire the pleasure of motherhood, and Abraham, though gray-haired, was young enough to wish to be a father. In an outward respect the marvel consists in the fact that it came to pass according to their expectation, in a deeper sense the miracle of faith consists in the fact that Abraham and Sarah were young enough to wish, and that faith had preserved their wish and therewith their youth. He accepted the fulfilment of the promise, he accepted it by faith, and it came to pass according to the promise and according to his faith – for Moses smote the rock with his rod, but he did not believe.

Then there was joy in Abraham's house, when Sarah became a bride on the day of their golden wedding.

But it was not to remain thus. Still once more Abraham was to be tried. He had fought with that cunning power which invents everything, with that alert enemy which never slumbers, with that old man who outlives all things – he had fought with Time and preserved his faith. Now all the terror of the strife was concentrated in one instant. "And God tempted Abraham and said unto him, Take Isaac, thine only son, whom thou lovest, and get thee into the land of Moriah, and offer him there for a burnt offering upon the mountain which I will show thee."

So all was lost – more dreadfully than if it had never come to pass! So the Lord was only making sport of Abraham! He made miraculously the preposterous actual, and now in turn He would annihilate it. It was indeed foolishness, but Abraham did not laugh at it like Sarah when the promise was announced. All was lost! Seventy years of faithful expectation, the brief joy at the fulfilment of faith. Who then is he that plucks away the old man's staff, who is it that requires that he himself shall break it? Who is he that would make a man's gray hairs comfortless, who is it that requires that he himself shall do it? Is there no compassion for the venerable oldling, none for the innocent child? And yet Abraham was God's elect, and it was the Lord who imposed the trial. All would now be lost. The glorious memory to be preserved by the human race, the promise in Abraham's seed – this was only a whim, a fleeting thought which the Lord had had, which Abraham should now obliterate. That glorious treasure which was just as old as faith in Abraham's heart, many, many years older than Isaac, the fruit of Abraham's life, sanctified by prayers, matured in conflict – the blessing upon Abraham's lips, this fruit was now to be plucked prematurely and remain without significance. For what significance had it when Isaac was to be sacrificed? That sad and yet blissful hour when Abraham was to take leave of all that was dear to him, when yet once more he was to lift up his head, when his countenance would shine like that of the Lord, when he would concentrate his whole soul in a blessing which was potent to make Isaac blessed all his days – this time would not come! For he would indeed take leave of Isaac, but in such a way that he himself would remain behind; death would separate them, but in such a way that Isaac remained its prey. The old man would not be joyful in death as he laid his hands in blessing upon Isaac, but he would be weary of life as he laid violent hands upon Isaac. And it was God who tried him. Yea, woe, woe unto the messenger who had come before Abraham with such tidings! Who would have ventured to be the emissary of this sorrow? But it was God who tried Abraham.

Yet Abraham believed, and believed for this life. Yea, if his faith had been only for a future life, he surely would have cast everything away in order to hasten out of this world to which he did not belong. But Abraham's faith was not of this sort, if there be such a faith; for really this is not faith but the furthest possibility of faith which has a presentiment of its object at the extremest limit of the horizon, yet is separated from it by a yawning abyss within which despair carries on its game. But Abraham believed precisely for this life, that he was to grow old in the land, honored by the people, blessed in his generation, remembered forever in Isaac, his dearest thing in life, whom he embraced with a love for which it would be a poor expression to say that he loyally fulfilled the father's duty of loving the son, as indeed is evinced in the words of the summons, "the son whom thou lovest." Jacob had twelve sons, and one of them he loved; Abraham had only one, the son whom he loved.

Yet Abraham believed and did not doubt, he believed the preposterous. If Abraham had doubted – then he would have done something else, something glorious; for how could Abraham do anything but what is great and glorious! He would have marched up to Mount Moriah, he would have cleft the firewood, lit the pyre, drawn the knife – he would have cried out to God, "Despise not this sacrifice, it is not the best thing I possess, that I know well, for what is an old man in comparison with the child of promise; but it is the best I am able to give Thee. Let Isaac never come to know this, that he may console himself with his youth." He would have plunged the knife into his own breast. He would have been admired in the world, and his name would not have been forgotten; but it is one thing to be admired, and another to be the guiding star which saves the anguished.

But Abraham believed. He did not pray for himself, with the hope of moving the Lord – it was only when the righteous punishment was decreed upon Sodom and Gomorrah that Abraham came forward with his prayers.

We read in those holy books: "And God tempted Abraham, and said unto him, Abraham, Abraham, where art thou? And he said, Here am I." Thou to whom my speech is addressed, was such the case with thee? When afar off thou didst see the heavy dispensation of providence approaching thee, didst thou not say to the mountains, Fall on me, and to the hills, Cover me? Or if thou wast stronger, did not thy foot move slowly along the way, longing as it were for the old path? When a call was issued to thee, didst thou answer, or didst thou not answer perhaps in a low voice, whisperingly? Not so Abraham: joyfully, buoyantly, confidently, with a loud voice, he answered, "Here am I." We read further: "And Abraham rose early in the morning" – as though it were to a festival, so he hastened, and early in the morning he had come to the place spoken of, to Mount Moriah.

He said nothing to Sarah, nothing to Eleazar. Indeed who could understand him? Had not the temptation by its very nature exacted of him an oath of silence? He cleft the wood, he bound Isaac, he lit the pyre, he drew the knife. My hearer, there was many a father who believed that with his son he lost everything that was dearest to him in the world, that he was deprived of every hope for the future, but yet there was none that was the child of promise in the sense that Isaac was for Abraham. There was many a father who lost his child; but then it was God, it was the unalterable, the unsearchable will of the Almighty, it was His hand took the child. Not so with Abraham. For him was reserved a harder trial, and Isaac's fate was laid along with the knife in Abraham's hand. And there he stood, the old man, with his only hope! But he did not doubt, he did not look anxiously to the right or to the left, he did not challenge heaven with his prayers. He knew that it was God the Almighty who was trying him, he knew that it was the hardest sacrifice that could be required of him; but he knew also that no sacrifice was too hard when God required it – and he drew the knife.

Who gave strength to Abraham's arm? Who held his right hand up so that it did not fall limp at his side? He who gazes at this becomes paralyzed. Who gave strength to Abraham's soul, so that his eyes did not grow dim, so that he saw neither Isaac nor the ram? He who gazes at this becomes blind. – And yet rare enough perhaps is the man who becomes paralyzed and blind, still more rare one who worthily recounts what happened. We all know it – it was only a trial.

If Abraham when he stood upon Mount Moriah had doubted, if he had gazed about him irresolutely, if before he drew the knife he had by chance discovered the ram, if God had permitted him to offer it instead of Isaac – then he would have betaken himself home, everything would have been the same, he has Sarah, he retained Isaac, and yet how changed! For his retreat would have been a flight, his salvation an accident, his reward dishonor, his future perhaps perdition. Then he would have borne witness neither to his faith nor to God's grace, but would have testified only how dreadful it is to march out to Mount Moriah. Then Abraham would not have been forgotten, nor would Mount Moriah, this mountain would then be mentioned, not like Ararat where the Ark landed, but would be spoken of as a consternation, because it was here that Abraham doubted.

Venerable Father Abraham! In marching home from Mount Moriah thou hadst no need of a panegyric which might console thee for thy loss; for thou didst gain all and didst retain Isaac. Was it not so? Never again did the Lord take him from thee, but thou didst sit at table joyfully with him in thy tent, as thou dost in the beyond to all eternity. Venerable Father Abraham! Thousands of years have run their course since those days, but thou hast need of no tardy lover to snatch the memorial of thee from the power of oblivion, for every language calls thee to remembrance – and yet thou dost reward thy lover more gloriously than does any other; hereafter thou dost make him blessed in thy bosom; here thou dost enthral his eyes and his heart by the marvel of thy deed. Venerable Father Abraham! Second Father of the human race! Thou who first wast sensible of and didst first bear witness to that prodigious passion which disdains the dreadful conflict with the rage of the elements and with the powers of creation in order to strive with God; thou who first didst know that highest passion, the holy, pure and humble expression of the divine madness[16] which the pagans admired – forgive him who would speak in praise of thee, if he does not do it fittingly. He spoke humbly, as if it were the desire of his own heart, he spoke briefly, as it becomes him to do, but he will never forget that thou hadst need of a hundred years to obtain a son of old age against expectation, that thou didst have to draw the knife before retaining Isaac: he will never forget that in a hundred and thirty years thou didst not get further than to faith.

PROBLEMATA:

PRELIMINARY EXPECTORATION

An old proverb fetched from the outward and visible world says: "Only the man that works gets the bread." Strangely enough this proverb does not aptly apply in that world to which it expressly belongs. For the outward world is subjected to the law of imperfection, and again and again the experience is repeated that he too who does not work gets the bread, and that he who sleeps gets it more abundantly than the man who works. In the outward world everything is made payable to the bearer, this world is in bondage to the law of indifference, and to him who has the ring, the spirit of the ring is obedient, whether he be Noureddin or Aladdin,[17] and he who has the world's treasure, has it, however he got it. It is different in the world of spirit. Here an eternal divine order prevails, here it does not rain both upon the just and upon the unjust, here the sun does not shine both upon the good and upon the evil, here it holds good that only he who works gets the bread, only he who was in anguish finds repose, only he who descends into the underworld rescues the beloved, only he who draws the knife gets Isaac. He who will not work does not get the bread but remains deluded, as the gods deluded Orpheus with an airy figure in place of the loved one, deluded him because he was effeminate, not courageous, because he was a cithara-player, not a man. Here it is of no use to have Abraham for one's father, nor to have seventeen ancestors – he who will not work must take note of what is written about the maidens of Israel,[18] for he gives birth to wind, but he who is willing to work gives birth to his own father.

There is a knowledge which would presumptuously introduce into the world of spirit the same law of indifference under which the external world sighs. It counts it enough to think the great – other work is not necessary. But therefore it doesn't get the bread, it perishes of hunger, while everything is transformed into gold. And what does it really know? There were many thousands of Greek contemporaries, and countless numbers in subsequent generations, who knew all the triumphs of Miltiades, but only one[19] was made sleepless by them. There were countless generations which knew by rote, word for word, the story of Abraham – how many were made sleepless by it?

Now the story of Abraham has the remarkable property that it is always glorious, however poorly one may understand it; yet here again the proverb applies, that all depends upon whether one is willing to labor and be heavy-laden. But they will not labor, and yet they would understand the story. They exalt Abraham – but how? They express the whole thing in perfectly general terms: "The great thing was that he loved God so much that he was willing to sacrifice to Him the best." That is very true, but "the best" is an indefinite expression. In the course of thought, as the tongue wags on, Isaac and "the best" are confidently identified, and he who meditates can very well smoke his pipe during the meditation, and the auditor can very well stretch out his legs in comfort. In case that rich young man whom Christ encountered on the road had sold all his goods and given to the poor, we should extol him, as we do all that is great, though without labor we would not understand him – and yet he would not have become an Abraham, in spite of the fact that he offered his best. What they leave out of Abraham's history is dread;[20] for to money I have no ethical obligation, but to the son the father has the highest and most sacred obligation. Dread, however, is a perilous thing for effeminate natures, hence they forget it, and in spite of that they want to talk about Abraham. So they talk – in the course of the oration they use indifferently the two terms, Isaac and "the best." All goes famously. However, if it chanced that among the auditors there was one who suffered from insomnia – then the most dreadful, the profoundest tragic and comic misunderstanding lies very close. He went home, he would do as Abraham did, for the son is indeed "the best."

If the orator got to know of it, he perhaps went to him, he summoned all his clerical dignity, he shouted, "O abominable man, offscouring of society, what devil possessed thee to want to murder thy son?" And the parson, who had not been conscious of warmth or perspiration in preaching about Abraham, is astonished at himself, at the earnest wrath which he thundered down upon that poor man. He was delighted with himself, for he had never spoken with such verve and unction. He said to himself and to his wife, "I am an orator. What I lacked was the occasion. When I talked about Abraham on Sunday I did not feel moved in the least." In case the same orator had a little superabundance of reason which might be lost, I think he would have lost it if the sinner were to say calmly and with dignity, "That in fact is what you yourself preached on Sunday." How could the parson be able to get into his head such a consequence? And yet it was so, and the mistake was merely that he didn't know what he was saying. Would there were a poet who might resolve to prefer such situations, rather than the stuff and nonsense with which comedies and novels are filled! The comic and the tragic here touch one another at the absolute point of infinity. The parson's speech was perhaps in itself ludicrous enough, but it became infinitely ludicrous by its effect, and yet this consequence was quite natural. Or if the sinner, without raising any objection, were to be converted by the parson's severe lecture, if the zealous clergyman were to go joyfully home, rejoicing in the consciousness that he not only was effective in the pulpit, but above all by his irresistible power as a pastor of souls, who on Sunday roused the congregation to enthusiasm, and on Monday like a cherub with a flaming sword placed himself before the man who by his action wanted to put to shame the old proverb, that "things don't go on in the world as the parson preaches."*

If on the other hand the sinner was not convinced, his situation is pretty tragic. Presumably he would be executed or sent to the lunatic asylum, in short, he would have become unhappy in relation to so-called reality – in another sense I can well think that Abraham made him happy, for he that labors does not perish.

How is one to explain the contradiction illustrated by that orator? Is it because Abraham had a prescriptive right to be a great man, so that what he did is great, and when another does the same it is sin, a heinous sin? In that case I do not wish to

*In the old days they said, "What a pity things don't go on in the world as the parson preaches" – perhaps the time is coming, especially with the help of philosophy, when they will say, "Fortunately things don't go on as the parson preaches; for after all there is some sense in life, but none at all in his preaching."

participate in such thoughtless eulogy. If faith does not make it a holy act to be willing to murder one's son, then let the same condemnation be pronounced upon Abraham as upon every other man. If a man perhaps lacks courage to carry his thought through, and to say that Abraham was a murderer, then it is surely better to acquire this courage, rather than waste time upon undeserved eulogies. The ethical expression for what Abraham did is, that he would murder Isaac; the religious expression is, that he would sacrifice Isaac; but precisely in this contradiction consists the dread which can well make a man sleepless, and yet Abraham is not what he is without this dread. Or perhaps he did not do at all what is related, but something altogether different, which is accounted for by the circumstances of his times – then let us forget him, for it is not worth while to remember that past which cannot become a present. Or had perhaps that orator forgotten something which corresponds to the ethical forgetfulness of the fact that Isaac was the son? For when faith is eliminated by becoming null or nothing, then there only remains the crude fact that Abraham wanted to murder Isaac – which is easy enough for anyone to imitate who has not faith, the faith, that is to say, which makes it hard for him.

For my part I do not lack the courage to think a thought whole. Hitherto there has been no thought I have been afraid of; if I should run across such a thought, I hope that I have at least the sincerity to say, "I am afraid of this thought, it stirs up something else in me, and therefore I will not think it. If in this I do wrong, the punishment will not fail to follow." If I had recognized that it was the verdict of truth that Abraham was a murderer, I do not know whether I would have been able to silence my pious veneration for him. However, if I had thought that, I presumably would have kept silent about it, for one should not initiate others into such thoughts. But Abraham is no dazzling illusion, he did not sleep into renown, it was not a whim of fate.

Can one then speak plainly about Abraham without incurring the danger that an individual might in bewilderment go ahead and do likewise? If I do not dare to speak freely, I will be completely silent about Abraham, above all I will not disparage him in such a way that precisely thereby he becomes a pitfall for the weak. For if one makes faith everything, that is, makes it what it is, then, according to my way of thinking, one may speak of it without danger in our age, which hardly extravagates in the matter of faith, and it is only by faith one attains likeness to Abraham, not by murder. If one makes love a transitory mood, a voluptuous emotion in a man, then one only lays pitfalls for the weak when one would talk about the exploits of love. Transient emotions every man surely has, but if as a consequence of such emotions one would do the terrible thing which love has sanctified as an immortal exploit, then all is lost, including the exploit and the bewildered doer of it.

So one surely can talk about Abraham, for the great can never do harm when it is apprehended in its greatness; it is like a two-edged sword which slays and saves. If it should fall to my lot to talk on the subject, I would begin by showing what a pious and God-fearing man Abraham was, worthy to be called God's elect. Only upon such a man is imposed such a test. But where is there such a man? Next I would describe how Abraham loved Isaac. To this end I would pray all good spirits to come to my aid, that my speech might be as glowing as paternal love is. I hope that I should be able to describe it in such a way that there would not be many a father in the realms and territories of the King who would dare to affirm that he loved his son in such a way. But if he does not love like Abraham, then every thought of offering Isaac would be not a trial but a base temptation [*Anfechtung*]. On this theme one could talk for several Sundays, one need be in no haste. The consequence would be that, if one spoke rightly, some few of the fathers would not require to hear more, but for the time being they would be joyful if they really succeeded in loving their sons as Abraham loved. If there was one who, after having heard about the greatness, but also about the dreadfulness of Abraham's deed, ventured to go forth upon that road, I would saddle my horse and ride with him. At every stopping-place till we came to Mount Moriah I would explain to him that he still could turn back, could repent the misunderstanding that he was called to be tried in such a conflict, that he could confess his lack of courage, so that God Himself must take Isaac, if He would have him. It is my conviction that such a man is not repudiated but may become blessed like all the others. But in time he does not become blessed. Would they not, even in the great ages of faith, have passed this judgment upon such a man? I knew a person who on one occasion could have saved my life if he[21] had been magnanimous. He said, "I see well enough what I could do, but I do not dare to. I am afraid that later I might lack strength and that I should regret it." He was not magnanimous, but who for this cause would not continue to love him?

Having spoken thus and moved the audience so that at least they had sensed the dialectical conflict of faith and its gigantic passion, I would not give rise to the error on the part of the audience that "he then has faith in such a high degree that it is enough for us to hold on to his skirts." For I would add, "I have no faith at all, I am by nature a shrewd pate, and every such person always has great difficulty in making the movements of faith – not that I attach, however, in and for itself, *any value to this difficulty which through the overcoming of it brought the clever head further than the point which the simplest and most ordinary man reaches more easily*."

After all, in the poets love has its priests, and sometimes one hears a voice which knows how to defend it; but of faith one hears never a word. Who speaks in honor of this passion? Philosophy goes further. Theology sits rouged at the window and courts its favor, offering to sell her charms to philosophy. It is supposed to be difficult to understand Hegel, but to understand Abraham is a trifle. To go beyond Hegel[22] is a miracle, but to get beyond Abraham is the easiest thing of all. I for my part have devoted a good deal of time to the understanding of the Hegelian philosophy, I believe also that I understand it tolerably well, but when in spite of the trouble I have taken there are certain passages I cannot understand, I am foolhardy enough to think that he himself has not been quite clear. All this I do easily and naturally, my head does not suffer from it. But on the other hand when I have to think of Abraham, I am as though annihilated. I catch sight every moment of that enormous paradox which is the substance of Abraham's life, every moment I am repelled, and my thought in spite of all its passion cannot get a hair's-breadth further. I strain every muscle to get a view of it – that very instant I am paralyzed.

I am not unacquainted with what has been admired as great

and noble in the world, my soul feels affinity with it, being convinced in all humility that it was in my cause the hero contended, and the instant I contemplate his deed I cry out to myself, *jam tua res agitur*.[23] I think myself into the hero, but into Abraham I cannot think myself; when I reach the height I fall down, for what I encounter there is the paradox. I do not however mean in any sense to say that faith is something lowly, but on the contrary that it is the highest thing, and that it is dishonest of philosophy to give something else instead of it and to make light of faith. Philosophy cannot and should not give faith, but it should understand itself and know what it has to offer and take nothing away, and least of all should fool people out of something as if it were nothing. I am not unacquainted with the perplexities and dangers of life, I do not fear them, and I encounter them buoyantly. I am not unacquainted with the dreadful, my memory is a faithful wife, and my imagination is (as I myself am not) a diligent little maiden who all day sits quietly at her work, and in the evening knows how to chat to me about it so prettily that I must look at it, though not always, I must say, is it landscapes, or flowers, or pastoral idylls she paints. I have seen the dreadful before my own eyes, I do not flee from it timorously, but I know very well that, although I advance to meet it, my courage is not the courage of faith, nor anything comparable to it. I am unable to make the movements of faith, I cannot shut my eyes and plunge confidently into the absurd, for me that is an impossibility ... but I do not boast of it. I am convinced that God is love,[24] this thought has for me a primitive lyrical validity. When it is present to me, I am unspeakably blissful, when it is absent, I long for it more vehemently than does the lover for his object; but I do not believe, this courage I lack. For me the love of God is, both in a direct and in an inverse sense, incommensurable with the whole of reality. I am not  cowardly enough to whimper and complain, but neither am I deceitful enough to deny that faith is something much higher. I can well endure living in my way, I am joyful and content, but my joy is not that of faith, and in comparison with that it is unhappy. I do not trouble God with my petty sorrows, the particular does not trouble me, I gaze only at my love, and I keep its virginal flame pure and clear. Faith is convinced that

God is concerned about the least things. I am content in this life with being married to the left hand, faith is humble enough to demand the right hand – for that this is humility I do not deny and shall never deny.

But really is everyone in my generation capable of making the movements of faith, I wonder? Unless I am very much mistaken, this generation is rather inclined to be proud of making what they do not even believe I am capable of making, viz. incomplete movements. It is repugnant to me to do as so often is done, namely, to speak inhumanly about a great deed, as though some thousands of years were an immense distance; I would rather speak humanly about it, as though it had occurred yesterday, letting only the greatness be the distance, which either exalts or condemns. So if (*in the quality of a tragic hero*, for I can get no higher) I had been summoned to undertake such a royal progress to Mount Moriah, I know well what I would have done. I would not have been cowardly enough to stay at home, neither would I have lain down or sauntered along the way, nor have forgotten the knife, so that there might be a little delay – I am pretty well convinced that I would have been there on the stroke of the clock and would have had everything in order, perhaps I would have arrived too early in order to get through with it sooner. But I also know what else I would have done. The very instant I mounted the horse I would have said to myself, "Now all is lost. God requires Isaac, I sacrifice him, and with him my joy – yet God is love and continues to be that for me; for in the temporal world God and I cannot talk together, we have no language in common." Perhaps one or another in our age will be foolish enough, or envious enough of the great, to want to make himself and me believe that if I really had done this, I would have done even a greater deed than Abraham; for my prodigious resignation was far more ideal and poetic than Abraham's narrow-mindedness. And yet this is the greatest falsehood, for my prodigious resignation was the surrogate for faith, nor could I do more than make the infinite movement, in order to find myself and again repose in myself. In that case I would not have loved Isaac as Abraham loved. That I was resolute in making the movement might prove my courage, humanly speaking; that I loved him with all my soul is the presumption apart from which the whole thing becomes a crime, but yet I did not love like Abraham, for in that case I would have held back even at the last minute, though not for this would I have arrived too late at Mount Moriah. Besides, by my behavior I would have spoiled the whole story; for if I had got Isaac back again, I would have been in embarrassment. What Abraham found easiest, I would have found hard, namely to be joyful again with Isaac; for he who with all the infinity of his soul, *propio motu et propiis auspiciis* [by his own power and on his own responsibility], has performed the infinite movement [of resignation] and cannot do more, only retains Isaac with pain.

But what did Abraham do? He arrived neither too soon nor too late. He mounted the ass, he rode slowly along the way. All that time he believed – he believed that God would not require Isaac of him, whereas he was willing nevertheless to sacrifice him if it was required. He believed by virtue of the absurd; for there could be no question of human calculation, and it was indeed the absurd that God who required it of him should the next instant recall the requirement. He climbed the mountain, even at the instant when the knife glittered he believed . . . that God would not require Isaac. He was indeed astonished at the outcome, but by a double-movement he had reached his first position, and therefore he received Isaac more gladly than the first time. Let us go further. We let Isaac be really sacrificed. Abraham believed. He did not believe that some day he would be blessed in the beyond, but that he would be happy here in the world. God could give him a new Isaac, could recall to life him who had been sacrificed. He believed by virtue of the absurd; for all human reckoning had long since ceased to function. That sorrow can derange a man's mind, that we see, and it is sad enough. That there is such a thing as strength of will which is able to haul up so exceedingly close to the wind that it saves a man's reason, even though he remains a little queer,[25] that too one sees. I have no intention of disparaging this; but to be able to lose one's reason, and therefore the whole of finiteness of which reason is the broker, and then by virtue of the absurd to gain precisely the same finiteness – that appalls my soul, but I do not for this cause say that it is something lowly, since on the contrary it is the only prodigy. Generally people are of the opinion that what faith produces is not a work of art, that it is coarse and common work, only for the more clumsy natures; but in fact this is far from the truth. The dialectic of faith is the finest and most remarkable of all; it possesses an elevation, of which indeed I can form a conception, but nothing more. I am able to make from the springboard the great leap whereby I pass into infinity, my back is like that of a tight-rope dancer, having been twisted in my childhood,[26] hence I find this easy; with a one-two-three! I can walk about existence on my head; but the next thing I cannot do, for I cannot perform the miraculous, but can only be astonished by it. Yes, if Abraham the instant he swung his leg over the ass's back had said to himself, "Now, since Isaac is lost, I might just as well sacrifice him here at home, rather than ride the long way to Moriah" – then I should have no need of Abraham, whereas now I bow seven times before his name and seventy times before his deed. For this indeed he did not do, as I can prove by the fact that he was glad at receiving Isaac, heartily glad, that he needed no preparation, no time to concentrate upon the finite and its joy. If this had not been the case with Abraham, then perhaps he might have loved God but not believed; for he who loves God without faith reflects upon himself, he who loves God believingly reflects upon God.

Upon this pinnacle stands Abraham. The last stage he loses sight of is the infinite resignation. He really goes further, and reaches faith; for all these caricatures of faith, the miserable lukewarm indolence which thinks, "There surely is no instant need, it is not worth while sorrowing before the time," the pitiful hope which says, "One cannot know what is going to happen ... it might possibly be after all" – these caricatures of faith are part and parcel of life's wretchedness, and the infinite resignation has already consigned them to infinite contempt.

Abraham I cannot understand,[27] in a certain sense there is nothing I can learn from him but astonishment. If people fancy that by considering the outcome of this story they might let themselves be moved to believe, they deceive themselves and want to swindle God out of the first movement of faith, the infinite resignation. They would suck worldly wisdom out of the paradox. Perhaps one or another may succeed in that, for our age is not willing to stop with faith, with its miracle of turning water into wine, it goes further, it turns wine into water.

Would it not be better to stop with faith, and is it not revolting that everybody wants to go further? When in our age (as indeed is proclaimed in various ways) they will not stop with love, where then are they going? To earthly wisdom, to petty calculation, to paltriness and wretchedness, to everything which can make man's divine origin doubtful. Would it not be better that they should stand still at faith, and that he who stands should take heed lest he fall? For the movements of faith must constantly be made by virtue of the absurd, yet in such a way, be it observed, that one does not lose the finite but gains it every inch. For my part I can well describe the movements of faith, but I cannot make them. When one would learn to make the motions of swimming one can let oneself be hung by a swimming-belt from the ceiling and go through the motions (describe them, so to speak, as we speak of describing a circle), but one is not swimming. In that way I can describe the movements of faith, but when I am thrown into the water, I swim, it is true (for I don't belong to the beach-waders), but I make other movements, I make the movements of infinity, whereas faith does the opposite: after having made the movements of infinity, it makes those of finiteness. Hail to him who can make those movements, he performs the marvellous, and I shall never grow tired of admiring him, whether he be Abraham or a slave in Abraham's house; whether he be a professor of philosophy or a servant-girl, I look only at the movements. But at them I do look, and do not let myself be fooled, either by myself or by any other man. The knights of the infinite resignation are easily recognized: their gait is gliding and assured. Those on the other hand who carry the jewel of faith are likely to be delusive, because their outward appearance bears a striking resemblance to that which both the infinite resignation and faith profoundly despise ... to Philistinism.

I candidly admit that in my practice I have not found any reliable example of the knight of faith, though I would not therefore deny that every second man may be such an example. I have been trying, however, for several years to get on the track of this, and all in vain. People commonly travel around the world to see rivers and mountains, new stars, birds of rare plumage, queerly deformed fishes, ridiculous breeds of men – they abandon themselves to the bestial stupor which gapes at existence, and they think they have seen something. This does not interest me. But if I knew where there was such a knight of faith, I would make a pilgrimage to him on foot, for this prodigy interests me absolutely. I would not let go of him for an instant, every moment I would watch to see how he managed to make the movements, I would regard myself as secured for life, and would divide my time between looking at him and practicing the exercises myself, and thus would spend all my time admiring him. As was said, I have not found any such person, but I can well think him. Here he is. Acquaintance made, I am introduced to him. The moment I set eyes on him I instantly push him from me, I myself leap backwards, I clasp my hands and say half aloud, "Good Lord, is this the man? Is it really he? Why, he looks like a tax-collector!" However, it is the man after all. I draw closer to him, watching his least movements to see whether there might not be visible a little heterogeneous fractional telegraphic message from the infinite, a glance, a look, a gesture, a note of sadness, a smile, which betrayed the infinite in its heterogeneity with the finite. No! I examine his figure from tip to toe to see if there might not be a cranny through which the infinite was peeping. No! He is solid through and through. His tread? It is vigorous, belonging entirely to finiteness; no smartly dressed townsman who walks out to Fresberg on a Sunday afternoon treads the ground more firmly, he belongs entirely to the world, no Philistine more so. One can discover nothing of that aloof and superior nature whereby one recognizes the knight of the infinite. He takes delight in everything, and whenever one sees him taking part in a particular pleasure, he does it with the persistence which is the mark of the earthly man whose soul is absorbed in such things. He tends to his work. So when one looks at him one might suppose that he was a clerk who had lost his soul in an intricate system of book-keeping, so precise is he. He takes a holiday on Sunday. He goes to church. No heavenly glance or any other token of the incommensurable betrays him; if one did not know him, it would be impossible to distinguish him from the rest of the congregation, for his healthy and vigorous hymn-singing proves at the most that he has a good chest. In the afternoon he walks to the forest. He takes delight in everything he sees, in the human swarm, in the new omnibuses,[28] in the water of the Sound; when one meets him on the Beach Road one might suppose he was a shopkeeper taking his fling, that's just the way he disports himself, for he is not a poet, and I have sought in vain to detect in him the poetic incommensurability. Toward evening he walks home, his gait is as indefatigable as that of the postman. On his way he reflects that his wife has surely a special little warm dish prepared for him, e.g. a calf's head roasted, garnished with vegetables. If he were to meet a man like-minded, he could continue as far as East Gate to discourse with him about that dish, with a passion befitting a hotel chef. As it happens, he hasn't four pence to his name, and yet he fully and firmly believes that his wife has that dainty dish for him. If she had it, it would then be an invidious sight for superior people and an inspiring one for the plain man, to see him eat; for his appetite is greater than Esau's. His wife hasn't it – strangely enough, it is quite the same to him. On the way he comes past a building-site and runs across another man. They talk together for a moment. In the twinkling of an eye he erects a new building, he has at his disposition all the powers necessary for it. The stranger leaves him with the thought that he certainly was a capitalist, while my admired knight thinks, "Yes, if the money were needed, I dare say I could get it." He lounges at an open window and looks out on the square on which he lives; he is interested in everything that goes on, in a rat which slips under the curb, in the children's play, and this with the nonchalance of a girl of sixteen. And yet he is no genius, for in vain I have sought in him the incommensurability of genius. In the evening he smokes his pipe; to look at him one would swear that it was the grocer over the way vegetating in the twilight. He lives as carefree as a ne'er-do-well, and yet he buys up the acceptable time at the dearest price, for he does not do the least thing except by virtue of the absurd. And yet, and yet – actually I could become furious over it, for envy if for no other reason – this man has made and every instant is making the movements of infinity. With infinite resignation he has drained the cup of life's profound sadness, he knows the bliss of the infinite, he senses the pain of renouncing everything, the dearest things he possesses in the world, and yet finiteness tastes to him just as good as to one who never knew anything higher, for his continuance in the finite did not bear a trace of the cowed and fearful spirit produced by the process of training; and yet he has this sense of security in enjoying it, as though the finite life were the surest thing of all. And yet, and yet the whole earthly form he exhibits is a new creation by virtue of the absurd. He resigned everything infinitely, and then he grasped everything again by virtue of the absurd. He constantly makes the movements of infinity, but he does this with such correctness and assurance that he constantly gets the finite out of it, and there is not a second when one has a notion of anything else. It is supposed to be the most difficult task for a dancer to leap into a definite posture in such a way that there is not a second when he is grasping after the posture, but by the leap itself he stands fixed in that posture. Perhaps no dancer can do it – that is what this knight does. Most people live dejectedly in worldly sorrow and joy; they are the ones who sit along the wall and do not join in the dance. The knights of infinity are dancers and possess elevation. They make the movements upward, and fall down again; and this too is no mean pastime, nor ungraceful to behold. But whenever they fall down they are not able at once to assume the posture, they vacillate an instant, and this vacillation shows that after all they are strangers in the world. This is more or less strikingly evident in proportion to the art they possess, but even the most artistic knights cannot altogether conceal this vacillation. One need not look at them when they are up in the air, but only the instant they touch or have touched the ground – then one recognizes them. But to be able to fall down in such a way that the same second it looks as if one were standing and walking, to transform the leap of life into a walk, absolutely to express the sublime in the pedestrian – that only the knight of faith can do – and this is the one and only prodigy.

But since the prodigy is so likely to be delusive, I will describe the movements in a definite instance which will serve to illustrate their relation to reality, for upon this everything turns. A young swain falls in love with a princess,[29] and the whole content of his life consists in this love, and yet the situation is such that it is impossible for it to be realized, impossible for it to be translated from ideality into reality.* The slaves of paltriness, the frogs in life's swamp, will naturally cry out, "Such a love is foolishness. The rich brewer's widow is a match fully as good and respectable." Let them croak in the swamp undisturbed. It is not so with the knight of infinite resignation, he does not give up his love, not for all the glory of the world. He is no fool. First he makes sure that this really is the content of his life, and his soul is too healthy and too proud to squander the least thing upon an inebriation. He is not cowardly, he is not afraid of letting love creep into his most secret, his most hidden thoughts, to let it twine in innumerable coils about every ligament of his consciousness – if the love becomes an unhappy love, he will never be able to tear himself loose from it. He feels a blissful rapture in letting love tingle through every nerve, and yet his soul is as solemn as that of the man who has drained the poisoned goblet and feels how the juice permeates every drop of blood – for this instant is life and death.[30] So when he has thus sucked into himself the whole of love and absorbed himself in it, he does not lack courage to make trial of everything and to venture everything. He surveys the situation of his life, he convokes the swift thoughts, which like tame doves obey his every bidding, he waves his wand over them, and they dart off in all directions. But when they all return, all as messengers of sorrow, and declare to him that it is an impossibility, then he becomes quiet, he dismisses them, he remains alone, and then he performs the movements. If what I am saying is to have any significance, it is requisite that the movement come about normally.† So for the first thing, the knight will have power to concentrate the whole content of life and the whole significance of reality in one single

*Of course any other instance whatsoever in which the individual finds that for him the whole reality of actual existence is concentrated, may, when it is seen to be unrealizable, be an occasion for the movement of resignation. However, I have chosen a love experience to make the movement visible, because this interest is doubtless easier to understand, and so relieves me from the necessity of making preliminary observations which in a deeper sense could be of interest only to a few.

†*To this end passion is necessary. Every movement of infinity comes about by passion, and no reflection can bring a movement about. This is the continual leap in existence which explains the movement, whereas mediation is a chimera which according to Hegel is supposed to explain everything, and at the same time this is the only thing he has never tried to explain.*

wish. If a man lacks this concentration, this intensity, if his soul from the beginning is dispersed in the multifarious, he never comes to the point of making the movement, he will deal shrewdly in life like the capitalists who invest their money in all sorts of securities, so as to gain on the one what they lose on the other – in short, he is not a knight. In the next place the knight will have the power to concentrate the whole result of the operations of thought in one act of consciousness. If he lacks this intensity, if his soul from the beginning is dispersed in the multifarious, he will never get time to make the movements, he will be constantly running errands in life, never enter into eternity, for even at the instant when he is closest to it he will suddenly discover that he has forgotten something for which he must go back. He will think that to enter eternity is possible the next instant, and that also is perfectly true, but by such considerations one never reaches the point of making the movements, but by their aid one sinks deeper and deeper into the mire.

So the knight makes the movement – but what movement? Will he forget the whole thing? (For in this too there is indeed a kind of concentration.) No! For the knight does not contradict himself, and it is a contradiction to forget the whole content of one's life and yet remain the same man. To become another man he feels no inclination, nor does he by any means regard this as greatness. Only the lower natures forget themselves and become something new. Thus the butterfly has entirely forgotten that it was a caterpillar, perhaps it may in turn so entirely forget it was a butterfly that it becomes a fish. The deeper natures never forget themselves and never become anything else than what they were. So the knight remembers everything, but precisely

---

Even to make the well-known Socratic distinction between what one understands and what one does not understand, passion is required, and of course even more to make the characteristic Socratic movement, the movement, namely, of ignorance. What our age lacks, however, is not reflection but passion. Hence in a sense our age is too tenacious of life to die, for dying is one of the most remarkable leaps, and a little verse of a poet has always attracted me much, because, after having expressed prettily and simply in five or six preceding lines his wish for good things in life, he concludes thus:[31]

Ein seliger Sprung in die Ewigkeit.

this remembrance is pain, and yet by the infinite resignation he is reconciled with existence. Love for that princess became for him the expression for an eternal love, assumed a religious character, was transfigured into a love for the Eternal Being, which did to be sure deny him the fulfilment of his love, yet reconciled him again by the eternal consciousness of its validity in the form of eternity, which no reality can take from him. Fools and young men prate about everything being possible for a man. That, however, is a great error. Spiritually speaking, everything is possible, but in the world of the finite there is much which is not possible. This impossible, however, the knight makes possible by expressing it spiritually, but he expresses it spiritually by waiving his claim to it. The wish which would carry him out into reality, but was wrecked upon the impossibility, is now bent inward, but it is not therefore lost, neither is it forgotten. At one moment it is the obscure emotion of the wish within him which awakens recollections, at another moment he awakens them himself; for he is too proud to be willing that what was the whole content of his life should be the thing of a fleeting moment. He keeps this love young, and along with him it increases in years and in beauty. On the other hand, he has no need of the intervention of the finite for the further growth of his love. From the instant he made the movement the princess is lost to him. He has no need of those erotic tinglings in the nerves at the sight of the beloved etc., nor does he need to be constantly taking leave of her in a finite sense, because he recollects her in an eternal sense,[32] and he knows very well that the lovers who are so bent upon seeing "her" yet once again, to say farewell for the last time, are right in being bent upon it, are right in thinking that it is the last time, for they forget one another the soonest. He has comprehended the deep secret that also in loving another person one must be sufficient unto oneself. He no longer takes a finite interest in what the princess is doing, and precisely this is proof that he has made the movement infinitely. Here one may have an opportunity to see whether the movement on the part of a particular person is true or fictitious. There was one who also believed that he had made the movement; but lo, time passed, the princess did something else, she married[33] – a prince, let us say – then his soul lost the elasticity of resignation. Thereby he knew that he had not made the movement rightly; for he who has made the act of resignation infinitely is sufficient unto himself. The knight does not annul his resignation, he preserves his love just as young as it was in its first moment, he never lets it go from him, precisely because he makes the movements infinitely. What the princess does, cannot disturb him, it is only the lower natures which find in other people the law for their actions, which find the premises for their actions outside themselves. If on the other hand the princess is like-minded, the beautiful consequence will be apparent. She will introduce herself into that order of knighthood into which one is not received by balloting, but of which everyone is a member who has courage to introduce himself, that order of knighthood which proves its immortality by the fact that it makes no distinction between man and woman. The two will preserve their love young and sound, she also will have triumphed over her pains, even though she does not, as it is said in the ballad, "lie every night beside her lord." These two will to all eternity remain in agreement with one another, with a well-timed *harmonia praestabilita*,[34] so that if ever the moment were to come, the moment which does not, however, concern them finitely (for then they would be growing older), if ever the moment were to come which offered to give love its expression in time, then they will be capable of beginning precisely at the point where they would have begun if originally they had been united. He who understands this, be he man or woman, can never be deceived, for it is only the lower natures which imagine they were deceived. No girl who is not so proud really knows how to love; but if she is so proud, then the cunning and shrewdness of all the world cannot deceive her.

In the infinite resignation there is peace and rest; every man who wills it, who has not abased himself by scorning himself (which is still more dreadful than being proud), can train himself to make this movement which in its pain reconciles one with existence. Infinite resignation is that shirt we read about in the old fable.[35] The thread is spun under tears, the cloth bleached with tears, the shirt sewn with tears; but then too it is a better protection than iron and steel. The imperfection in the fable is that a third party can manufacture this shirt. The secret in life is that everyone must sew it for himself, and the astonishing thing is that a man can sew it fully as well as a woman. In the infinite resignation there is peace and rest and comfort in sorrow – that is, if the movement is made normally. It would not be difficult for me, however, to write a whole book, were I to examine the various misunderstandings, the preposterous attitudes, the deceptive movements, which I have encountered in my brief practice. People believe very little in spirit, and yet making this movement depends upon spirit, it depends upon whether this is or is not a one-sided result of a *dira necessitas*, and if this is present, the more dubious it always is whether the movement is normal. If one means by this that the cold, unfruitful necessity must necessarily be present, one thereby affirms that no one can experience death before he actually dies, and that appears to me a crass materialism. However, in our time people concern themselves rather little about making pure movements. In case one who was about to learn to dance were to say, "For centuries now one generation after another has been learning positions, it is high time I drew some advantage out of this and began straightway with the French dances" – then people would laugh at him; but in the world of spirit they find this exceedingly plausible. What is education? I should suppose that education was the curriculum one had to run through in order to catch up with oneself, and he who will not pass through this curriculum is helped very little by the fact that he was born in the most enlightened age.

The infinite resignation is the last stage prior to faith, so that one who has not made this movement has not faith; for only in the infinite resignation do I become clear to myself with respect to my eternal validity, and only then can there be any question of grasping existence by virtue of faith.

Now we will let the knight of faith appear in the role just described. He makes exactly the same movements as the other knight, infinitely renounces claim to the love which is the content of his life, he is reconciled in pain; but then occurs the prodigy, he makes still another movement more wonderful than all, for he says, "I believe nevertheless that I shall get her, in virtue, that is, of the absurd, in virtue of the fact that with God all things are possible."[36] The absurd is not one of the factors which can be discriminated within the proper compass of the understanding: it is not identical with the improbable, the unexpected, the unforeseen. At the moment when the knight made the act of resignation,[37] he was convinced, humanly speaking, of the impossibility. This was the result reached by the understanding, and he had sufficient energy to think it. On the other hand, in an infinite sense it was possible, namely, by renouncing it; but this sort of possessing is at the same time a relinquishing, and yet there is no absurdity in this for the understanding, for the understanding continued to be in the right in affirming that in the world of the finite where it holds sway this was and remained an impossibility. This is quite as clear to the knight of faith, so the only thing that can save him is the absurd, and this he grasps by faith. So he recognizes the impossibility, and that very instant he believes the absurd; for, if without recognizing the impossibility with all the passion of his soul and with all his heart, he should wish to imagine that he has faith, he deceives himself, and his testimony has no bearing, since he has not even reached the infinite resignation.

Faith therefore is not an aesthetic emotion but something far higher, precisely because it has resignation as its presupposition; it is not an immediate instinct of the heart, but is the paradox of life and existence. So when in spite of all difficulties a young girl still remains convinced that her wish will surely be fulfilled, this conviction is not the assurance of faith, even if she was brought up by Christian parents, and for a whole year perhaps has been catechized by the parson. She is convinced in all her childish naiveté and innocence, this conviction also ennobles her nature and imparts to her a preternatural greatness, so that like a thaumaturge she is able to conjure the finite powers of existence and make the very stones weep, while on the other hand in her flurry she may just as well run to Herod as to Pilate and move the whole world by her tears. Her conviction is very lovable, and one can learn much from her, but one thing is not to be learned from her, one does not learn the movements, for her conviction does not dare in the pain of resignation to face the impossibility.

So I can perceive that it requires strength and energy and freedom of spirit to make the infinite movement of resignation, I can also perceive that it is feasible. But the next thing astonishes me, it makes my head swim, for after having made the movement of resignation, then by virtue of the absurd to get everything, to get the wish whole and uncurtailed – that is beyond human power, it is a prodigy. But this I can perceive, that the young girl's conviction is mere levity in comparison with the firmness faith displays notwithstanding it has perceived the impossibility. Whenever I essay to make this movement, I turn giddy, the very instant I am admiring it absolutely a prodigious dread grips my soul – for what is it to tempt God? And yet this movement is the movement of faith and remains such, even though philosophy, in order to confuse the concepts, would make us believe that it has faith, and even though theology would sell out faith at a bargain price.

For the act of resignation faith is not required, for what I gain by resignation is my eternal consciousness, and this is a purely philosophical movement which I dare say I am able to make if it is required, and which I can train myself to make, for whenever any finiteness would get the mastery over me, I starve myself until I can make the movement, for my eternal consciousness is my love to God, and for me this is higher than everything. For the act of resignation faith is not required, but it is needed when it is the case of acquiring the very least thing more than my eternal consciousness, for this is the paradoxical. The movements are frequently confounded, for it is said that one needs faith to renounce the claim to everything, yea, a stranger thing than this may be heard, when a man laments the loss of his faith, and when one looks at the scale to see where he is, one sees, strangely enough, that he has only reached the point where he should make the infinite movement of resignation. In resignation I make renunciation of everything, this movement I make by myself, and if I do not make it, it is because I am cowardly and effeminate and without enthusiasm and do not feel the significance of the lofty dignity which is assigned to every man, that of being his own censor, which is a far prouder title than that of Censor General to the whole Roman Republic. This movement I make by myself, and what I gain is myself in my eternal consciousness, in blissful agreement with my love for the Eternal Being. By faith I make renunciation of nothing, on the contrary, by faith I acquire everything, precisely in the sense in which it is said that he who has faith like a grain of mustard can remove mountains. A purely human courage is required to renounce the whole of the temporal to gain the eternal; but this I gain, and to all eternity I cannot renounce it – that is a self-contradiction. But a paradoxical and humble courage is required to grasp the whole of the temporal by virtue of the absurd, and this is the courage of faith. By faith Abraham did not renounce his claim upon Isaac, but by faith he got Isaac. By virtue of resignation that rich young man should have given away everything, but then when he had done that, the knight of faith should have said to him, "By virtue of the absurd thou shalt get every penny back again. Canst thou believe that?" And this speech ought by no means to have been indifferent to the aforesaid rich young man, for in case he gave away his goods because he was tired of them, his resignation was not much to boast of.

It is about the temporal, the finite, everything turns in this case. I am able by my own strength to renounce everything, and then to find peace and repose in pain. I can stand everything – even though that horrible demon, more dreadful than death, the king of terrors, even though madness were to hold up before my eyes the motley of the fool, and I understood by its look that it was I who must put it on, I still am able to save my soul, if only it is more to me than my earthly happiness that my love to God should triumph in me. A man may still be able at the last instant to concentrate his whole soul in a single glance toward that heaven from which cometh every good gift, and his glance will be intelligible to himself and also to Him whom it seeks as a sign that he nevertheless remained true to his love. Then he will calmly put on the motley garb. He whose soul has not this romantic enthusiasm has sold his soul, whether he got a kingdom for it or a paltry piece of silver. But by my own strength I am not able to get the least of the things which belong to finiteness, for I am constantly using my strength to renounce everything. By my own strength I am able to give up the princess, and I shall not become a grumbler, but shall find joy and repose in my pain; but by my own strength I am not able to get her again, for I am employing all my strength to be resigned. But by faith, says that marvellous knight, by faith I shall get her in virtue of the absurd.

So this movement I am unable to make. As soon as I would

begin to make it everything turns around dizzily, and I flee back to the pain of resignation. I can swim in existence, but for this mystical soaring I am too heavy. To exist in such a way that my opposition to existence is expressed as the most beautiful and assured harmony with it, is something I cannot do. And yet it must be glorious to get the princess, that is what I say every instant, and the knight of resignation who does not say it is a deceiver, he has not had one wish only, and he has not kept the wish young by his pain. Perhaps there was one who thought it fitting enough that the wish was no longer vivid, that the barb of pain was dulled, but such a man is no knight. A free-born soul who caught himself entertaining such thoughts would despise himself and begin over again, above all he would not permit his soul to be deceived by itself. And yet it must be glorious to get the princess, and yet the knight of faith is the only happy one, the heir apparent to the finite, whereas the knight of resignation is a stranger and a foreigner. Thus to get the princess, to live with her joyfully and happily day in and day out (for it is also conceivable that the knight of resignation might get the princess, but that his soul had discerned the impossibility of their future happiness), thus to live joyfully and happily every instant by virtue of the absurd, every instant to see the sword hanging over the head of the beloved, and yet not to find repose in the pain of resignation, but joy by virtue of the absurd – this is marvellous. He who does it is great, the only great man. The thought of it stirs my soul, which never was niggardly in the admiration of greatness.

In case then everyone in my generation who will not stop at faith is really a man who has comprehended life's horror, who has understood what Daub[38] means when he says that a soldier who stands alone at his post with a loaded gun in a stormy night beside a powder-magazine ... will get strange thoughts into his head – in case then everyone who will not stop at faith is a man who had strength of soul to comprehend that the wish was an impossibility, and thereupon gave himself time to remain alone with this thought, in case everyone who will not stop at faith is a man who is reconciled in pain and is reconciled to pain, in case everyone who will not stop at faith is a man who in the next place (and if he has not done all the foregoing, there is no need of his troubling himself about faith) – in the next place did the marvellous thing, grasped the whole of existence by virtue of the absurd ... then what I write is the highest eulogy of my contemporaries by one of the lowliest among them, who was able only to make the movement of resignation. But why will they not stop at faith, why does one sometimes hear that people are ashamed to acknowledge that they have faith? This I cannot comprehend. If ever I contrive to be able to make this movement, I shall in the future ride in a coach and four.

If it is really true that all the Philistinism I behold in life (which I do not permit my word but my actions to condemn) is not what it seems to be – is it the miracle? That is conceivable, for the hero of faith had in fact a striking resemblance to it – for that hero of faith was not so much an ironist or a humorist, but something far higher. Much is said in our age about irony and humor, especially by people who have never been capable of engaging in the practice of these arts, but who nevertheless know how to explain everything. I am not entirely unacquainted with these two passions,[39] I know a little more about them than what is to be found in German and German-Danish compendiums. I know therefore that these two passions are essentially different from the passion of faith. Irony and humor reflect also upon themselves, and therefore belong within the sphere of the infinite resignation, their elasticity due to the fact that the individual is incommensurable with reality.

The last movement, the paradoxical movement of faith, I cannot make (be that a duty or whatever it may be), in spite of the fact that I would do it more than gladly. Whether a man has a right to make this affirmation, must be left to him, it is a question between him and the Eternal Being who is the object of faith whether in this respect he can hit upon an amicable compromise. What every man can do is to make the movement of infinite resignation, and I for my part would not hesitate to pronounce everyone cowardly who wishes to make himself believe he cannot do it. With faith it is a different matter. But what every man has not a right to do, is to make others believe that faith is something lowly, or that it is an easy thing, whereas it is the greatest and the hardest.

People construe the story of Abraham in another way. They

extol God's grace in bestowing Isaac upon him again – the whole thing was only a trial. A trial – that word may say much or little, and yet the whole thing is over as quickly as it is said. One mounts a winged horse, the same instant one is at Mount Moriah, the same instant one sees the ram; one forgets that Abraham rode only upon an ass, which walks slowly along the road, that he had a journey of three days, that he needed some time to cleave the wood, to bind Isaac, and to sharpen the knife.

And yet they extol Abraham. He who is to deliver the discourse can very well sleep till a quarter of an hour before he has to preach, the auditor can well take a nap during the discourse, for all goes smoothly, without the least trouble from any quarter. If there was a man present who suffered from insomnia, perhaps he then went home and sat in a corner and thought: "It's an affair of a moment, this whole thing; if only you wait a minute, you see the ram, and the trial is over." If the orator were to encounter him in this condition, he would, I think, confront him with all his dignity and say, "Wretched man, that thou couldst let thy soul sink into such foolishness! No miracle occurs. The whole of life is a trial." In proportion as the orator proceeds with his outpouring, he would get more and more excited, would become more and more delighted with himself, and whereas he had noticed no congestion of the blood while he talked about Abraham, he now felt how the vein swelled in his forehead. Perhaps he would have lost his breath as well as his tongue if the sinner had answered calmly and with dignity, "But it was about this you preached last Sunday."

Let us then either consign Abraham to oblivion, or let us learn to be dismayed by the tremendous paradox which constitutes the significance of Abraham's life, that we may understand that our age, like every age, can be joyful if it has faith. In case Abraham is not a nullity, a phantom, a show one employs for a pastime, then the fault can never consist in the fact that the sinner wants to do likewise, but the point is to see how great a thing it was that Abraham did, in order that man may judge for himself whether he has the call and the courage to be subjected to such a test. The comic contradiction in the behavior of the orator is that he reduced Abraham to an insignificance, and yet would admonish the other to behave in the same way.

Should not one dare then to talk about Abraham? I think one should. If I were to talk about him, I would first depict the pain of his trial. To that end I would like a leech suck all the dread and distress and torture out of a father's sufferings, so that I might describe what Abraham suffered, whereas all the while he nevertheless believed. I would remind the audience that the journey lasted three days and a good part of the fourth, yea, that these three and a half days were infinitely longer than the few thousand years which separate me from Abraham. Then I would remind them that, in my opinion, every man should dare still turn around ere he begins such an undertaking, and every instant he can repentantly turn back. If one does this, I fear no danger, nor am I afraid of awakening in people an inclination to be tried like Abraham. But if one would dispose of a cheap edition of Abraham, and yet admonish everyone to do likewise, then it is ludicrous.

It is now my intention to draw out from the story of Abraham the dialectical consequences inherent in it, expressing them in the form of *problemata*, in order to see what a tremendous paradox faith is, a paradox which is capable of transforming a murder into a holy act well-pleasing to God, a paradox which gives Isaac back to Abraham, which no thought can master, because faith begins precisely there where thinking leaves off.

PROBLEM I

Is there such a thing as a teleological suspension of the ethical?

The ethical as such is the universal, and as the universal it applies to everyone, which may be expressed from another point of view by saying that it applies every instant. It reposes immanently in itself, it has nothing without itself which is its *telos*,[40] but is itself *telos* for everything outside it, and when this has been incorporated by the ethical it can go no further. Conceived immediately as physical and psychical, the particular individual is the individual who has his *telos* in the universal, and his ethical task is to express himself constantly in it, to abolish his particularity in order to become the universal. As soon as the individual would assert himself in his particularity over against the universal he sins, and only by recognizing this can he again reconcile himself with the universal. Whenever the individual after he has entered the universal feels an impulse to assert himself as the particular, he is in temptation [*Anfechtung*], and he can labor himself out of this only by penitently abandoning himself as the particular in the universal. If this be the highest thing that can be said of man and of his existence, then the ethical has the same character as man's eternal blessedness, which to all eternity and at every instant is his *telos*, since it would be a contradiction to say that this might be abandoned (i.e. teleologically suspended), inasmuch as this is no sooner suspended than it is forfeited, whereas in other cases what is suspended is not forfeited but is preserved precisely in that higher thing which is its *telos*.[41]

If such be the case, then Hegel is right when in his chapter on "The Good and the Conscience,"[42] he characterizes man merely as the particular and regards this character as "a moral form of evil" which is to be annulled in the teleology of the moral, so that the individual who remains in this stage is either sinning or subjected to temptation [*Anfechtung*]. On the other hand, Hegel is wrong in talking of faith, wrong in not protesting loudly and clearly against the fact that Abraham enjoys honor and glory as the father of faith, whereas he ought to be prosecuted and convicted of murder.

For faith is this paradox, that the particular is higher than the universal – yet in such a way, be it observed, that the movement repeats itself, and that consequently the individual, after having been in the universal, now as the particular isolates himself as higher than the universal. If this be not faith, then Abraham is lost, then faith has never existed in the world ... because it has always existed. For if the ethical (i.e. the moral) is the highest thing, and if nothing incommensurable remains in man in any other way but as the evil (i.e. the particular which has to be expressed in the universal), then one needs no other categories besides those which the Greeks possessed or which by consistent thinking can be derived from them. This fact Hegel ought not to have concealed, for after all he was acquainted with Greek thought.

One not infrequently hears it said by men, who for lack of losing themselves in studies are absorbed in phrases, that a light shines upon the Christian world whereas a darkness broods over paganism. This utterance has always seemed strange to me, inasmuch as every profound thinker and every serious artist is even in our day rejuvenated by the eternal youth of the Greek race. Such an utterance may be explained by the consideration that people do not know what they ought to say but only that they must say something. It is quite right for one to say that paganism did not possess faith, but if with this one is to have said something, one must be a little clearer about what one understands by faith, since otherwise one falls back into such phrases. To explain the whole of existence and faith along with it, without having a conception of what faith is, is easy, and that man does not make the poorest calculation in life who reckons upon admiration when he possesses such an explanation; for, as Boileau says, "*un sot trouve toujours un plus sot qui l'admire.*"

Faith is precisely this paradox, that the individual as the particular is higher than the universal, is justified over against it, is not subordinate but superior – yet in such a way, be it observed, that it is the particular individual who, after he has been subordinated as the particular to the universal, now through the universal becomes the individual who as the particular is superior to the universal, for the fact that the individual as the particular stands in an absolute relation to the absolute. This position cannot be mediated, for all mediation comes about precisely by virtue of the universal; it is and remains to all eternity a paradox, inaccessible to thought. And yet faith is this paradox – or else (these are the logical deductions which I would beg the reader to have *in mente* at every point, though it would be too prolix for me to reiterate them on every occasion) – or else there never has been faith ... precisely because it always has been. In other words, Abraham is lost.

That for the particular individual this paradox may easily be mistaken for a temptation [*Anfechtung*] is indeed true, but one ought not for this reason to conceal it. That the whole constitution of many persons may be such that this paradox repels them is indeed true, but one ought not for this reason to make faith something different in order to be able to possess it, but ought rather to admit that one does not possess it, whereas those who possess faith should take care to set up certain criteria so that one might distinguish the paradox from a temptation [*Anfechtung*].

Now the story of Abraham contains such a teleological suspension of the ethical. There have not been lacking clever pates and profound investigators who have found analogies to it. Their wisdom is derived from the pretty proposition that at bottom everything is the same. If one will look a little more closely, I have not much doubt that in the whole world one will not find a single analogy (except a later instance which proves nothing), if it stands fast that Abraham is the representative of faith, and that faith is normally expressed in him whose life is not merely the most paradoxical that can be thought but so paradoxical that it cannot be thought at all. He acts by virtue of the absurd, for it is precisely absurd that he as the particular is higher than the universal. This paradox cannot be mediated; for as soon as he begins to do this he has to admit that he was in temptation [*Anfechtung*], and if such was the case, he never gets to the point of sacrificing Isaac, or, if he has sacrificed Isaac, he must turn back repentantly to the universal. By virtue of the absurd he gets Isaac again. Abraham is therefore at no instant a tragic hero but something quite different, either a murderer or a believer. The middle term which saves the tragic hero, Abraham has not. Hence it is that I can understand the tragic hero but cannot understand Abraham, though in a certain crazy sense I admire him more than all other men.

Abraham's relation to Isaac, ethically speaking, is quite simply expressed by saying that a father shall love his son more dearly than himself. Yet within its own compass the ethical has various gradations. Let us see whether in this story there is to be found any higher expression for the ethical such as would ethically explain his conduct, ethically justify him in suspending the ethical obligation toward his son, without in this search going beyond the teleology of the ethical.

When an undertaking in which a whole nation is concerned is hindered,[43] when such an enterprise is brought to a standstill by the disfavor of heaven, when the angry deity sends a calm which mocks all efforts, when the seer performs his heavy task and proclaims that the deity demands a young maiden as a sacrifice – then will the father heroically make the sacrifice. He will magnanimously conceal his pain, even though he might wish that he were "the lowly man who dares to weep,"[44] not the king who must act royally. And though solitary pain forces its way into his breast, he has only three confidants among the people, yet soon the whole nation will be cognizant of his pain, but also cognizant of his exploit, that for the welfare of the whole he was willing to sacrifice her, his daughter, the lovely young maiden. O charming bosom! O beautiful cheeks! O bright golden hair! (v.687). And the daughter will affect him by her tears, and the father will turn his face away, but the hero will raise the knife. – When the report of this reaches the ancestral home, then will the beautiful maidens of Greece blush with enthusiasm, and if the daughter was betrothed, her true love will not be angry but be proud of sharing in the father's deed, because the maiden belonged to him more feelingly than to the father.

When the intrepid judge[45] who saved Israel in the hour of need in one breath binds himself and God by the same vow, then heroically the young maiden's jubilation, the beloved daughter's joy, he will turn to sorrow, and with her all Israel will lament her maiden youth; but every free-born man will understand, and every stout-hearted woman will admire Jephtha, and every maiden in Israel will wish to act as did his daughter. For what good would it do if Jephtha were victorious by reason of his vow if he did not keep it? Would not the victory again be taken from the nation?

When a son is forgetful of his duty,[46] when the state entrusts the father with the sword of justice, when the laws require punishment at the hand of the father, then will the father heroically forget that the guilty one is his son, he will magnanimously conceal his pain, but there will not be a single one among the people, not even the son, who will not admire the father, and whenever the law of Rome is interpreted, it will be remembered that many interpreted it more learnedly, but none so gloriously as Brutus.

If, on the other hand, while a favorable wind bore the fleet on with swelling sails to its goal, Agamemnon had sent that messenger who fetched Iphigenia in order to be sacrificed; if Jephtha, without being bound by any vow which decided the fate of the nation, had said to his daughter, "Bewail now thy virginity for the space of two months, for I will sacrifice thee"; if Brutus had had a righteous son and yet would have ordered the lictors to execute him – who would have understood them? If these three men had replied to the query why they did it by saying, "It is a trial in which we are tested," would people have understood them better?

When Agamemnon, Jephtha, Brutus at the decisive moment heroically overcome their pain, have heroically lost the beloved and have merely to accomplish the outward sacrifice, then there never will be a noble soul in the world who will not shed tears of compassion for their pain and of admiration for their exploit. If, on the other hand, these three men at the decisive moment were to adjoin to their heroic conduct this little word, "But for all that it will not come to pass," who then would understand them? If as an explanation they added, "This we believe by virtue of the absurd," who would understand them better? For who would not easily understand that it was absurd, but who would understand that one could then believe it?

The difference between the tragic hero and Abraham is clearly evident. The tragic hero still remains within the ethical.

He lets one expression of the ethical find its *telos* in a higher expression of the ethical; the ethical relation between father and son, or daughter and father, he reduces to a sentiment which has its dialectic in its relation to the idea of morality. Here there can be no question of a teleological suspension of the ethical itself.

With Abraham the situation was different. By his act he overstepped the ethical entirely and possessed a higher *telos* outside of it, in relation to which he suspended the former. For I should very much like to know how one would bring Abraham's act into relation with the universal, and whether it is possible to discover any connection whatever between what Abraham did and the universal ... except the fact that he transgressed it. It was not for the sake of saving a people, not to maintain the idea of the state, that Abraham did this, and not in order to reconcile angry deities. If there could be a question of the deity being angry, he was angry only with Abraham, and Abraham's whole action stands in no relation to the universal, is a purely private undertaking. Therefore, whereas the tragic hero is great by reason of his moral virtue, Abraham is great by reason of a purely personal virtue. In Abraham's life there is no higher expression for the ethical than this, that the father shall love his son. Of the ethical in the sense of morality there can be no question in this instance. In so far as the universal was present, it was indeed cryptically present in Isaac, hidden as it were in Isaac's loins, and must therefore cry out with Isaac's mouth, "Do it not! Thou art bringing everything to naught."

Why then did Abraham do it? For God's sake, and (in complete identity with this) for his own sake. He did it for God's sake because God required this proof of his faith; for his own sake he did it in order that he might furnish the proof. The unity of these two points of view is perfectly expressed by the word which has always been used to characterize this situation: it is a trial, a temptation [*Fristelse*].[47] A temptation – but what does that mean? What ordinarily tempts a man is that which would keep him from doing his duty, but in this case the temptation is itself the ethical ... which would keep him from doing God's will. But what then is duty? Duty is precisely the expression for God's will.

Here is evident the necessity of a new category if one would understand Abraham. Such a relationship to the deity paganism did not know. The tragic hero does not enter into any private relationship with the deity, but for him the ethical is the divine, hence the paradox implied in his situation can be mediated in the universal.

Abraham cannot be mediated, and the same thing can be expressed also by saying that he cannot talk. So soon as I talk I express the universal, and if I do not do so, no one can understand me. Therefore if Abraham would express himself in terms of the universal, he must say that his situation is a temptation [*Anfechtung*], for he has no higher expression for that universal which stands above the universal which he transgresses.

Therefore, though Abraham arouses my admiration, he at the same time appals me. He who denies himself and sacrifices himself for duty gives up the finite in order to grasp the infinite, and that man is secure enough. The tragic hero gives up the certain for the still more certain, and the eye of the beholder rests upon him confidently. But he who gives up the universal in order to grasp something still higher which is not the universal – what is he doing? Is it possible that this can be anything else but a temptation [*Anfechtung*]? And if it be possible ... but the individual was mistaken – what can save him? He suffers all the pain of the tragic hero, he brings to naught his joy in the world, he renounces everything ... and perhaps at the same instant debars himself from the sublime joy which to him was so precious that he would purchase it at any price. Him the beholder cannot understand nor let his eye rest confidently upon him. Perhaps it is not possible to do what the believer proposes, since it is indeed unthinkable. Or if it could be done, but if the individual had misunderstood the deity – what can save him? The tragic hero has need of tears and claims them, and where is the envious eye which would be so barren that it could not weep with Agamemnon; but where is the man with a soul so bewildered that he would have the presumption to weep for Abraham? The tragic hero accomplishes his act at a definite instant in time, but in the course of time he does something not less significant, he visits the man whose soul is beset with sorrow, whose breast for stifled sobs cannot draw breath, whose thoughts pregnant with tears weigh heavily upon him, to him he makes his appearance, dissolves the sorcery of sorrow, loosens his corslet, coaxes forth his tears by the fact that in his sufferings the sufferer forgets his own. One cannot weep over Abraham. One approaches him with a *horror religiosus*, as Israel approached Mount Sinai. – If then the solitary man who ascends Mount Moriah, which with its peak rises heaven-high above the plain of Aulis, if he be not a somnambulist who walks securely above the abyss while he who is stationed at the foot of the mountain and is looking on trembles with fear and out of reverence and dread dare not even call to him – if this man is disordered in his mind, if he had made a mistake! Thanks and thanks again to him who proffers to the man whom the sorrows of life have assaulted and left naked – proffers to him the fig-leaf of the word with which he can cover his wretchedness. Thanks be to thee, great Shakespeare, who art able to express everything, absolutely everything, precisely as it is – and yet why didst thou never pronounce this pang? Didst thou perhaps reserve it to thyself – like the loved one whose name one cannot endure that the world should mention? For the poet purchases the power of words, the power of uttering all the dread secrets of others, at the price of a little secret he is unable to utter . . . and a poet is not an apostle, he casts out devils only by the power of the devil.

But now when the ethical is thus teleologically suspended, how does the individual exist in whom it is suspended? He exists as the particular in opposition to the universal. Does he then sin? For this is the form of sin, as seen in the idea. Just as the infant, though it does not sin, because it is not as such yet conscious of its existence, yet its existence is sin, as seen in the idea, and the ethical makes its demands upon it every instant. If one denies that this form can be repeated [in the adult] in such a way that it is not sin, then the sentence of condemnation is pronounced upon Abraham. How then did Abraham exist? He believed. This is the paradox which keeps him upon the sheer edge and which he cannot make clear to any other man, for the paradox is that he as the individual puts himself in an absolute relation to the absolute. Is he justified in doing this? His justification is once more the paradox; for if he is justified, it is not by virtue of anything universal, but by virtue of being the particular individual.

How then does the individual assure himself that he is

justified? It is easy enough to level down the whole of existence to the idea of the state or the idea of society. If one does this, one can also mediate easily enough, for then one does not encounter at all the paradox that the individual as the individual is higher than the universal – which I can aptly express also by the thesis of Pythagoras, that the uneven numbers are more perfect than the even. If in our age one occasionally hears a rejoinder which is pertinent to the paradox, it is likely to be to the following effect: "It is to be judged by the result." A hero who has become a *σκάνδαλν*[48] to his contemporaries because they are conscious that he is a paradox who cannot make himself intelligible, will cry out defiantly to his generation, "The result will surely prove that I am justified." In our age we hear this cry rather seldom, for as our age, to its disadvantage, does not produce heroes, it has also the advantage of producing few caricatures. When in our age one hears this saying, "It is to be judged according to the result," a man is at once clear as to who it is he has the honor of talking with. Those who talk thus are a numerous tribe, whom I will denominate by the common name of *Docents*.[49] In their thoughts they live secure in existence, they have a *solid* position and sure prospects in a well-ordered state, they have centuries and even millenniums between them and the concussions of existence, they do not fear that such things could recur – for what would the police say to that! and the newspapers! Their lifework is to judge the great, and to judge them according to the result. Such behavior toward the great betrays a strange mixture of arrogance and misery: of arrogance because they think they are called to be judges; of misery because they do not feel that their lives are even in the remotest degree akin to the great. Surely a man who possesses even a little *erectioris ingenii* [of the higher way of thinking] has not become entirely a cold and clammy mollusk, and when he approaches what is great it can never escape his mind that from the creation of the world it has been customary for the result to come last, and that, if one would truly learn anything from great actions, one must pay attention precisely to the beginning. In case he who should act were to judge himself according to the result, he would never get to the point of beginning. Even though the result may give joy to the whole world, it cannot help the hero, for he would get to know the result only when the whole thing was over, and it was not by this he became a hero, but he was such for the fact that he began.

Moreover, the result (inasmuch as it is the answer of finiteness to the infinite query) is in its dialectic entirely heterogeneous with the existence of the hero. Or is it possible to prove that Abraham was justified in assuming the position of the individual with relation to the universal . . . for the fact that he got Isaac by *miracle*? If Abraham had actually sacrificed Isaac, would he then have been less justified?

But people are curious about the result, as they are about the result in a book – they want to know nothing about dread, distress, the paradox. They flirt aesthetically with the result, it comes just as unexpectedly but also just as easily as a prize in the lottery; and when they have heard the result they are edified. And yet no robber of temples condemned to hard labor behind iron bars, is so base a criminal as the man who pillages the holy, and even Judas who sold his Master for thirty pieces of silver is not more despicable than the man who sells greatness.

It is abhorrent to my soul to talk inhumanly about greatness, to let it loom darkly at a distance in an indefinite form, to make out that it is great without making the human character of it evident – wherewith it ceases to be great. For it is not what happens to me that makes me great, but it is what I do, and there is surely no one who thinks that a man became great because he won the great prize in the lottery. Even if a man were born in humble circumstances, I would require of him nevertheless that he should not be so inhuman toward himself as not to be able to think of the King's castle except at a remote distance, dreaming vaguely of its greatness and wanting at the same time to exalt it and also to abolish it by the fact that he exalted it meanly. I require of him that he should be man enough to step forward confidently and worthily even in that place. He should not be unmanly enough to desire impudently to offend everybody by rushing straight from the street into the King's hall. By that he loses more than the King. On the contrary, he should find joy in observing every rule of propriety with a glad and confident enthusiasm which will make him frank and fearless. This is only a symbol, for the difference here remarked upon is only a very imperfect expression for spiritual distance. I require of every man that he should not think so inhumanly of himself as not to dare to enter those palaces where not merely the memory of the elect abides but where the elect themselves abide. He should not press forward impudently and impute to them kinship with himself; on the contrary, he should be blissful every time he bows before them, but he should be frank and confident and always be something more than a charwoman, for if he will not be more, he will never gain entrance. And what will help him is precisely the dread and distress by which the great are tried, for otherwise, if he has a bit of pith in him, they will merely arouse his justified envy. And what distance alone makes great, what people would make great by empty and hollow phrases, that they themselves reduce to naught.

Who was ever so great as that blessed woman, the Mother of God, the Virgin Mary? And yet how do we speak of her? We say that she was highly favored among women. And if it did not happen strangely that those who hear are able to think as inhumanly as those who talk, every young girl might well ask, "Why was not I too the highly favored?" And if I had nothing else to say, I would not dismiss such a question as stupid, for when it is a matter of favor, abstractly considered, everyone is equally entitled to it. What they leave out is the distress, the dread, the paradox. My thought is as pure as that of anyone, and the thought of the man who is able to think such things will surely become pure – and if this be not so, he may expect the dreadful; for he who once has evoked these images cannot be rid of them again, and if he sins against them, they avenge themselves with quiet wrath, more terrible than the vociferousness of ten ferocious reviewers. To be sure, Mary bore the child miraculously, but it came to pass with her after the manner of women, and that season is one of dread, distress and paradox. To be sure, the angel was a ministering spirit, but it was not a servile spirit which obliged her by saying to the other young maidens of Israel, "Despise not Mary. What befalls her is the extraordinary." But the Angel came only to Mary, and no one could understand her. After all, what woman was so mortified as Mary? And is it not true in this instance also that one whom God blesses He curses in the same breath? This is the spirit's interpretation of Mary, and she is not (as it shocks me to say, but shocks me still more to think that they have thoughtlessly and coquettishly interpreted her thus) – she is not a fine lady who sits in state and plays with an infant god. Nevertheless, when she says, "Behold the handmaid of the Lord" – then she is great, and I think it will not be found difficult to explain why she became the Mother of God. She has no need of worldly admiration, any more than Abraham has need of tears, for she was not a heroine, and he was not a hero, but both of them became greater than such, not at all because they were exempted from distress and torment and paradox, but they became great through these.[50]

It is great when the poet, presenting his tragic hero before the admiration of men, dares to say, "Weep for him, for he deserves it." For it is great to deserve the tears of those who are worthy to shed tears. It is great that the poet dares to hold the crowd in check, dares to castigate men, requiring that every man examine himself whether he be worthy to weep for the hero. For the waste-water of blubberers is a degradation of the holy. – But greater than all this it is that the knight of faith dares to say even to the noble man who would weep for him, "Weep not for me, but weep for thyself."

One is deeply moved, one longs to be back in those beautiful times, a sweet yearning conducts one to the desired goal, to see Christ wandering in the promised land. One forgets the dread, the distress, the paradox. Was it so easy a matter not to be mistaken? Was it not dreadful that this man who walks among the others – was it not dreadful that He was God? Was it not dreadful to sit at table with Him? Was it so easy a matter to become an Apostle? But the result, eighteen hundred years – that is a help, it helps to the shabby deceit wherewith one deceives oneself and others. I do not feel the courage to wish to be contemporary with such events, but hence I do not judge severely those who were mistaken, nor think meanly of those who saw aright.

I return, however, to Abraham. Before the result, either Abraham was every minute a murderer, or we are confronted by a paradox which is higher than all mediation.

The story of Abraham contains therefore a teleological suspension of the ethical. As the individual he became higher than the universal. This is the paradox which does not permit of mediation. It is just as inexplicable how he got into it as it is inexplicable how he remained in it. If such is not the position of Abraham, then he is not even a tragic hero but a murderer. To want to continue to call him the father of faith, to talk of this to people who do not concern themselves with anything but words, is thoughtless. A man can become a tragic hero by his own powers – but not a knight of faith. When a man enters upon the way, in a certain sense the hard way of the tragic hero, many will be able to give him counsel; to him who follows the narrow way of faith no one can give counsel, him no one can understand. Faith is a miracle, and yet no man is excluded from it; for that in which all human life is unified is passion,* and faith is a passion.

*Lessing has somewhere given expression to a similar thought from a purely aesthetic point of view. What he would show expressly in this passage is that sorrow too can find a witty expression. To this end he quotes a rejoinder of the unhappy English king, Edward II. In contrast to this he quotes from Diderot a story of a peasant woman and a rejoinder of hers. Then he continues: "That too was wit, and the wit of a peasant at that; but the situation made it inevitable. Consequently one must not seek to find the excuse for the witty expressions of pain and of sorrow in the fact that the person who uttered them was a superior person, well educated, intelligent, and witty withal, *for the passions make all men again equal* – but the explanation is to be found in the fact that in all probability everyone would have said the same thing in the same situation. The thought of a peasant woman a queen could have had and must have had, just as what the king said in that instance a peasant too would have been able to say and doubtless would have said." Cf. *Sämtliche Werke*, XXX, p. 223.[51]

PROBLEM II

Is there such a thing as an absolute duty toward God?

The ethical is the universal, and as such it is again the divine. One has therefore a right to say that fundamentally every duty is a duty toward God; but if one cannot say more, then one affirms at the same time that properly I have no duty toward God. Duty becomes duty by being referred to God, but in duty itself I do not come into relation with God. Thus it is a duty to love one's neighbor, but in performing this duty I do not come into relation with God but with the neighbor whom I love. If I say then in this connection that it is my duty to love God, I am really uttering only a tautology, inasmuch as "God" is in this instance used in an entirely abstract sense as the divine, i.e. the universal, i.e. duty. So the whole existence of the human race is rounded off completely like a sphere, and the ethical is at once its limit and its content. God becomes an invisible vanishing-point, a powerless thought, His power being only in the ethical which is the content of existence. If in any way it might occur to any man to want to love God in any other sense than that here indicated, he is romantic, he loves a phantom which, if it had merely the power of being able to speak, would say to him, "I do not require your love. Stay where you belong." If in any way it might occur to a man to want to love God otherwise, this love would be open to suspicion, like that of which Rousseau speaks, referring to people who love the Kaffirs instead of their neighbors.

So in case what has been expounded here is correct, in case there is no incommensurability in a human life, and what there is of the incommensurable is only such by an accident from which no consequences can be drawn, in so far as existence is regarded in terms of the idea, Hegel is right; but he is not right in talking about faith or in allowing Abraham to be regarded as the father of it; for by the latter he has pronounced judgment both upon Abraham and upon faith. In the Hegelian philosophy[52] *das*

Äussere (*die Entäusserung*) is higher than *das Innere*. This is frequently illustrated by an example. The child is *das Innere*, the man *das Äussere*. Hence it is that the child is defined by the outward, and conversely, the man, as *das Äussere*, is defined precisely by *das Innere*. Faith, on the contrary, is the paradox that inwardness is higher than outwardness – or, to recall an expression used above, the uneven number is higher than the even.

In the ethical way of regarding life it is therefore the task of the individual to divest himself of the inward determinants and express them in an outward way. Whenever he shrinks from this, whenever he is inclined to persist in or to slip back again into the inward determinants of feeling, mood, etc., he sins, he is in a temptation [*Anfechtung*]. The paradox of faith is this, that there is an inwardness which is incommensurable for the outward, an inwardness, be it observed, which is not identical with the first but is a new inwardness. This must not be overlooked. Modern philosophy[53] has permitted itself without further ado to substitute in place of "faith" the immediate. When one does that it is ridiculous to deny that faith has existed in all ages. In that way faith comes into rather simple company along with feeling, mood, idiosyncrasy, vapors, etc. To this extent philosophy may be right in saying that one ought not to stop there. But there is nothing to justify philosophy in using this phrase with regard to faith. Before faith there goes a movement of infinity, and only then, *necopinate*,[54] by virtue of the absurd, faith enters upon the scene. This I can well understand without maintaining on that account that I have faith. If faith is nothing but what philosophy makes it out to be, then Socrates already went further, much further, whereas the contrary is true, that he never reached it. In an intellectual respect he made the movement of infinity. His ignorance is infinite resignation. This task in itself is a match for human powers, even though people in our time disdain it; but only after it is done, only when the individual has evacuated himself in the infinite, only then is the point attained where faith can break forth.

The paradox of faith is this, that the individual is higher than the universal, that the individual (to recall a dogmatic distinction now rather seldom heard) determines his relation to the universal by his relation to the absolute, not his relation to the absolute by his relation to the universal. The paradox can also be expressed by saying that there is an absolute duty toward God; for in this relationship of duty the individual as an individual stands related absolutely to the absolute. So when in this connection it is said that it is a duty to love God, something different is said from that in the foregoing; for if this duty is absolute, the ethical is reduced to a position of relativity. From this, however, it does not follow that the ethical is to be abolished, but it acquires an entirely different expression, the paradoxical expression – that, for example, love to God may cause the knight of faith to give his love to his neighbor the opposite expression to that which, ethically speaking, is required by duty.

If such is not the case, then faith has no proper place in existence, then faith is a temptation [*Anfechtung*], and Abraham is lost, since he gave in to it.

This paradox does not permit of mediation, for it is founded precisely upon the fact that the individual is only the individual. As soon as this individual [who is aware of a direct command from God] wishes to express his absolute duty in [terms of] the universal [i.e. the ethical, and] is sure of his duty in that [i.e. the universal or ethical precept], he recognizes that he is in temptation [i.e. a trial of faith], and, if in fact he resists [the direct indication of God's will], he ends by not fulfilling the absolute duty so called [i.e. what here has been called the absolute duty]; and, if he doesn't do this, [i.e. doesn't put up a resistance to the direct intimation of God's will], he sins, even though *realiter* his deed were that which it was his absolute duty to do.* So what should Abraham do? If he would say to another person, "Isaac I love more dearly than everything in the world, and hence it is so

*The translator has ventured to render this muddy sentence very liberally (though he has bracketed his explanatory additions), in order to bring out the meaning this sentence must have if it is to express the anguishing paradox of a "teleological suspension of the ethical." This is the meaning Niels Thulstrup gets out of it, and he tells me that this is the translation of Emanuel Hirsch. As S.K.'s sentence stands, without explanatory additions, it reminds me of a rigmarole I have often recited to the mystification of my hearers: "If a man were to signify, which he were not, if he had the power, which being denied him, he were to endeavor anyhow – merely because he don't, would you?" Much as I love Kierkegaard, I sometimes hate him for keeping me awake at night. Only between sleeping and waking am I able to unravel some of his most complicated sentences.

hard for me to sacrifice him"; then surely the other would have shaken his head and said, "Why will you sacrifice him then?" – or if the other had been a sly fellow, he surely would have seen through Abraham and perceived that he was making a show of feelings which were in strident contradiction to his act.

In the story of Abraham we find such a paradox. His relation to Isaac, ethically expressed, is this, that the father should love the son. This ethical relation is reduced to a relative position in contrast with the absolute relation to God. To the question, "Why?" Abraham has no answer except that it is a trial, a temptation [*Fristelse*] – terms which, as was remarked above, express the unity of the two points of view: that it is for God's sake and for his own sake. In common usage these two ways of regarding the matter are mutually exclusive. Thus when we see a man do something which does not comport with the universal, we say that he scarcely can be doing it for God's sake, and by that we imply that he does it for his own sake. The paradox of faith has lost the intermediate term, i.e. the universal. On the one side it has the expression for the extremest egoism (doing the dreadful thing it does for one's own sake); on the other side the expression for the most absolute self-sacrifice (doing it for God's sake). Faith itself cannot be mediated into the universal, for it would thereby be destroyed. Faith is this paradox, and the individual absolutely cannot make himself intelligible to anybody. People imagine maybe that the individual can make himself intelligible to another individual in the same case. Such a notion would be unthinkable if in our time people did not in so many ways seek to creep slyly into greatness. The one knight of faith can render no aid to the other. Either the individual becomes a knight of faith by assuming the burden of the paradox, or he never becomes one. In these regions partnership is unthinkable. Every more precise explication of what is to be understood by Isaac the individual can give only to himself. And even if one were able, generally speaking,[55] to define ever so precisely what should be intended by Isaac (which moreover would be the most ludicrous self-contradiction, i.e. that the particular individual who definitely stands outside the universal is subsumed under universal categories precisely when he has to act as the individual who stands outside the universal), the individual nevertheless will never be able to assure himself by the aid of others that this application is appropriate, but he can do so only by himself as the individual. Hence even if a man were cowardly and paltry enough to wish to become a knight of faith on the responsibility of an outsider, he will never become one; for only the individual becomes a knight of faith as the particular individual, and this is the greatness of this knighthood, as I can well understand without entering the order, since I lack courage; but this is also its terror, as I can comprehend even better.

In Luke 14:26, as everybody knows, there is a striking doctrine taught about the absolute duty toward God: "If any man cometh unto me and hateth not his own father and mother and wife and children and brethren and sisters, yea, and his own life also, he cannot be my disciple." This is a hard saying, who can bear to hear it? For this reason it is heard very seldom. This silence, however, is only an evasion which is of no avail. Nevertheless, the student of theology learns to know that these words occur in the New Testament, and in one or another exegetical aid[56] he finds the explanation that *μισεῖν* in this passage and a few others is used in the sense of *μείσειν*, signifying *minus diligo*, *posthabeo*, *non colo*, *nihili facio*. However, the context in which these words occur does not seem to strengthen this tasteful explanation. In the verse immediately following there is a story about a man who desired to build a tower but first sat down to calculate whether he was capable of doing it, lest people might laugh at him afterwards. The close connection of this story with the verse here cited seems precisely to indicate that the words are to be taken in as terrible a sense as possible, to the end that everyone may examine himself as to whether he is able to erect the building.

In case this pious and kindly exegete, who by abating the price thought he could smuggle Christianity into the world, were fortunate enough to convince a man that grammatically, linguistically and *κατ᾽ ἀναλογίαν* [analogically] this was the meaning of that passage, it is to be hoped that the same moment he will be fortunate enough to convince the same man that Christianity is one of the most pitiable things in the world. For the doctrine which in one of its most lyrical outbursts, where the consciousness of its eternal validity swells in it most strongly, has nothing else to say but a noisy word which means nothing but only signifies that one is to be less kindly, less attentive, more indifferent; the doctrine which at the moment when it makes as if it would give utterance to the terrible ends by driveling instead of terrifying – that doctrine is not worth taking off my hat to.

The words are terrible, yet I fully believe that one can understand them without implying that he who understands them has courage to do them. One must at all events be honest enough to acknowledge what stands written and to admit that it is great, even though one has not the courage for it. He who behaves thus will not find himself excluded from having part in that beautiful story which follows, for after all it contains consolation of a sort for the man who had not courage to begin the tower. But we must be honest, and not interpret this lack of courage as humility, since it is really pride, whereas the courage of faith is the only humble courage.

One can easily perceive that if there is to be any sense in this passage, it must be understood literally. God it is who requires absolute love. But he who in demanding a person's love thinks that this love should be proved also by becoming lukewarm to everything which hitherto was dear – that man is not only an egoist but stupid as well, and he who would demand such love signs at the same moment his own death-warrant, supposing that his life was bound up with this coveted love. Thus a husband demands that his wife shall leave father and mother, but if he were to regard it as a proof of her extraordinary love for him that she for his sake became an indolent, lukewarm daughter etc., then he is the stupidest of the stupid. If he had any notion of what love is, he would wish to discover that as daughter and sister she was perfect in love, and would see therein the proof that she would love him more than anyone else in the realm. What therefore in the case of a man one would regard as a sign of egoism and stupidity, that one is to regard by the help of an exegete as a worthy conception of the Deity.

But how hate them? I will not recall here the human distinction between loving and hating – not because I have much to object to in it (for after all it is passionate), but because it is egoistic and is not in place here. However, if I regard the problem as a paradox, then I understand it, that is, I understand it in such a way as one can understand a paradox. The absolute duty may cause one to do what ethics would forbid, but by no means can it cause the knight of faith to cease to love. This is shown by Abraham. The instant he is ready to sacrifice Isaac the ethical expression for what he does is this: he hates Isaac. But if he really hates Isaac, he can be sure that God does not require this, for Cain and Abraham are not identical. Isaac he must love with his whole soul; when God requires Isaac he must love him if possible even more dearly, and only on this condition can he *sacrifice* him; for in fact it is this love for Isaac which, by its paradoxical opposition to his love for God, makes his act a sacrifice. But the distress and dread in this paradox is that, humanly speaking, he is entirely unable to make himself intelligible. Only at the moment when his act is in absolute contradiction to his feeling is his act a sacrifice, but the reality of his act is the factor by which he belongs to the universal, and in that aspect he is and remains a murderer.

Moreover, the passage in Luke must be understood in such a way as to make it clearly evident that the knight of faith has no higher expression of the universal (i.e. the ethical) by which he can save himself. Thus, for example, if we suppose that the Church requires such a sacrifice of one of its members, we have in this case only a tragic hero. For the idea of the Church is not qualitatively different from that of the State, in so far as the individual comes into it by a simple mediation, and in so far as the individual comes into the paradox he does not reach the idea of the Church; he does not come out of the paradox, but in it he must find either his blessedness or his perdition. Such an ecclesiastical hero expresses in his act the universal, and there will be no one in the Church – not even his father and mother etc. – who fails to understand him. On the other hand, he is not a knight of faith, and he has also a different answer from that of Abraham: he does not say that it is a trial or a temptation in which he is tested.

People commonly refrain from quoting such a text as this in Luke. They are afraid of giving men a free rein, are afraid that the worst will happen as soon as the individual takes it into his head to comport himself as the individual. Moreover, they think that to exist as the individual is the easiest thing of all, and that therefore people have to be compelled to become the universal. I cannot share either this fear or this opinion, and both for the same reason. He who has learned that to exist as the individual is the most terrible thing of all will not be fearful of saying that it is great, but then too he will say this in such a way that his words will scarcely be a snare for the bewildered man, but rather will help him into the universal, even though his words do to some extent make room for the great. The man who does not dare to mention such texts will not dare to mention Abraham either, and his notion that it is easy enough to exist as the individual implies a very suspicious admission with regard to himself; for he who has a real respect for himself and concern for his soul is convinced that the man who lives under his own supervision, alone in the whole world, lives more strictly and more secluded than a maiden in her lady's bower. That there may be some who need compulsion, some who, if they were free-footed, would riot in selfish pleasures like unruly beasts, is doubtless true; but a man must prove precisely that he is not of this number by the fact that he knows how to speak with dread and trembling; and out of reverence for the great one is bound to speak, lest it be forgotten for fear of the ill effect, which surely will fail to eventuate when a man talks in such a way that one knows it for the great, knows its terror – and apart from the terror one does not know the great at all.

Let us consider a little more closely the distress and dread in the paradox of faith. The tragic hero renounces himself in order to express the universal, the knight of faith renounces the universal in order to become the individual. As has been said, everything depends upon how one is placed. He who believes that it is easy enough to be the individual can always be sure that he is not a knight of faith, for vagabonds and roving geniuses are not men of faith. The knight of faith knows, on the other hand, that it is glorious to belong to the universal. He knows that it is beautiful and salutary to be the individual who translates himself into the universal, who edits as it were a pure and elegant edition of himself, as free from errors as possible and which everyone can read. He knows that it is refreshing to become intelligible to oneself in the universal so that he understands it and so that every individual who understands him understands through him in turn the universal, and both rejoice in the security of the universal. He knows that it is beautiful to be born as the individual who has the universal as his home, his friendly abiding-place, which at once welcomes him with open arms when he would tarry in it. But he knows also that higher than this there winds a solitary path, narrow and steep; he knows that it is terrible to be born outside the universal, to walk without meeting a single traveller. He knows very well where he is and how he is related to men. Humanly speaking, he is crazy and cannot make himself intelligible to anyone. And yet it is the mildest expression, to say that he is crazy. If he is not supposed to be that, then he is a hypocrite, and the higher he climbs on this path, the more dreadful a hypocrite he is.

The knight of faith knows that to give up oneself for the universal inspires enthusiasm, and that it requires courage, but he also knows that security is to be found in this, precisely because it is for the universal. He knows that it is glorious to be understood by every noble mind, so glorious that the beholder is ennobled by it, and he feels as if he were bound; he could wish it were this task that had been allotted to him. Thus Abraham could surely have wished now and then that the task were to love Isaac as becomes a father, in a way intelligible to all, memorable throughout all ages; he could wish that the task were to sacrifice Isaac for the universal, that he might incite the fathers to illustrious deeds – and he is almost terrified by the thought that for him such wishes are only temptations and must be dealt with as such, for he knows that it is a solitary path he treads and that he accomplishes nothing for the universal but only himself is tried and examined. Or what did Abraham accomplish for the universal? Let me speak humanly about it, quite humanly. He spent seventy years in getting a son of his old age. What other men get quickly enough and enjoy for a long time he spent seventy years in accomplishing. And why? Because he was tried and put to the test. Is not that crazy? But Abraham believed, and Sarah wavered and got him to take Hagar as a concubine – but therefore he also had to drive her away. He gets Isaac, then he has to be tried again. He knew that it is glorious to express the universal, glorious to live with Isaac. But this is not the task. He knew that it is a kingly thing to sacrifice such a son for the universal, he himself would have found repose in that, and all would have reposed in the commendation of his deed, as a vowel reposes in its consonant,[57] but that is not the task – he is tried. That Roman general who is celebrated by his name of Cunctator[58] checked the foe by procrastination – but what a procrastinator Abraham is in comparison with him! ... yet he did not save the state. This is the content of one hundred and thirty years. Who can bear it? Would not his contemporary age, if we can speak of such a thing, have said of him, "Abraham is eternally procrastinating. Finally he gets a son. That took long enough. Now he wants to sacrifice him. So is he not mad? And if at least he could explain why he wants to do it – but he always says that it is a trial." Nor could Abraham explain more, for his life is like a book placed under a divine attachment and which never becomes *publici juris*.[59]

This is the terrible thing. He who does not see it can always be sure that he is no knight of faith, but he who sees it will not deny that even the most tried of tragic heroes walks with a dancing step compared with the knight of faith, who comes slowly creeping forward. And if he has perceived this and assured himself that he has not courage to understand it, he will at least have a presentiment of the marvellous glory this knight attains in the fact that he becomes God's intimate acquaintance, the Lord's friend, and (to speak quite humanly) that he says "Thou" to God in heaven, whereas even the tragic hero only addresses Him in the third person.

The tragic hero is soon ready and has soon finished the fight, he makes the infinite movement and then is secure in the universal. The knight of faith, on the other hand, is kept sleepless, for he is constantly tried, and every instant there is the possibility of being able to return repentantly to the universal, and this possibility can just as well be a temptation as the truth. He can derive evidence from no man which it is, for with that query he is outside the paradox.

So the knight of faith has first and foremost the requisite passion to concentrate upon a single factor the whole of the ethical which he transgresses, so that he can give himself the assurance that he really loves Isaac with his whole soul.* If he cannot do that, he is in temptation [*Anfechtung*]. In the next place, he has enough passion to make this assurance available in the twinkling of an eye and in such a way that it is as completely valid as it was in the first instance. If he is unable to do this, he can never budge from the spot, for he constantly has to begin all over again. The tragic hero also concentrated in one factor the ethical which he teleologically surpassed, but in this respect he had support in the universal. The knight of faith has only himself alone, and this constitutes the dreadfulness of the situation. Most men live in such a way under an ethical obligation that they can let the sorrow be sufficient for the day, but they never reach this passionate concentration, this energetic consciousness. The universal may in a certain sense help the tragic hero to attain this, but the knight of faith is left all to himself. The hero does the deed and finds repose in the universal, the knight of faith is kept in constant tension. Agamemnon gives up Iphigenia and thereby has found repose in the universal, then he takes the step of sacrificing her. If Agamemnon does not make the infinite movement, if his soul at the decisive instant, instead of having passionate concentration, is absorbed by the common twaddle that he had several daughters and *vielleicht* [perhaps] the *Ausserordentliche* [extraordinary] might occur – then he is of course not a hero but a hospital-case. The hero's concentration Abraham

*I would elucidate yet once more the difference between the collisions which are encountered by the tragic hero and by the knight of faith. The tragic hero assures himself that the ethical obligation [i.e. the lower ethical obligation, which he puts aside for the higher; in the present case, accordingly, it is the obligation to spare his daughter's life] is totally present in him by the fact that he transforms it into a wish. Thus Agamemnon can say, "The proof that I do not offend against my parental duty is that my duty is my only wish." So here we have wish and duty face to face with one another. The fortunate chance in life is that the two correspond, that my wish is my duty and vice versa, and the task of most men in life is precisely to remain within their duty and by their enthusiasm to transform it into their wish. The tragic hero gives up his wish in order to accomplish his duty. For the knight of faith wish and duty are also identical, but he is required to give up both. Therefore when he would resign himself to giving up his wish he does not find repose, for that is after all his duty. If he would remain within his duty and his wish, he is not a knight of faith, for the absolute duty requires precisely that he should give them up. The tragic hero apprehends a higher expression of duty but not an absolute duty.

also has, even though in his case it is far more difficult, since he has no support in the universal; but he makes one more movement by which he concentrates his soul upon the miracle. If Abraham did not do that, he is only an Agamemnon – if in any way it is possible to explain how he can be justified in sacrificing Isaac when thereby no profit accrues to the universal.

Whether the individual is in temptation [*Anfechtung*] or is a knight of faith only the individual can decide. Nevertheless it is possible to construct from the paradox several criteria which he too can understand who is not within the paradox. The true knight of faith is always absolute isolation, the false knight is sectarian. This sectarianism is an attempt to leap away from the narrow path of the paradox and become a tragic hero at a cheap price. The tragic hero expresses the universal and sacrifices himself for it. The sectarian punchinello, instead of that, has a private theatre, i.e. several good friends and comrades who represent the universal just about as well as the beadles in *The Golden Snuffbox*[60] represent justice. The knight of faith, on the contrary, is the paradox, is the individual, absolutely nothing but the individual, without connections or pretensions. This is the terrible thing which the sectarian manikin cannot endure. For instead of learning from this terror that he is not capable of performing the great deed and then plainly admitting it (an act which I cannot but approve, because it is what I do) the manikin thinks that by uniting with several other manikins he will be able to do it. But that is quite out of the question. In the world of spirit no swindling is tolerated. A dozen sectaries join arms with one another, they know nothing whatever of the lonely temptations which await the knight of faith and which he dares not shun precisely because it would be still more dreadful if he were to press forward presumptuously. The sectaries deafen one another by their noise and racket, hold the dread off by their shrieks, and such a hallooing company of sportsmen think they are storming heaven and think they are on the same path as the knight of faith who in the solitude of the universe never hears any human voice but walks alone with his dreadful responsibility.

The knight of faith is obliged to rely upon himself alone, he feels the pain of not being able to make himself intelligible to others, but he feels no vain desire to guide others. The pain is his assurance that he is in the right way, this vain desire he does not know, he is too serious for that. The false knight of faith readily betrays himself by this proficiency in guiding which he has acquired in an instant. He does not comprehend what it is all about, that if another individual is to take the same path, he must become entirely in the same way the individual and have no need of any man's guidance, least of all the guidance of a man who would obtrude himself. At this point men leap aside, they cannot bear the martyrdom of being uncomprehended, and instead of this they choose conveniently enough the worldly admiration of their proficiency. The true knight of faith is a witness, never a teacher, and therein lies his deep humanity, which is worth a good deal more than this silly participation in others' weal and woe which is honored by the name of sympathy, whereas in fact it is nothing but vanity. He who would only be a witness thereby avows that no man, not even the lowliest, needs another man's sympathy or should be abased that another may be exalted. But since he did not win what he won at a cheap price, neither does he sell it out at a cheap price, he is not petty enough to take men's admiration and give them in return his silent contempt, he knows that what is truly great is equally accessible to all.

Either there is an absolute duty toward God, and if so it is the paradox here described, that the individual as the individual is higher than the universal and as the individual stands in an absolute relation to the absolute/or else faith never existed, because it has always existed, or, to put it differently, Abraham is lost, or one must explain the passage in the fourteenth chapter of Luke as did that tasteful exegete, and explain in the same way the corresponding passages and similar ones.[61]

PROBLEM III

Was Abraham ethically defensible in keeping silent about his purpose before Sarah, before Eleazar, before Isaac?

The ethical as such is the universal, again, as the universal it is the manifest, the revealed. The individual regarded as he is immediately, that is, as a physical and psychical being, is the hidden, the concealed. So his ethical task is to develop out of this concealment and to reveal himself in the universal. Hence whenever he wills to remain in concealment he sins and lies in temptation [*Anfechtung*], out of which he can come only by revealing himself.

With this we are back again at the same point. If there is not a concealment which has its ground in the fact that the individual as the individual is higher than the universal, then Abraham's conduct is indefensible, for he paid no heed to the intermediate ethical determinants. If on the other hand there is such a concealment, we are in the presence of the paradox which cannot be mediated inasmuch as it rests upon the consideration that the individual as the individual is higher than the universal, but it is the universal precisely which is mediation. The Hegelian philosophy holds that there is no justified concealment, no justified incommensurability. So it is self-consistent when it requires revelation, but it is not warranted in regarding Abraham as the father of faith and in talking about faith. For faith is not the first immediacy but a subsequent immediacy. The first immediacy is the aesthetical, and about this the Hegelian philosophy may be in the right. But faith is not the aesthetical – or else faith has never existed because it has always existed.

It will be best to regard the whole matter from a purely aesthetical point of view, and with that intent to embark upon an aesthetic deliberation, to which I beg the reader to abandon himself completely for the moment, while I, to contribute my share, will modify my presentation in conformity with the subject. The category I would consider a little more closely is the interesting, a category which especially in our age (precisely because our age lives *in discrimine rerum*) [at a turning-point in history] has acquired great importance, for it is properly the category of the turning-point. Therefore we, after having loved this category *pro virili* [with all our power], should not scorn it as some do because we have outgrown it, but neither should we be too greedy to attain it, for certain it is that to be interesting or to have an interesting life is not a task for industrial art but a fateful privilege, which like every privilege in the world of spirit is bought only by deep pain. Thus, for example, Socrates was the most interesting man that ever lived, his life the most interesting that has been recorded, but this existence was allotted to him by the Deity, and in so far as he himself had to acquire it he was not unacquainted with trouble and pain. To take such a life in vain does not beseem a man who takes life seriously, and yet it is not rare to see in our age examples of such an endeavor. Moreover the interesting is a border-category, a boundary between aesthetics and ethics. For this reason our deliberation must constantly glance over into the field of ethics, while in order to be able to acquire significance it must grasp the problem with aesthetic intensity and concupiscence. With such matters ethics seldom deals in our age. The reason is supposed to be that there is no appropriate place for it in the System. Then surely one might do it in a monograph, and moreover, if one would not do it prolixly, one might do it briefly and yet attain the same end – if, that is to say, a man has the predicate in his power, for one or two predicates can betray a whole world. Might there not be some place in the System for a little word like the predicate?

In his immortal *Poetics* (Chapter 11) Aristotle says,[62] *δύο μεν οὖν τοῦ μύθου μέρη περὶ ταῦτ' ἐστί, περιπέτεια καὶ ἀναγνώρισις*. I am of course concerned here only with the second factor, *ἀναγνώρισις*, recognition. Where there can be question of a recognition there is implied *eo ipso* a previous concealment. So just as recognition is the relieving, the relaxing factor in the dramatic life, so is concealment the factor of tension. What Aristotle has to say in the same chapter about the merits of tragedy which are variously appraised in proportion as *περιπέτεια* and *ἀναγνώρισις* impinge[63] upon one another, and also what he says about the "individual" and the "double recognition," I cannot take into consideration here, although by its inwardness and quiet concentration what he says is peculiarly tempting to one who is weary of the superficial omniscience of encyclopedic scholars. A more general observation may be appropriate here. In Greek tragedy concealment (and consequently recognition) is an epic survival grounded upon a fate in which the dramatic action disappears from view and from which it derives its obscure and enigmatic origin. Hence it is that the effect produced by a Greek tragedy is like the impression of a marble statue which lacks the power of the eye. Greek tragedy is blind. Hence a certain abstraction is necessary in order to appreciate it properly. A son[64] murders his father, but only afterwards does he learn that it was his father. A sister[65] wants to sacrifice her brother, but at the decisive moment she learns who he is. This dramatic motive is not so apt to interest our *reflective* age. Modern drama has given up fate, has emancipated itself dramatically, sees with its eyes, scrutinizes itself, resolves fate in its dramatic consciousness. Concealment and revelation are in this case the hero's free act for which he is responsible.

Recognition and concealment are also present as an essential element in modern drama. To adduce examples of this would be too prolix. I am courteous enough to assume that everybody in our age, which is so aesthetically wanton, so potent and so enflamed that the act of conception comes as easy to it as to the partridge hen, which, according to Aristotle's affirmation,[66] needs only to hear the voice of the cock or the sound of its flight overhead – I assume that everyone, merely upon hearing the word "concealment," will be able to shake half a score of romances and comedies out of his sleeve. Wherefore I express myself briefly and so will throw out at once a general observation. In case one who plays hide and seek (and thereby introduces into the play the dramatic ferment) hides something nonsensical, we get a comedy; if on the other hand he stands in relation to the idea, he may come near being a tragic hero. I give here merely an example of the comic. A man rouges his face and wears a periwig. The same man is eager to try his fortune with the fair sex, he is perfectly sure of conquering by the aid of the rouge and the periwig which make him absolutely irresistible. He captures a girl and is at the acme of happiness. Now comes the gist of the matter: if he is able to admit this embellishment, he does not lose all of his infatuating power; when he reveals himself as a plain ordinary man, and bald at that, he does not thereby lose the loved one. – Concealment is his free act, for which aesthetics also holds him responsible. This science is no friend of bald hypocrites, it abandons him to the mercy of laughter. This must suffice as a mere hint of what I mean – the comical cannot be a subject of interest for this investigation.

It is incumbent upon me to examine dialectically the part played by concealment in aesthetics and ethics, for the point is to show the absolute difference between the aesthetic concealment and the paradox.

A couple of examples. A girl is secretly in love with a man, although they have not definitely avowed their love to one another. Her parents compel her to marry another (there may be moreover a consideration of filial piety which determines her), she obeys her parents, she conceals her love, "so as not to make the other unhappy, and no one will ever know what she suffers." – A young man is able by a single word to get possession of the object of his longings and his restless dreams. This little word, however, will compromise, yea, perhaps (who knows?) bring to ruin a whole family, he resolves magnanimously to remain in his concealment, "the girl shall never get to know it, so that she may perhaps become happy by giving her hand to another." What a pity that these two persons, both of whom were concealed from their respective beloveds, were also concealed from one another, otherwise a remarkable higher unity might have been brought about. – Their concealment is a free act, for which they are responsible also to aesthetics. Aesthetics, however, is a courteous and sentimental science which knows of more expedients than a pawnbroker. So what does it do? It makes everything possible for the lovers. By the help of a chance the partners to the projected marriage get a hint of the magnanimous resolution of the other part, it comes to an explanation, they get one another and at the same time attain rank with real heroes. For in spite of the fact that they did not even get time to sleep over their resolution, aesthetics treats them nevertheless as if they had courageously fought for their resolution during many years. For aesthetics does not trouble itself greatly about time, whether in jest or seriousness time flies equally fast for it.

But ethics knows nothing about that chance or about that sentimentality, nor has it so speedy a concept of time. Thereby the matter receives a different aspect. It is no good arguing with ethics, for it has pure categories. It does not appeal to experience, which of all ludicrous things is the most ludicrous, and which so far from making a man wise rather makes him mad if he knows nothing higher than this. Ethics has in its possession no chance, and so matters do not come to an explanation, it does not jest with dignities, it lays a prodigious responsibility upon the shoulders of the puny hero, it denounces as presumption his wanting to play providence by his actions, but it also denounces him for wanting to do it by his suffering. It bids a man believe in reality and have courage to fight against all the afflictions of reality, and still more against the bloodless sufferings he has assumed on his own responsibility. It warns against believing the calculations of the understanding, which are more perfidious than the oracles of ancient times. It warns against every untimely magnanimity. Let reality decide – then is the time to show courage, but then ethics itself offers all possible assistance. If, however, there was something deeper which moved in these two, if there was seriousness to see the task, seriousness to commence it, then something will come of them; but ethics cannot help, it is offended, for they keep a secret from it, a secret they hold at their own peril.

So aesthetics required concealment and rewarded it, ethics required revelation and punished concealment.

At times, however, even aesthetics requires revelation. When the hero ensnared in the aesthetic illusion thinks by his silence to save another man, then it requires silence and rewards it. On the other hand, when the hero by his action intervenes disturbingly in another man's life, then it requires revelation. I am now on the subject of the tragic hero. I would consider for a moment Euripides' *Iphigenia in Aulis*. Agamemnon must sacrifice Iphigenia. Now aesthetics requires silence of Agamemnon inasmuch as it would be unworthy of the hero to seek comfort from any other man, and out of solicitude for the women too he ought to conceal this from them as long as possible. On the other hand, the hero, precisely in order to be a hero, must be tried by dreadful temptations which the tears of Clytemnestra and Iphigenia provide for him. What does aesthetics do? It has an expedient, it has in readiness an old servant who reveals everything to Clytemnestra. Then all is as it should be.

Ethics, however, has at hand no chance and no old servant. The aesthetical idea contradicts itself as soon as it must be carried out in reality. Hence ethics requires revelation. The tragic hero displays his ethical courage precisely by the fact that it is he who, without being ensnared in any aesthetic illusion, himself announces to Iphigenia her fate. If the tragic hero does this, then he is the beloved son of ethics in whom it is well pleased. If he keeps silent, it may be because he thinks thereby to make it easier for others, but it may also be because thereby he makes it easier for himself. However, he knows that he is not influenced by this latter motive. If he keeps silent, he assumes as the individual a serious responsibility inasmuch as he ignores an argument which may come from without. As a tragic hero he cannot do this, for ethics loves him precisely because he constantly expresses the universal. His heroic action demands courage, but it belongs to this courage that he shall shun no argumentation. Now it is certain that tears are a dreadful *argumentum ad hominem*, and doubtless there are those who are moved by nothing yet are touched by tears. In the play Iphigenia had leave to weep, really she ought to have been allowed like Jephthah's daughter two months for weeping, not in solitude but at her father's feet, allowed to employ all her art "which is but tears," and to twine about his knees instead of presenting the olive branch of the suppliant.

Aesthetics required revelation but helped itself out by a chance; ethics required revelation and found in the tragic hero its satisfaction.

In spite of the severity with which ethics requires revelation, it cannot be denied that secrecy and silence really make a man great precisely because they are characteristics of inwardness. When Amor leaves Psyche he says to her, "Thou shalt give birth to a child which will be a divine infant if thou dost keep silence, but a human being if thou dost reveal the secret." The tragic hero who is the favorite of ethics is the purely human, and him I can understand, and all he does is in the light of the revealed. If I go further, then I stumble upon the paradox, either the divine or the demoniac, for silence is both. Silence is the snare of the demon, and the more one keeps silent, the more terrifying the demon becomes; but silence is also the mutual understanding between the Deity and the individual.

Before going on to the story of Abraham, however, I would call before the curtain several poetic personages. By the power of dialectic I keep them upon tiptoe, and by wielding over them the scourge of despair I shall surely keep them from standing still, in order that in their dread they may reveal one thing and another.*

In his *Poetics*[67] Aristotle relates a story of a political disturbance at Delphi which was provoked by a question of marriage. *The bridegroom, when the augurs*[68] *foretell to him that a misfortune would follow his marriage, suddenly changes his plan at the decisive moment when he comes to fetch the bride* – he will not celebrate the wedding. I have no need of more.† In Delphi this event hardly passed

*These movements and attitudes might well be a subject for further aesthetic treatment. However, I leave it undecided to what extent faith and the whole life of faith might be a fit subject for such treatment. Only, because it is always a joy to me to thank him to whom I am indebted, I would thank Lessing for some hints of a Christian drama which is found in his *Hamburgische Dramaturgie*.[69] He, however, fixed his glance upon the purely divine side of the Christian life (the consummated victory) and hence he had misgivings; perhaps he would have expressed a different judgment if he had paid more attention to the purely human side (*theologia viatorum*).[70] Doubtless what he says is very brief, in part evasive, but since I am always glad to have the company of Lessing, I seize it at once. Lessing was not merely one of the most comprehensive minds Germany has had, he not only was possessed of rare exactitude in his learning (for which reason one can securely rely upon him and upon his autopsy without fear of being duped by inaccurate quotations which can be traced nowhere, by half-understood phrases which are drawn from untrustworthy compendiums, or to be disoriented by a foolish trumpeting of novelties which the ancients have expounded far better) but he possessed at the same time an exceedingly uncommon gift of explaining what he himself had understood. There he stopped. In our age people go further and explain more than they have understood.

†According to Aristotle the historic catastrophe was as follows. To avenge themselves the family of the bride introduced a temple-vessel among his household goods, and he is sentenced as a temple-robber. This, however, is of no consequence, for the question is not whether the family is shrewd or stupid in

without tears; if a poet were to have adopted it as his theme, he might have dared to count very surely upon sympathy. Is it not dreadful that love, which in human life often enough was cast into exile, is now deprived of the support of heaven? Is not the old proverb that "marriages are made in heaven" here put to shame? Usually it is all the afflictions and difficulties of the finite which like evil spirits separate the lovers, but love has heaven on its side, and therefore this holy alliance overcomes all enemies. In this case it is heaven itself which separates what heaven itself has joined together. And who would have guessed such a thing? The young bride least of all. Only a moment before she was sitting in her chamber in all her beauty, and the lovely maidens had conscientiously adorned her so that they could justify before all the world what they had done, so that they not merely derived joy from it but envy, yea, joy for the fact that it was not possible for them to become more envious, because it was not possible for her to become more beautiful. She sat alone in her chamber and was transformed from beauty unto beauty, for every means was employed that feminine art was capable of to adorn worthily the worthy. But there still was lacking something which the young maidens had not dreamed of: a veil finer, lighter and yet more impenetrable than that in which the young maidens had enveloped her, a bridal dress which no young maiden knew of or could help her to obtain, yea, even the bride herself did not know how to obtain it. It was an invisible, a friendly power, taking pleasure in adorning a bride, which enveloped her in it without her knowledge; for she saw only how the bridegroom passed by and went up to the temple. She saw the door shut behind him, and she became even more calm and blissful, for she only knew that he now belonged to her more than ever. The door of the temple opened, he stepped out, but maidenly she cast down her eyes and therefore did not see that his countenance was troubled, but he saw that heaven was jealous of the bride's loveliness and of his good fortune. The door

---

taking revenge. The family has an ideal significance only in so far as it is drawn into the dialectic of the hero. Besides it is fateful enough that he, when he would shun danger by not marrying, plunges into it, and also that his life comes into contact with the divine in a double way: first by the saying of the augurs, and then by being condemned for sacrilege.

of the temple opened, and the young maidens saw the bridegroom step out, but they did not see that his countenance was troubled, they were busy fetching the bride. Then forth she stepped in all her maidenly modesty and yet like a queen surrounded by her maids of honor, who bowed before her as the young maiden always bows before a bride. Thus she stood at the head of her lovely band and waited – it was only an instant, for the temple was near at hand – and the bridegroom came ... but he passed by her door.

But here I break off – I am not a poet, I go about things only dialectically. It must be remembered first of all that it is at the decisive instant the hero gets this elucidation, so he is pure and blameless, has not lightmindedly tied himself to the fiancée. In the next place, he has a divine utterance for him, or rather against him,[71] he is therefore not guided like those puny lovers by his own conceit. Moreover, it goes without saying that this utterance makes him just as unhappy as the bride, yea, a little more so, since he after all is the occasion of her unhappiness. It is true enough that the augurs only foretold a misfortune to *him*, but the question is whether this misfortune is not of such a sort that in injuring him it would also affect injuriously their conjugal happiness. What then is he to do? (1) Shall he preserve silence and celebrate the wedding? – with the thought that "perhaps the misfortune will not come at once, at any rate I have upheld love and have not feared to make myself unhappy. But keep silent I must, for otherwise even the short moment is wasted." This seems plausible, but it is not so by any means, for in doing this he has insulted the girl. He has in a way made the girl guilty by his silence, for in case she had known the truth she never would have consented to such a union. So in the hour of need he would not only have to bear the misfortune but also the responsibility for having kept silent and her justified indignation that he had kept silent. Or (2) shall he keep silent and give up celebrating the wedding? In this case he must embroil himself in a mystification by which he reduces himself to naught in relation to her. Aesthetics would perhaps approve of this. The catastrophe might then be fashioned like that of the real story, except that at the last instant an explanation would be forthcoming – however, that would be after it was all over, since aesthetically viewed it is a necessity to let him die . . . unless this science should see its way to annul the fateful prophecy. Still, this behavior, magnanimous as it is, implies an offense against the girl and against the reality of her love. Or (3) shall he speak? One of course must not forget that our hero is a little too poetical for us to suppose that to sign away his love might not have for him a significance very different from the result of an unsuccessful business speculation. If he speaks, the whole thing becomes a story of unhappy love in the style of Axel and Valborg.* This is a pair which heaven itself separates.[72] However, in the present case the separation is to be conceived somewhat differently since it results at the same time from the free act of the individuals. What is so very difficult in the dialectic of this case is that the misfortune is to fall only upon him. So the two lovers do not find like Axel and Valborg a common expression for their suffering, inasmuch as heaven levels its decree equally against Axel and Valborg because they are equally near of kin to one another. If this were the case here, a way out would be thinkable. For since heaven does not employ any visible power to separate them but leaves this to them, it is

*Moreover, from this point one might conduct the dialectical movements in another direction. Heaven foretells a misfortune consequent upon his marriage, so in fact he might give up the wedding but not for this reason give up the girl, rather live with her in a romantic union which for the lovers would be more than satisfactory. This implies, however, an offense against the girl because in his love for her he does not express the universal. However, this would be a theme both for a poet and for an ethicist who would defend marriage. On the whole, if poetry were to pay attention to the religious and to the inwardness of personalities, it would find themes of far greater importance than those with which it now busies itself. In poetry one hears again and again this story: a man is bound to a girl whom he once loved – or perhaps never sincerely loved, for now he has seen another girl who is the ideal. A man makes a mistake in life, it was in the right street but it was in the wrong house, for opposite, on the second floor, dwells the ideal – this people think a theme for poetry. A lover has made a mistake, he saw his fiancée by lamplight and thought she had dark hair, but, lo, on closer inspection she is blonde – but her sister, she is the ideal! This they think is a theme for poetry! My opinion is that every such man is a lout who may be intolerable enough in real life but ought instantly to be hissed off the stage when he would give himself airs in poetry. Only passion against passion provides a poetic collision, not the rumpus of these particulars within the same passion. If, for example, a girl in the Middle Ages, after having fallen in love, convinces herself that all earthly love is a sin and prefers a heavenly, here is a poetic collision, and the girl is poetic, for her life is in the idea.

thinkable that they might resolve between them to defy heaven and its misfortune too.

Ethics, however, will require him to speak. His heroism then is essentially to be found in the fact that he gives up aesthetic magnanimity, which in this case, however, could not easily be thought to have any admixture of the vanity which consists in being hidden, for it must indeed be clear to him that he makes the girl unhappy. The reality of this heroism depends, however, upon the fact that he had had his opportunity [for a genuine love] and annulled it; for if such heroism could be acquired without this, we should have plenty of heroes in our age, in our age which has attained an unparalleled proficiency in forgery and does the highest things by leaping over the intermediate steps.

But then why this sketch, since I get no further after all than the tragic hero? Well, because it is at least possible that it might throw light upon the paradox. Everything depends upon how this man stands related to the utterance of the augurs which is in one way or another decisive for his life. Is this utterance *publici juris*, or is it a *privatissimum*? The scene is laid in Greece, the utterance of the augur is intelligible to all. I do not mean merely that the ordinary man is able to understand its content lexically, but that the ordinary man can understand that an augur announces to the individual the decision of heaven. So the utterance of the augur is not intelligible only to the hero but to all, and no private relationship to the deity results from it. Do what he will, that which is foretold will come to pass, and neither by doing nor by leaving undone does he come into closer relationship with the deity, or become either the object of its grace or of its wrath. The result foretold is a thing which any ordinary man will be just as well able as the hero to understand, and there is no secret writing which is legible to the hero only. Inasmuch as he would speak, he can do so perfectly well, for he is able to make himself intelligible; inasmuch as he would keep silent, it is because by virtue of being the individual he would be higher than the universal, would delude himself with all sorts of fantastic notions about how she will soon forget the sorrow, etc. On the other hand, in case the will of heaven had not been announced to him by an augur, in case it had come to his knowledge in an entirely private way, in case it had put itself into an entirely private relationship with him, then we encounter the paradox (supposing there is such a thing – for my reflection takes the form of a dilemma), then he could not speak, however much he might wish to.[73] He did not then enjoy himself in the silence but suffered pain – but this precisely was to him the assurance that he was justified. So the reason for his silence is not that he as the individual would place himself in an absolute relation to the *universal*, but that he as the individual was placed in an absolute relation to the *absolute*. In this then he would also be able to find repose (as well as I am able to figure it to myself), whereas his magnanimous silence would constantly have been disquieted by the requirements of the ethical. It is very much to be desired that aesthetics would for once essay to begin at the point where for so many years it has ended, with the illusory magnanimity. Once it were to do this it would work directly in the interest of the religious, for religion is the only power which can deliver the aesthetical out of its conflict with the ethical. Queen Elizabeth[74] sacrificed to the State her love for Essex by signing his death-warrant. This was a heroic act, even if there was involved a little personal grievance for the fact that he had not sent her the ring. He had in fact sent it, as we know, but it was kept back by the malice of a lady of the court. Elizabeth received intelligence of this (so it is related, *ni fallor*), thereupon she sat for ten days with one finger in her mouth and bit it without saying a word, and thereupon she died. This would be a theme for a poet who knew how to wrench the mouth open – without this condition it is at the most serviceable to a conductor of the ballet, with whom in our time the poet too often confuses himself.

I will follow this with a sketch which involves the demoniacal. The legend of *Agnes and the Merman* will serve my purpose. The merman is a seducer who shoots up from his hiding-place in the abyss, with wild lust grasps and breaks the innocent flower which stood in all its grace on the seashore and pensively inclined its head to listen to the howling of the ocean. This is what the poets hitherto have meant by it. Let us make an alteration. The merman was a seducer. He had called to Agnes, had by his smooth speech enticed from her the hidden sentiments, she has found in the merman what she sought, what she was gazing after down at the bottom of the sea. Agnes would like to follow him. The merman has lifted her up in his arms, Agnes twines about his neck, with her whole soul she trustingly abandons herself to the stronger one; he already stands upon the brink, he leans over the sea, about to plunge into it with his prey – then Agnes looks at him once more, not timidly, not doubtingly, not proud of her good fortune, not intoxicated by pleasure, but with absolute faith in him, with absolute humility, like the lowly flower she conceived herself to be; by this look she entrusts to him with absolute confidence her whole fate.[75] And, behold, the sea roars no more, its voice is mute, nature's passion which is the merman's strength leaves him in the lurch, a dead calm ensues – and still Agnes continues to look at him thus. Then the merman collapses, he is not able to resist the power of innocence, his native element is unfaithful to him, he cannot seduce Agnes. He leads her back again, he explains to her that he only wanted to show her how beautiful the sea is when it is calm, and Agnes believes him. – Then he turns back alone and the sea rages, but despair in the merman rages more wildly. He is able to seduce Agnes, he is able to seduce a hundred Agneses, he is able to infatuate every girl – but Agnes has conquered, and the merman has lost her. Only as a prey can she become his, he cannot belong faithfully to any girl, for in fact he is only a merman. Here I have taken the liberty of making a little alteration* in the merman; substantially I have also altered Agnes a little, for in the legend Agnes is not entirely without fault – and generally speaking it is nonsense and coquetry and an

*One might also treat this legend in another way. The merman does not want to seduce Agnes, although previously he had seduced many. He is no longer a merman, or, if one so will, he is a miserable merman who already has long been sitting on the floor of the sea and sorrowing. However, he knows (as the legend in fact teaches),[76] that he can be delivered by the love of an innocent girl. But he has a bad conscience with respect to girls and does not dare to approach them. Then he sees Agnes. Already many a time when he was hidden in the reeds he had seen her walking on the shore.[77] Her beauty, her quiet occupation with herself, fixes his attention upon her; but only sadness prevails in his soul, no wild desire stirs in it. And so when the merman mingles his sighs with the soughing of the reeds she turns her ear thither, and then stands still and falls to dreaming, more charming than any woman and yet beautiful as a liberating angel which

insult to the feminine sex to imagine a case of seduction where the girl is not the least bit to blame. In the legend Agnes is (to modernize my expression a little) a woman who craves "the interesting," and every such woman can always be sure that there is a merman in the offing, for with half an eye mermen discover the like of that and steer for it like a shark after its prey. It is therefore very stupid to suppose (or is it a rumor which a merman has spread abroad?) that the so-called culture protects a girl against seduction. No, existence is more righteous and fair: there is only one protection, and that is innocence.

We will now bestow upon the merman a human consciousness and suppose that the fact of his being a merman indicates a human pre-existence in the consequences of which his life is entangled. There is nothing to prevent him from becoming a hero, for the step he now takes is one of reconciliation. He is saved by Agnes, the seducer is crushed, he has bowed to the power of innocence, he can never seduce again. But at the same instant two powers are striving for possession of him: repentance; and Agnes and repentance. If repentance alone takes possession of him, then he is hidden; if Agnes and repentance take possession of him, then he is revealed.

Now in case repentance grips the merman and he remains concealed, he has clearly made Agnes unhappy, for Agnes loved him in all her innocence, she believed that at the instant when even to her he seemed changed, however well he hid it, he was telling the truth in saying that he only wanted to show her the beautiful calmness of the sea. However, with respect to passion the merman himself becomes still more unhappy, for he loved Agnes with a multiplicity of passions and had besides a new guilt

---

inspires the merman with confidence. The merman plucks up courage, he approaches Agnes, he wins her love, he hopes for his deliverance. But Agnes was no quiet maiden, she was fond of the roar of the sea, and the sad sighing beside the inland lake pleased her only because then she seethed more strongly within. She would be off and away, she would rush wildly out into the infinite with the merman whom she loved – so she incites the merman. She disdained his humility, now pride awakens. And the sea roars and the waves foam and the merman embraces Agnes and plunges with her into the deep. Never had he been so wild, never so full of desire, for he had hoped by this girl to find deliverance. He soon became tired of Agnes, yet no one ever found her corpse, for she became a mermaid who tempted men by her songs.

to bear. The demoniacal element in repentance will now explain to him that this is precisely his punishment [for the faults of his pre-existent state], and that the more it tortures him the better.

If he abandons himself to this demoniacal influence, he then perhaps makes still another attempt to save Agnes, in such a way as one can, in a certain sense, save a person by means of the evil. He knows that Agnes loves him. If he could wrest from Agnes this love, then in a way she is saved. But how? The merman has too much sense to depend upon the notion that an open-hearted confession would awaken her disgust. He will therefore try perhaps to incite in her all dark passions, will scorn her, mock her, hold up her love to ridicule, if possible he will stir up her pride. He will not spare himself any torment; for this is the profound contradiction in the demoniacal, and in a certain sense there dwells infinitely more good in a demoniac than in a trivial person. The more selfish Agnes is, the easier the deceit will prove for him (for it is only very inexperienced people who suppose that it is easy to deceive innocence; existence is very profound, and it is in fact the easiest thing for the shrewd to fool the shrewd) – but all the more terrible will be the merman's sufferings. The more cunningly his deceit is planned, the less will Agnes bashfully hide from him her suffering; she will resort to every means, nor will they be without effect – not to shake his resolution, I mean, but to torture him.

So by help of the demoniacal the merman desires to be the individual who as the individual is higher than the universal. The demoniacal has the same characteristic as the divine inasmuch as the individual can enter into an absolute relation to it. This is the analogy, the counterpart, to that paradox of which we are talking. It has therefore a certain resemblance which may deceive one. Thus the merman has apparently the proof that his silence is justified for the fact that by it he suffers all his pain. However, there is no doubt that he can talk. He can thus become a tragic hero, to my mind a grandiose tragic hero, if he talks. Some, perhaps, will only understand wherein this is grandiose.*

*Aesthetics sometimes treats a similar subject with its customary coquetry. The merman is saved by Agnes, and the whole thing ends in a happy marriage. A happy marriage! That's easy enough. On the other hand, if ethics were to

He will then be able to wrest from his mind every self-deceit about his being able to make Agnes happy by his trick, he will have courage, humanly speaking, to crush Agnes. Here I would make in conclusion only one psychological observation. The more selfishly Agnes has been developed, the more dazzling will the self-deception be, indeed it is not inconceivable that in reality it might come to pass that a merman by his demoniac shrewdness has, humanly speaking, not only saved an Agnes but brought something extraordinary out of her; for a demon knows how to torture powers out of even the weakest person, and in his way he may have the best intentions toward a human being.

The merman stands at the dialectical turning-point. If he is delivered out of the demoniacal into repentance there are two paths open to him. He may hold back, remain in his concealment, but not rely upon his shrewdness. He does not come as the individual into an absolute relationship with the demoniacal but finds repose in the counter-paradox that the deity will save Agnes. (So it is the Middle Ages would perform the movement, for according to its conception the merman is absolutely dedicated to the cloister.) Or else he may be saved along with Agnes. Now this is not to be understood to mean that by the love of Agnes for him he might be saved from being henceforth a deceiver (this is the aesthetic way of performing a rescue, which always goes around the main point, which is the continuity of the merman's life); for so far as that goes he is already saved, he is saved inasmuch as he becomes revealed. Then he marries Agnes. But still he must have recourse to the paradox. For when the individual by his guilt has gone outside the universal he can return to it only by virtue of having come as the individual into

deliver the address at the wedding service, it would be quite another thing, I imagine. Aesthetics throws the cloak of love over the merman, and so everything is forgotten. It is also careless enough to suppose that at a wedding things go as they do at an auction where everything is sold in the state it is in when the hammer falls. All it cares for is that the lovers get one another, it doesn't trouble about the rest. If only it could see what happens afterwards – but for that it has no time, it is at once in full swing with the business of clapping together a new pair of lovers. Aesthetics is the most faithless of all sciences. Everyone who has deeply loved it becomes in a certain sense unhappy, but he who has never loved it is and remains a pecus.

an absolute relationship with the absolute. Here I will make an observation by which I say more than was said at any point in the foregoing discussion.* Sin is not the first immediacy, sin is a later immediacy. By sin the individual is already higher (in the direction of the demoniacal paradox) than the universal, because it is a contradiction on the part of the universal to impose itself upon a man who lacks the *conditio sine qua non.* If philosophy among other vagaries were also to have the notion that it could occur to a man to act in accordance with its teaching, one might make out of that a queer comedy. An ethics which disregards sin is a perfectly idle science; but if it asserts sin, it is *eo ipso* well beyond itself. Philosophy teaches that the immediate must be annulled [*aufgehoben*]. That is true enough; but what is not true in this is that sin is as a matter of course the immediate, for that is no more true than that faith as a matter of course is the immediate.

As long as I move in these spheres everything goes smoothly, but what is said here does not by any means explain Abraham; for it was not by sin Abraham became the individual, on the contrary, he was a righteous man, he is God's elect. So the analogy to Abraham will not appear until after the individual has been brought to the point of being able to accomplish the universal, and then the paradox repeats itself.

The movements of the merman I can understand, whereas I cannot understand Abraham; for it is precisely through the paradox that the merman comes to the point of realizing the universal. For if he remains hidden and initiates himself into all the torments of repentance, then he becomes a demon and as such is brought to naught. If he remains concealed but does not think cunningly that being himself tormented in the bondage of repentance he could work Agnes loose, then he finds peace indeed but is lost for this world. If he becomes revealed and allows himself to be saved by Agnes, then he is the greatest man I

*In the foregoing discussion I have intentionally refrained from any consideration of sin and its reality. The whole discussion points to Abraham, and him I can still approach by immediate categories – in so far, that is to say, as I am able to understand him. As soon as sin makes its appearance ethics comes to grief precisely upon repentance; for repentance is the highest ethical expression, but precisely as such it is the deepest ethical self-contradiction.

can picture to myself; for it is only the aesthetic writer who thinks lightmindedly that he extols the power of love by letting the lost man be loved by an innocent girl and thereby saved, it is only the aesthetic writer who sees amiss and believes that the girl is the heroine, instead of the man being the hero. So the merman cannot belong to Agnes unless, after having made the infinite movement, the movement of repentance, he makes still one more movement by virtue of the absurd. By his own strength he can make the movement of repentance, but for that he uses up absolutely all his strength and hence he cannot by his own strength return and grasp reality. If a man has not enough passion to make either the one movement or the other, if he loiters through life, repenting a little, and thinks that the rest will take care of itself, he has once and for all renounced the effort to live in the idea – and then he can very easily reach and help others to reach the highest attainments, i.e. delude himself and others with the notion that in the world of spirit everything goes as in a well-known game of cards where everything depends on haphazard. One can therefore divert oneself by reflecting how strange it is that precisely in our age when everyone is able to accomplish the highest things doubt about the immortality of the soul could be so widespread, for the man who has really made even so much as the movement of infinity is hardly a doubter. The conclusions of passion are the only reliable ones, that is, the only convincing conclusions. Fortunately existence is in this instance more kindly and more faithful than the wise maintain, for it excludes no man, not even the lowliest, it fools no one, for in the world of spirit only he is fooled who fools himself.

It is the opinion of all, and so far as I dare permit myself to pass judgment it is also my opinion, that it is not the highest thing to enter the monastery; but for all that it is by no means my opinion that in our age when nobody enters the monastery everybody is greater than the deep and earnest souls who found repose in a monastery. How many are there in our age who have passion enough to think this thought and then to judge themselves honestly? This mere thought of taking time upon one's conscience, of giving it time to explore with its sleepless vigilance every secret thought, with such effect that, if every instant one does not make the movement by virtue of the highest and holiest there is in a man, one is able with dread and horror to discover* and by dread itself, if in no other way, to lure forth the obscure *libido*[78] which is concealed after all in every human life, whereas on the contrary when one lives in society with others one so easily forgets, is let off so easily, is sustained in so many ways, gets opportunity to start afresh – this mere thought, conceived with proper respect, I would suppose, must chasten many an individual in our age which imagines it has already reached the highest attainment. But about this people concern themselves very little in our age which has reached the highest attainment, whereas in truth no age has so fallen victim to the comic as this has, and it is incomprehensible that this age has not already by a *generatio aequivoca* [breeding without mating] given birth to its hero, the demon who would remorselessly produce the dreadful spectacle of making the whole age laugh and making it forget that it was laughing at itself. Or what is existence for but to be laughed at if men in their twenties have already attained the utmost? And for all that, what loftier emotion has the age found since men gave up entering the monastery? Is it not a pitiable prudence, shrewdness, faintheartedness, it has found, which sits in high places and cravenly makes men believe they have accomplished the greatest things and insidiously withholds them from attempting to do even the lesser things? The man who has performed the cloister-movement has only one movement more to make, that is, the movement of the absurd. How many in our age understand what the absurd is? How many of our contemporaries so live that they have renounced all or have gained all? How many are even so honest with themselves that they know what they can do and what they cannot? And is it not true that in so far as one finds such people one finds them rather among the less cultured and in part among women? The age in a kind of clairvoyance reveals its weak point, as a demoniac always reveals himself without understanding himself, for over and over again

*People do not believe this in our serious age, and yet it is remarkable that even in paganism, more easy-going and less given to reflection, the two outstanding representatives of the Greek *γνῶθι σαυτόν* [know thyself] as a conception of existence intimated each in his way that by delving deep into oneself one would first of all discover the disposition to evil. I surely do not need to say that I am thinking of Pythagoras and Socrates.

it is demanding the comic. If it really were this the age needed, the theater might perhaps need a new play in which it was made a subject of laughter that a person died of love – or would it not rather be salutary for this age if such a thing were to happen among us, if the age were to witness such an occurrence, in order that for once it might acquire courage to believe in the power of spirit, courage to stop quenching cravenly the better impulses in oneself and quenching enviously the better impulses in others ... by laughter? Does the age really need a ridiculous exhibition by a religious enthusiast in order to get something to laugh at, or does it not need rather that such an enthusiastic figure should remind it of that which has been forgotten?

If one would like to have a story written on a similar theme but more touching for the fact that the passion of repentance was not awakened, one might use to this effect a tale which is narrated in the book of Tobit. The young Tobias wanted to marry Sarah the daughter of Raguel and Edna. But a sad fatality hung over this young girl. She had been given to seven husbands, all of whom had perished in the bride-chamber. With a view to my plan this feature is a blemish in the narrative, for almost irresistibly a comic effect is produced by the thought of seven fruitless attempts to get married notwithstanding she was very near to it – just as near as a student who seven times failed to get his diploma. In the book of Tobit the accent falls on a different spot, therefore the high figure is significant and in a certain sense is contributory to the tragic effect, for it enhances the courage of Tobias, which was the more notable because he was the only son of his parents (6:14) and because the deterrent was so striking. So this feature must be left out. Sarah is a maiden who has never been in love, who treasures still a young maiden's bliss, her enormous first mortgage upon life, her *Vollmachtbrief zum Glücke*,[79] the privilege of loving a man with her whole heart. And yet she is the most unhappy maiden, for she knows that the evil demon who loves her will kill the bridegroom the night of the wedding. I have read of many a sorrow, but I doubt if there is anywhere to be found so deep a sorrow as that which we discover in the life of this girl. However, if the misfortune comes from without, there is some consolation to be found after all.

Although existence did not bring one that which might have made one happy, there is still consolation in the thought that one would have been able to receive it. But the unfathomable sorrow which time can never divert, which time can never heal: To be aware that it was of no avail though existence were to do everything! A Greek writer conceals so infinitely much by his simple naiveté when he says: *πάντως γὰρ οὐδεὶς ἔρωτα ἔφυγεν ἢ φεύξεται, μέχτις ἂν κάλλος ᾖ καὶ ὀφθαλμοὶ βλέπωσιν* (cf. *Longi Pastoralia*).[80] There has been many a girl who became unhappy in love, but after all she became so, Sarah was so before she became so. It is hard not to find the man to whom one can surrender oneself devotedly, but it is *unspeakably* hard not to be able to surrender oneself. A young girl surrenders herself, and then they say, "Now she is no longer free"; but Sarah was never free, and yet she had never surrendered herself. It is hard if a girl surrendered herself and then was cheated,[81] but Sarah was cheated before she surrendered herself. What a world of sorrow is implied in what follows, when finally Tobias wishes to marry Sarah! What wedding ceremonies! What preparations! No maiden has ever been so cheated as Sarah, for she was cheated out of the most sacred thing of all, the absolute wealth which even the poorest girl possesses, cheated out of the secure, boundless, unrestrained, unbridled devotion of surrender – for first there had to be a fumigation by laying the heart of the fish and its liver upon glowing coals. And think of how the mother had to take leave of her daughter, who having herself been cheated out of all, in continuity with this must cheat the mother out of her most beautiful possession. Just read the narrative. "Edna prepared the chamber and brought Sarah thither and wept and received the tears of her daughter. And she said unto her, Be of good comfort, my child, the Lord of heaven and earth give thee joy for this thy sorrow! Be of good courage, my daughter." And then the moment of the nuptials! Let one read it if one can for tears. "But after they were both shut in together Tobias rose up from the bed and said, Sister, arise, and let us pray that the Lord may have mercy upon us" (8:4).

In case a poet were to read this narrative, in case he were to make use of it, I wager a hundred to one that he would lay all the emphasis upon the young Tobias. His heroic courage in being willing to risk his life in such evident danger – which the narrative recalls once again, for the morning after the nuptials Raguel says to Edna, "Send one of the maidservants and let her see whether he be alive; but if not, that we may bury him and no man know of it" (8:12) – this heroic courage would be the poet's theme. I take the liberty of proposing another. Tobias acted bravely, stoutheartedly and chivalrously, but any man who has not the courage for this is a molly-coddle who does not know what love is, or what it is to be a man, or what is worth living for; he had not even comprehended the little mystery, that it is better to give than to receive, and has no inkling of the great one, that it is far more difficult to receive than to give – that is, if one has had courage to do without and in the hour of need did not become cowardly. No, it is Sarah that is the heroine. I desire to draw near to her as I never have drawn near to any girl or felt tempted in thought to draw near to any girl I have read about. For what love to God it requires to be willing to let oneself be healed when from the beginning one has been thus bungled without one's fault, from the beginning has been an abortive specimen of humanity![82] What ethical maturity was required for assuming the responsibility of allowing the loved one to do such a daring deed! What humility before the face of another person! What faith in God to believe that the next instant she would not hate the husband to whom she owed everything!

Let Sarah be a man, and with that the demoniacal is close at hand. The proud and noble nature can endure everything, but one thing it cannot endure, it cannot endure pity. In that there is implied an indignity which can only be inflicted upon one by a higher power, for by oneself one can never become an object of pity. If a man has sinned, he can bear the punishment for it without despairing; but without blame to be singled out from his mother's womb as a sacrifice to pity, as a sweet-smelling savor in its nostrils, that he cannot put up with. Pity has a strange dialectic, at one moment it requires guilt, the next moment it will not have it, and so it is that to be predestinated to pity is more and more dreadful the more the individual's misfortune is in the direction of the spiritual. But Sarah had no blame attaching to her, she is cast forth as a prey to every suffering and in addition to this has to endure the torture of pity – for even I who admire her more than Tobias loved her, even I cannot mention her name without saying, "Poor girl." Put a man in Sarah's place, let him know that in case he were to love a girl a spirit of hell would come and murder his loved one – it might well be possible that he would choose the demoniacal part, that he would shut himself up within himself and say in the way a demoniacal nature talks in secret, "Many thanks, I am no friend of courteous and prolix phrases, I do not absolutely need the pleasure of love, I can become a Blue Beard, finding my delight in seeing maidens perish during the night of their nuptials." Commonly one hears little about the demoniacal, notwithstanding that this field, particularly in our time, has a valid claim to be explored, and notwithstanding that the observer, in case he knows how to get a little in *rapport* with the demon, can, at least occasionally, make use of almost every man for this purpose. As such an explorer Shakespeare is and constantly remains a hero. That horrible demon, the most demoniacal figure Shakespeare has depicted and depicted incomparably, the Duke of Gloucester (afterwards to become Richard III) – what made him a demon? Evidently the fact that he could not bear the pity he had been subjected to since childhood. His monologue in the first act of *Richard III* is worth more than all the moral systems which have no inkling of the terrors of existence or of the explanation of them.

> I, that am rudely stamped, and want love's majesty
> To strut before a wanton ambling nymph;
> I, that am curtail'd of this fair proportion,
> Cheated of feature by dissembling nature,
> Deformed, unfinished, sent before my time
> Into this breathing world, scarce half made up,
> And that so lamely and unfashionable
> That dogs bark at me as I halt by them.

Such natures as that of Gloucester one cannot save by mediating them into an idea of society. Ethics in fact only makes game of them, just as it would be a mockery of Sarah if ethics were to say to her, "Why dost thou not express the universal and get married?" Essentially such natures are in the paradox and are no more imperfect than other men, but are either lost in the demoniacal paradox or saved in the divine. Now from time out of mind people have been pleased to think that witches, hobgoblins, gnomes, etc. were deformed, and undeniably every man on seeing a deformed person has at once an inclination to associate this with the notion of moral depravity. What a monstrous injustice! For the situation must rather be inverted, in the sense that existence itself has corrupted them, in the same way that a stepmother makes the children wicked. The fact of being originally set outside of the universal, by nature or by a historical circumstance, is the beginning of the demoniacal, for which the individual himself however is not to blame. Thus Cumberland's Jew[83] is also a demon notwithstanding he does what is good. Thus too the demoniacal may express itself as contempt for men – a contempt, be it observed, which does not cause a man to behave contemptibly, since on the contrary he counts it his forte that he is better than all who condemn him. – In view of such cases the poets ought to lose no time in sounding the alarm. God knows what books are read now by the younger generation of verse makers! Their study likely consists in learning rhymes by rote. God knows what significance in existence these men have! At this moment I do not know what use they are except to furnish an edifying proof of the immortality of the soul, for the fact that one can say of them as Baggesen says[84] of the poet of our town, Kildevalle, "If he is immortal, then we all are." – What has here been said about Sarah, almost as a sort of poetic production and therefore with a fantastic presupposition, acquires its full significance if one with psychological interest will delve deep into the meaning of the old saying: *Nullum unquam exstitit magnum ingenium sine aliqua dementia.*[85] For this *dementia* is the suffering allotted to genius in existence, it is the expression, if I may say so, of the divine jealousy, whereas the gift of genius is the expression of the divine favor. So from the start the genius is disoriented in relation to the universal and is brought into relation with the paradox – whether it be that in despair at his limitation (which in his eyes transforms his omnipotence into impotence) he seeks a demoniacal reassurance and therefore will not admit such limitation either before God or men, or whether he reassures himself religiously by love to the Deity. Here are implied psychological topics to which, it seems to me, one might gladly sacrifice a whole life – and yet one so seldom hears a word about them.[86] What relation has madness to genius? Can we construct the one out of the other? In what sense and how far is the genius master of his madness? For it goes without saying that to a certain degree he is master of it, since otherwise he would be actually a madman. For such observations, however, ingenuity in a high degree is requisite, and love; for to make observation upon a superior mind is very difficult. If with due attention to this difficulty one were to read through the works of particular authors most celebrated for their genius, it might in barely a single instance perhaps be possible, though with much pains, to discover a little.

I would consider still another case, that of an individual who by being hidden and by his silence would save the universal. To this end I make use of the legend of Faust.[87] Faust is a doubter,* an apostate against the spirit, who takes the path of the flesh. This is what the poets mean by it, and whereas again and again it is repeated that every age has its Faust, yet one poet after another follows indefatigably the same beaten track. Let us make a little alteration. Faust is the doubter *par excellence*, but he is a sympathetic nature. Even in Goethe's interpretation of Faust

*If one would prefer not to make use of a doubter, one might choose a similar figure, an ironist, for example, whose sharp sight has discovered fundamentally the ludicrousness of existence, who by a secret understanding with the forces of life ascertains what the patient wishes. He knows that he possesses the power of laughter if he would use it, he is sure of his victory, yea, also of his good fortune. He knows that an individual voice will be raised in resistance, but he knows that he is stronger, he knows that for an instant one can still cause men to seem serious, but he knows also that privately they long to laugh with him; he knows that for an instant one can still cause a woman to hold a fan before her eyes when he talks, but he knows that she is laughing behind the fan, that the fan is not absolutely impervious to vision, he knows that one can write on it an invisible inscription, he knows that when a woman strikes at him with her fan it is because she has understood him, he knows without the least danger of deception how laughter sneaks in, and how when once it has taken up its lodging it lies in ambush and waits. Let us imagine such an Aristophanes, such a Voltaire, a little altered, for he is at the same time a sympathetic nature, he loves existence, he loves men, and he knows that even though the reproof of laughter will perhaps educate a saved young race, yet in the contemporary generation a multitude of men will be ruined. So he keeps silent and as far as possible forgets how to laugh. But dare he keep silent? Perhaps there are sundry persons who do not in the least understand the difficulty I have in mind. They are likely of the opinion that it is

I sense the lack of a deeper psychological insight into the secret conversations of doubt with itself. In our age, when indeed all have experienced doubt, no poet has yet made a step in this direction. So I think I might well offer them Royal Securities[88] to write on, so that they could write down all they have experienced in this respect – they would hardly write more than there is room for on the left-hand margin.

Only when one thus deflects Faust back into himself, only then can doubt appear poetic, only then too does he himself discover in reality all its sufferings. He knows that it is spirit which sustains existence, but he knows then too that the security and joy in which men live is not founded upon the power of spirit but is easily explicable as an unreflected happiness. As a doubter, as the doubter, he is higher than all this, and if anyone would deceive him by making him believe that he has passed through a course of training in doubt, he readily sees through the deception; for the man who has made a movement in the world of spirit, hence an infinite movement, can at once hear through the spoken word whether it is a tried and experienced man who is speaking or a Münchhausen. What a Tamberlane is able to accomplish by means of his Huns, that Faust is able to accomplish by means of his doubt: to frighten men up in dismay, to cause existence to quake beneath their feet, to disperse men abroad, to cause the shriek of dread to be heard on all sides. And if he does it, he is nevertheless no Tamberlane, he is in a certain sense warranted and has the warranty of thought. But Faust is a sympathetic nature, he loves existence, his soul is acquainted with no envy, he perceives that he is unable to check the raging

---

an admirable act of magnanimity to keep silent. That is not at all my opinion, for I think that every such character, if he has not had the magnanimity to keep silent, is a traitor against existence. So I require of him this magnanimity; but when he possesses it, dare he then keep silent? Ethics is a dangerous science, and it might be possible that Aristophanes was determined by purely ethical considerations in resolving to reprove by laughter his misguided age. Aesthetical magnanimity does not help [to solve the question whether one ought to keep silent], for on the credit of that one does not take such a risk. If he is to keep silent, then into the paradox he must go. – I will suggest still another plan for a story. Suppose e.g. that a man possessed a explanation of a heroic life which explained it in a sorry way, and yet a whole generation reposes securely in an absolute belief in this hero, without suspecting anything of the sort.

he is well able to arouse, he desires no Herostratic honor[89] – he keeps silent, he hides the doubt in his soul more carefully than the girl who hides under her heart the fruit of a sinful love, he endeavors as well as he can to walk in step with other men, but what goes on within him he consumes within himself, and thus he offers himself a sacrifice for the universal.

When an eccentric pate raises a whirlwind of doubt one may sometimes hear people say, "Would that he had kept silent." Faust realizes this idea. He who has a conception of what it means to live upon spirit knows also what the hunger of doubt is, and that the doubter hungers just as much for the daily bread of life as for the nutriment of the spirit. Although all the pain Faust suffers may be a fairly good argument that it was not pride possessed him, yet to test this further I will employ a little precautionary expedient which I invent with great ease. For as Gregory of Rimini was called *tortor infantium*[90] because he espoused the view of the damnation of infants, so I might be tempted to call myself *tortor heroum*; for I am very inventive when it is a question of putting heroes to the torture. Faust sees Marguerite – not after he had made the choice of pleasure, for my Faust does not choose pleasure – he sees Marguerite, not in the concave mirror of Mephistopheles but in all her lovable innocence, and as his soul has preserved love for mankind he can perfectly well fall in love with her. But he is a doubter, his doubt has annihilated reality for him; for so ideal is my Faust that he does not belong to these scientific doubters who doubt one hour every semester in the professorial chair, but at other times are able to do everything else, as indeed they do this, without the support of spirit or by virtue of spirit. He is a doubter, and the doubter hungers just as much for the daily bread of joy as for the food of the spirit. He remains, however, true to his resolution and keeps silent, and he talks to no man of his doubt, nor to Marguerite of his love.

It goes without saying that Faust is too ideal a figure to be content with the tattle that if he were to talk he would give occasion to an ordinary discussion and the whole thing would pass off without any consequences – or perhaps, and perhaps. . . . (Here, as every poet will easily see, the comic is latent in the plan, threatening to bring Faust into an ironical relation to these fools of low comedy who in our age run after doubt, produce an external argument, e.g. a doctor's diploma, to prove that they really have doubted, or take their oath that they have doubted everything, or prove it by the fact that on a journey they met a doubter – these express-messengers and foot-racers in the world of spirit, who in the greatest haste get from one man a little hint of doubt, from another a little hint of faith, and then turn it to account as best they can, according as the congregation wants to have fine sand or coarse sand.)[91] Faust is too ideal a figure to go about in carpet-slippers. He who has not an infinite passion is not the ideal, and he who has an infinite passion has long ago saved his soul out of such nonsense. He keeps silent and sacrifices himself/or he talks with the consciousness that he will confound everything.

If he keeps silent, ethics condemns him, for it says, "Thou shalt acknowledge the universal, and it is precisely by speaking thou dost acknowledge it, and thou must not have compassion upon the universal." One ought not to forget this consideration when sometimes one judges a doubter severely for talking. I am not inclined to judge such conduct leniently, but in this case as everywhere all depends upon whether the movements occur normally. If worse comes to worst, a doubter, even though by talking he were to bring down all possible misfortune upon the world, is much to be preferred to these miserable sweet-tooths who taste a little of everything, and who would heal doubt without being acquainted with it, and who are therefore usually the proximate cause of it when doubt breaks out wildly and with ungovernable rage. – If he speaks, then he confounds everything – for though this does not actually occur, he does not get to know it till afterwards, and the upshot cannot help a man either at the moment of action or with regard to his responsibility.

If he keeps silent on his own responsibility, he may indeed be acting magnanimously, but to his other pains he adds a little temptation [*Anfechtung*], for the universal will constantly torture him and say, "You ought to have talked. Where will you find the certainty that it was not after all a hidden pride which governed your resolution?"

If on the other hand the doubter is able to become the particular individual who as the individual stands in an absolute relation to the absolute, then he can get a warrant for his silence. In this case he must transform his doubt into guilt. In this case he is within the paradox, but in this case his doubt is cured, even though he may get another doubt.

Even the New Testament would approve of such a silence. There are even passages in the New Testament which commend irony – if only it is used to conceal something good. This movement, however, is as properly a movement of irony as is any other which has its ground in the fact that subjectivity is higher than reality. In our age people want to hear nothing about this, generally they want to know no more about irony than Hegel has said about it[92] – who strangely enough had not much understanding of it, and bore a grudge against it, which our age has good reason not to give up, for it had better beware of irony. In the Sermon on the Mount it is said, "When thou fastest, anoint thy head and wash thy face, that thou be not seen of men to fast." This passage bears witness directly to the truth that subjectivity is incommensurable with reality, yea, that it has leave to deceive. If only the people who in our age go gadding about with vague talk about the congregational idea[93] were to read the New Testament, they would perhaps get other ideas into their heads.

But now as for Abraham – how did he act? For I have not forgotten, and the reader will perhaps be kind enough to remember, that it was with the aim of reaching this point I entered into the whole foregoing discussion – not as though Abraham would thereby become more intelligible, but in order that the unintelligibility might become more desultory.[94] For, as I have said, Abraham I cannot understand, I can only admire him. It was also observed that the stages I have described do none of them contain an analogy to Abraham. The examples were simply educed in order that while they were shown in their own proper sphere they might at the moment of variation [from Abraham's case] indicate as it were the boundary of the unknown land. If there might be any analogy, this must be found in the paradox of sin, but this again lies in another sphere and cannot explain Abraham and is itself far easier to explain than Abraham.

So then, Abraham did not speak, he did not speak to Sarah, nor to Eleazar, nor to Isaac, he passed over three ethical authorities; for the ethical had for Abraham no higher expression than the family life.

Aesthetics permitted, yea, required of the individual silence, when he knew that by keeping silent he could save another. This is already sufficient proof that Abraham does not lie within the circumference of aesthetics. His silence has by no means the intention of saving Isaac, and in general his whole task of sacrificing Isaac for his own sake and for God's sake is an offense to aesthetics, for aesthetics can well understand that I sacrifice myself, but not that I sacrifice another for my own sake. The aesthetic hero was silent. Ethics condemned him, however, because he was silent by virtue of his accidental particularity. His human foreknowledge was what determined him to keep silent. This ethics cannot forgive, every such human knowledge is only an illusion, ethics requires an infinite movement, it requires revelation. So the aesthetic hero *can* speak but will not.

The genuine tragic hero sacrifices himself and all that is his for the universal, his deed and every emotion with him belong to the universal, he is revealed, and in this self-revelation he is the beloved son of ethics. This does not fit the case of Abraham: he does nothing for the universal, and he is concealed.

Now we reach the paradox. Either the individual as the individual is able to stand in an absolute relation to the absolute (and then the ethical is not the highest) /or Abraham is lost – he is neither a tragic hero, nor an aesthetic hero.

Here again it may seem as if the paradox were the easiest and most convenient thing of all. However, I must repeat that he who counts himself convinced of this is not a knight of faith, for distress and anguish are the only legitimations that can be thought of, and they cannot be thought in general terms, for with that the paradox is annulled.

Abraham keeps silent – but he *cannot* speak. Therein lies the distress and anguish. For if I when I speak am unable to make myself intelligible, then I am not speaking – even though I were to talk uninterruptedly day and night. Such is the case with Abraham. He is able to utter everything, but one thing he cannot say, i.e. say it in such a way that another understands it, and so he is not speaking. The relief of speech is that it translates me into the universal. Now Abraham is able to say the most beautiful things any language can express about how he loves Isaac. But it is not this he has at heart to say, it is the profounder thought that he would sacrifice him because it is a trial. This latter thought no one can understand, and hence everyone can only misunderstand the former. This distress the tragic hero does not know. He has first of all the comfort that every counter-argument has received due consideration, that he has been able to give to Clytemnestra, to Iphigenia, to Achilles, to the chorus, to every living being, to every voice from the heart of humanity, to every cunning, every alarming, every accusing, every compassionate thought, opportunity to stand up against him. He can be sure that everything that can be said against him has been said, unsparingly, mercilessly – and to strive against the whole world is a comfort, to strive with oneself is dreadful. He has no reason to fear that he has overlooked anything, so that afterwards he must cry out as did King Edward the Fourth at the news of the death of Clarence:[95]

> Who su'd to me for him? who, in my wrath,
> Kneel'd at my feet and bade me be advised?
> Who spoke of brotherhood? who spoke of love?

The tragic hero does not know the terrible responsibility of solitude. In the next place he has the comfort that he can weep and lament with Clytemnestra and Iphigenia – and tears and cries are assuaging, but unutterable sighs are torture. Agamemnon can quickly collect his soul into the certainty that he will act, and then he still has time to comfort and exhort. This Abraham is unable to do. When his heart is moved, when his words would contain a blessed comfort for the whole world, he does not dare to offer comfort, for would not Sarah, would not Eleazar, would not Isaac say, "Why wilt thou do it? Thou canst refrain"? And if in his distress he would give vent to his feelings and would embrace all his dear ones before taking the final step, this might perhaps bring about the dreadful consequence that Sarah, that Eleazar, that Isaac would be offended in him and would believe he was a hypocrite. He is unable to speak, he speaks no human language. Though he himself understood all the tongues of the world, though his loved ones also understood them, he nevertheless cannot speak – he speaks a divine language ... he "speaks with tongues."

This distress I can well understand, I can admire Abraham, I am not afraid that anyone might be tempted by this narrative lightheartedly to want to be the individual, but I admit also that I have not the courage for it, and that I renounce gladly any prospect of getting further – if only it were possible that in any way, however late, I might get so far. Every instant Abraham is able to break off, he can repent the whole thing as a temptation [*Anfechtung*], then he can speak, then all could understand him – but then he is no longer Abraham.

Abraham cannot speak, for he cannot utter the word which explains all (that is, not so that it is intelligible), he cannot say that it is a test, and a test of such a sort, be it noted, that the ethical is the temptation [*Versuchung*]. He who is so situated is an emigrant from the sphere of the universal. But the next word he is still less able to utter. For, as was sufficiently set forth earlier, Abraham makes two movements: he makes the infinite movement of resignation and gives up Isaac (this no one can understand because it is a private venture); but in the next place, he makes the movement of faith every instant. This is his comfort, for he says: "But yet this will not come to pass, or, if it does come to pass, then the Lord will give me a new Isaac, by virtue viz. of the absurd." The tragic hero does at last get to the end of the story. Iphigenia bows to her father's resolution, she herself makes the infinite movement of resignation, and now they are on good terms with one another. She can understand Agamemnon because his undertaking expresses the universal. If on the other hand Agamemnon were to say to her, "In spite of the fact that the deity demands thee as a sacrifice, it might yet be possible that he did not demand it – by virtue viz. of the absurd," he would that very instant become unintelligible to Iphigenia. If he could say this by virtue of human calculation, Iphigenia would surely understand him, but from that it would follow that Agamemnon had not made the infinite movement of resignation, and so he is not a hero, and so the utterance of the seer is a sea-captain's tale and the whole occurrence a vaudeville.

Abraham did not speak. Only one word of his has been preserved, the only reply to Isaac, which also is sufficient proof that he had not spoken previously. Isaac asks Abraham where the lamb is for the burnt offering. "And Abraham said, God will provide Himself the lamb for the burnt offering, my son."

This last word of Abraham I shall consider a little more closely. If there were not this word, the whole event would have lacked something; if it were to another effect, everything perhaps would be resolved into confusion.

I have often reflected upon the question whether a tragic hero, be the culmination of his tragedy a suffering or an action, ought to have a last rejoinder. In my opinion it depends upon the life-sphere to which he belongs, whether his life has intellectual significance, whether his suffering or his action stands in relation to spirit.

It goes without saying that the tragic hero, like every other man who is not deprived of the power of speech, can at the instant of his culmination utter a few words, perhaps a few appropriate words, but the question is whether it is appropriate for him to utter them. If the significance of his life consists in an outward act, then he has nothing to say, since all he says is essentially chatter whereby he only weakens the impression he makes, whereas the ceremonial of tragedy requires that he perform his task in silence, whether this consists in action or in suffering. Not to go too far afield, I will take an example which lies nearest to our discussion. If Agamemnon himself and not Calchas had had to draw the knife against Iphigenia, then he would have only demeaned himself by wanting at the last moment to say a few words, for the significance of his act was notorious, the juridical procedure of piety, of compassion, of emotion, of tears was completed, and moreover his life had no relation to spirit, he was not a teacher or a witness to the spirit. On the other hand, if the significance of a hero's life is in the direction of spirit, then the lack of a rejoinder would weaken the impression he makes. What he has to say is not a few appropriate words, a little piece of declamation, but the significance of his rejoinder is that in the decisive moment he carries himself through. Such an intellectual tragic hero ought to have what in other circumstances is too often striven for in ludicrous ways, he ought to have and he ought to keep the last word. One requires of him the same exalted bearing which is seemly in every tragic hero, but in addition to this there is required of him one word. So when such an intellectual tragic hero has his culmination in suffering (in death), then by his last word he becomes immortal before he dies, whereas the ordinary tragic hero on the other hand does not become immortal till after his death.

One may take Socrates as an example. He was an intellectual tragic hero. His death sentence was announced to him. That instant he dies – for one who does not understand that the whole power of the spirit is required for dying, and that the hero always dies before he dies, that man will not get so very far with his conception of life. So as a hero it is required of Socrates that he repose tranquilly in himself, but as an intellectual tragic hero it is required of him that he at the last moment have spiritual strength sufficient to carry himself through. So he cannot like the ordinary tragic hero concentrate upon keeping himself face to face with death, but he must make this movement so quickly that at the same instant he is consciously well over and beyond this strife and asserts himself. If Socrates had been silent in the crisis of death, he would have weakened the effect of his life and aroused the suspicion that in him the elasticity of irony was not an elemental power but a game, the flexibility of which he had to employ at the decisive moment to sustain him emotionally.*

What is briefly suggested here has to be sure no application to Abraham in case one might think it possible to find out by analogy an appropriate word for Abraham to end with, but it does apply to this extent, that one thereby perceives how necessary it is that Abraham at the last moment must carry himself through, must not silently draw the knife, but must have a word to say, since as the father of faith he has absolute significance in a spiritual sense. As to what he must say, I can

*Opinions may be divided as to which rejoinder of Socrates is to be regarded as the decisive one, inasmuch as Socrates has been in so many ways volatilized by Plato. I propose the following. The sentence of death is announced to him, the same instant he dies, the same instant he overcomes death and carries himself through in the famous reply which expresses surprise that he had been condemned by a majority of three votes.[96] With no vague and idle talk in the marketplace, with no foolish remark of an idiot, could he have jested more ironically than with the sentence which condemned him to death.

form no conception beforehand; after he has said it I can maybe understand it, maybe in a certain sense can understand Abraham in what he says, though without getting any closer to him than I have been in the foregoing discussion. In case no last rejoinder of Socrates had existed, I should have been able to think myself into him and formulate such a word; if I were unable to do it, a poet could, but no poet can catch up with Abraham.

Before I go on to consider Abraham's last word more closely I would call attention to the difficulty Abraham had in saying anything at all. The distress and anguish in the paradox consisted (as was set forth above) in silence – Abraham cannot speak.* So in view of this fact it is a contradiction to require him to speak, unless one would have him out of the paradox again, in such a sense that at the last moment he suspends it, whereby he ceases to be Abraham and annuls all that went before. So then if Abraham at the last moment were to say to Isaac, "To thee it applies," this would only have been a weakness. For if he could speak at all, he ought to have spoken long before, and the weakness in this case would consist in the fact that he did not possess the maturity of spirit and the concentration to think in advance the whole pain but had thrust something away from him, so that the actual pain contained a plus over and above the thought pain. Moreover, by such a speech he would fall out of the role of the paradox, and if he really wanted to speak to Isaac, he must transform his situation into a temptation [*Anfechtung*], for otherwise he could say nothing, and if he were to do that, then he is not even so much as a tragic hero.

However, a last word of Abraham has been preserved, and in so far as I can understand the paradox I can also apprehend the total presence of Abraham in this word. First and foremost, he does not say anything, and it is in this form he says what he has to say. His reply to Isaac has the form of irony, for it always is irony when I say something and do not say anything. Isaac

*If there can be any question of an analogy, the circumstance of the death of Pythagoras furnishes it, for the silence which he had always maintained he had to carry through in his last moment, and therefore [being compelled to speak] he said, "It is better to be put to death than to speak" (cf. Diogenes Laertius, viii. 39).

interrogates Abraham on the supposition that Abraham knows. So then if Abraham were to have replied, "I know nothing," he would have uttered an untruth. He cannot say anything, for what he knows he cannot say. So he replies, "God will provide Himself the lamb for the burnt offering, my son." Here the double movement in Abraham's soul is evident, as it was described in the foregoing discussion. If Abraham had merely renounced his claim to Isaac and had done no more, he would in this last word be saying an untruth, for he knows that God demands Isaac as a sacrifice, and he knows that he himself at that instant precisely is ready to sacrifice him. We see then that after making this movement he made every instant the next movement, the movement of faith by virtue of the absurd. Because of this he utters no falsehood, for in virtue of the absurd it is of course possible that God could do something entirely different. Hence he is speaking no untruth, but neither is he saying anything, for he speaks a foreign language. This becomes still more evident when we consider that it was Abraham himself who must perform the sacrifice of Isaac. Had the task been a different one, had the Lord commanded Abraham to bring Isaac out to Mount Moriah and then would Himself have Isaac struck by lightning and in this way receive him as a sacrifice, then, taking his words in a plain sense, Abraham might have been right in speaking enigmatically as he did, for he could not himself know what would occur. But in the way the task was prescribed to Abraham he himself had to act, and at the decisive moment he must know what he himself would do, he must know that Isaac will be sacrificed. In case he did not know this definitely, then he has not made the infinite movement of resignation, then, though his word is not indeed an untruth, he is very far from being Abraham, he has less significance than the tragic hero, yea, he is an irresolute man who is unable to resolve either on one thing or another, and for this reason will always be uttering riddles. But such a hesitator is a sheer parody of a knight of faith.

Here again it appears that one may have an understanding of Abraham, but can understand him only in the same way as one understands the paradox. For my part I can in a way understand Abraham, but at the same time I apprehend that I have not the courage to speak, and still less to act as he did – but by this I do not by any means intend to say that what he did was insignificant, for on the contrary it is the one only marvel.

And what did the contemporary age think of the tragic hero? They thought that he was great, and they admired him. And that honorable assembly of nobles, the jury which every generation impanels to pass judgment upon the foregoing generation, passed the same judgment upon him. But as for Abraham there was no one who could understand him. And yet think what he attained! He remained true to his love. But he who loves God has no need of tears, no need of admiration, in his love he forgets his suffering, yea, so completely has he forgotten it that afterwards there would not even be the least inkling of his pain if God Himself did not recall it, for God sees in secret and knows the distress and counts the tears and forgets nothing.

So either there is a paradox, that the individual as the individual stands in an absolute relation to the absolute/or Abraham is lost.

EPILOGUE

One time in Holland when the market was rather dull for spices the merchants had several cargoes dumped into the sea to peg up prices. This was a pardonable, perhaps a necessary device for deluding people. Is it something like that we need now in the world of spirit? Are we so thoroughly convinced that we have attained the highest point that there is nothing left for us but to make ourselves believe piously that we have not got so far – just for the sake of having something left to occupy our time? Is it such a self-deception the present generation has need of, does it need to be trained to virtuosity in self-deception, or is it not rather sufficiently perfected already in the art of deceiving itself? Or rather is not the thing most needed an honest seriousness which dauntlessly and incorruptibly points to the tasks, an honest seriousness which lovingly watches over the tasks, which does not frighten men into being over hasty in getting the highest tasks accomplished, but keeps the tasks young and beautiful and charming to look upon and yet difficult withal and appealing to noble minds. For the enthusiasm of noble natures is aroused only by difficulties. Whatever the one generation may learn from the other, that which is genuinely human no generation learns from the foregoing. In this respect every generation begins primitively, has no different task from that of every previous generation, nor does it get further, except in so far as the preceding generation shirked its task and deluded itself. This authentically human factor is passion, in which also the one generation perfectly understands the other and understands itself. Thus no generation has learned from another to love, no generation begins at any other point than at the beginning, no generation has a shorter task assigned to it than had the preceding generation, and if here one is not willing like the previous generations to stop with love but would go further, this is but idle and foolish talk.

But the highest passion in a man is faith, and here no generation begins at any other point than did the preceding generation, every generation begins all over again, the subsequent generation gets no further than the foregoing – in so far as this remained faithful to its task and did not leave it in the lurch. That this should be wearisome is of course something the generation cannot say, for the generation has in fact the task to perform and has nothing to do with the consideration that the foregoing generation had the same task – unless the particular generation or the particular individuals within it were presumptuous enough to assume the place which belongs by right only to the Spirit which governs the world and has patience enough not to grow weary. If the generation begins that sort of thing, it is upside down, and what wonder then that the whole of existence seems to it upside down, for there surely is no one who has found the world so upside down as did the tailor in the fairy tale[97] who went up in his lifetime to heaven and from that standpoint contemplated the world. If the generation would only concern itself about its task, which is the highest thing it can do, it cannot grow weary, for the task is always sufficient for a human life. When the children on a holiday have already got through playing all their games before the clock strikes twelve and say impatiently, "Is there nobody can think of a new game?" does this prove that these children are more developed and more advanced than the children of the same generation or of a previous one who could stretch out the familiar games, to last the whole day long? Or does it not prove rather that these children lack what I would call the lovable seriousness which belongs essentially to play?

Faith is the highest passion in a man. There are perhaps many in every generation who do not even reach it, but no one gets further. Whether there be many in our age who do not discover it, I will not decide, I dare only appeal to myself as a witness who makes no secret that the prospects for him are not the best, without for all that wanting to delude himself and to betray the great thing which is faith by reducing it to an insignificance, to an ailment of childhood which one must wish to get over as soon as possible. But for the man also who does not so much as reach faith life has tasks enough, and if one loves them sincerely, life will by no means be wasted, even though it never is comparable to the life of those who sensed and grasped the highest. But he who reached faith (it makes no difference whether he be a man of distinguished talents or a simple man) does not remain standing at faith, yea, he would be offended if anyone were to say this of him, just as the lover would be indignant if one said that he remained standing at love, for he would reply, "I do not remain standing by any means, my whole life is in this." Nevertheless he does not get further, does not reach anything different, for if he discovers this, he has a different explanation for it.

"One must go further, one must go further." This impulse to go further is an ancient thing in the world. Heraclitus the obscure, who deposited his thoughts in his writings and his writings in the Temple of Diana (for his thoughts had been his armor during his life, and therefore he hung them up in the temple of the goddess),[98] Heraclitus the obscure said, "One cannot pass twice through the same stream."* Heraclitus the obscure had a disciple who did not stop with that, he went further and added, "One cannot do it even once."† Poor Heraclitus, to have such a disciple! By this amendment the thesis of Heraclitus was so improved that it became an Eleatic thesis which denies movement, and yet that disciple desired only to be a disciple of Heraclitus ... and to go further – not back to the position Heraclitus had abandoned.

*Plato's *Cratyllus*, §402.

†Cf. Tennemann, *Geschichte der Philosophie*, I, p. 220.

ON AUTHORITY AND REVELATION
THE BOOK ON ADLER

or A CYCLE OF ETHICO-RELIGIOUS ESSAYS

INTRODUCTION

1846.

Since, as says the barber (and one who has no opportunity of keeping abreast of the age by the aid of newspapers may well rest satisfied with the barber, who in olden times when there were as yet no newspapers was what the newspapers are now: universal intelligence, "our age is the age of movement," it is not improbable that the lives of many men go on in such a way that they have indeed premises for living but reach no conclusions – quite like this stirring age which has set in movement many premises but also has reached no conclusion. Such a man's life goes on till death comes and puts an end to life, but without bringing with it an end in the sense of a conclusion. For it is one thing that a life is over, and a different thing that a life is finished by reaching its conclusion. In the degree that such a man has talents he can go ahead and become an author, as he understands it. But such an understanding is an illusion. For that matter (since here we may hypothetically admit everything possible, so long as we hold fast the decisive point), he may have extraordinary talents and remarkable learning, but an author he is not, in spite of the fact that he produces books. Like his life, his book must be material. Perhaps this material may be worth its weight in gold, but it is only material. Here is no poet who poetically rounds out the thing as a whole, no psychologist who organizes the individual trait and the individual person within a total apprehension, no dialectician who prescribes the place within the life-view which he has at his disposition. No, in spite of the fact that the man writes, he is not essentially an author; he will be capable of writing the first part, but he cannot write the second part, or (to avoid any misunderstanding) he can write the first and also the second part, but he cannot write the third part – the last part he cannot write. If he goes ahead naively (led astray by the reflection that every book must have a last part) and so writes the last part, he will make it thoroughly clear by writing the last part that he makes a written renunciation to all claim to be an author. For though it is indeed by writing that one justifies the claim to be an author, it is also, strangely enough, by writing that one virtually renounces this claim. If he had been thoroughly aware of the inappropriateness of the third part – well, one may say, *si tacuisset, philosophus mansisset.*

To find the conclusion, it is necessary first of all to observe that it is lacking, and then in turn to feel quite vividly the lack of it. It might therefore be imagined that an essential author, just to make evident the misfortune that men are living without a conclusion, might write a fragment (but by calling it that he would avoid all misapprehension), though in another sense he provided the conclusion by providing the necessary life-view. And after all a world-view, a life-view, is the only true condition of every literary production. Every poetic conclusion is an illusion. If a life-view is developed, if it stands out whole and clear in its necessary coherence, one has no need to put the hero to death, one may as well let him live: the premise is nevertheless resolved and satisfied in the conclusion, the development is complete. But if there is lacking a life-view (which of course must be in the first part and everywhere, though the lack of it only becomes evident in the second part or the third, that is to say, the conclusion), it is of no avail to let the hero die, no, it avails nothing that the writer, to make quite sure that he is dead, even has him buried in the course of the story – with this the development is by no means complete. If death had that power, nothing would be easier than to be a poet, and poetry would not be needed at all. For in reality it is indeed true that every man dies, his life comes to an end; but from this it does not follow that his life has an end in the sense of a conclusion, "that it *came* to an end" – precisely this past tense shows that death is not the decisive thing, that the conclusion may fall within a man's lifetime, and that to regard death as a conclusion is a deceitful evasion, for death is related quite indifferently to the premise of a man's life, and therefore is not a conclusion of any sort.

But the more the time for development is lacking, and the more individuals there are who lack a conclusion, all the more active men seem to be in multiplying premises. This in turn has the result that to get a conclusion becomes more and more difficult, because, instead of the decisiveness of the conclusion, there results a stoppage which, spiritually understood, is what constipation is in the animal organism, while the augmentation of premises is just as dangerous as overloading oneself with food when one suffers from constipation, though for a moment it may seem an alleviation. Gradually the movement of time changes it into an unhealthy fermentation. So the individuals whose life contains only premises may make use of this sickness of our age by becoming authors, and their productions will be precisely what the age demands. Under these circumstances an essential author would naturally prescribe a diet, but the premise-authors are better off.

As opportunity makes thieves, so does this fermentation make 'mad' authors (in the sense that we speak of 'mad money' in times of serious inflation), for the lack of a conclusion in our age obscures the fact that the authors lack it. The relative differences of premise-authors among themselves, with respect to talents and such like, may be very great, but they have in common this essential mark, that they are not real authors. On the surface of such a fermentation there may be floating many clever pates, but even the most insignificant pates may aspire to writing at least a little premise-contribution for a newspaper. In this way there is prospect of advancement for the most insignificant pates, and consequently there is a great number, a multitude of authors, so that by reason of their number they may best be likened to sulphur-matches which are sold in bundles. Such an author, upon whose head is deposited something phosphorescent (the suggestion of a project, a hint), one takes up by the legs and strikes him upon a newspaper, and out there come three to four columns. And the premise-authors have really a striking resemblance to sulphur-matches – both explode with a puff.

But in spite of this explosion, or perhaps precisely because of it, all premise-authors, whatever their relative differences may be, have one thing in common: they all have a *purpose*, they all wish to produce an effect, they all wish that their works may have an extraordinary diffusion and may be read if possible by all mankind. This curious trait is reserved for men in such an age of fermentation: to have a purpose, for the sake of this purpose to be on the move in the sweat of their brow, and not really to know in themselves whither this purpose tends; for knowing *that*, one must also have the conclusion. This, as the proverb says, is to see that a town is called Little Run, but not to know whither it is running. Instead of having, each man for himself, a clear conception of what one wills *in concreto* before one begins to express one's views, one has a superstitious notion about the utility of starting a discussion, one has the superstition that, while the individuals themselves do not know what they will, the spirit of the age should be able by its dialectic to make it clear what one really wills, so that by this these purposeful gentlemen may get to know what their purpose really is. Everyone in his own way is busily engaged in kindling the fire under the boiler with these combustible premises – but nobody seems to think how dangerous this is with no engineer at hand.

The premise-author is easily recognized and easily described, if only one will remember that he is the exact opposite to the essential author, that while the former is outwardly directed, the latter is inwardly directed. Now it may be a social problem. The premise-author has absolutely no precise and clear notion of what is to be done, how the pressure can be relieved. He thinks thus: "If only an outcry is raised, then surely it will turn out all right." Now it may be a religious problem. The premise-writer has neither time nor patience to think it out more precisely. His notion is: "If only an outcry is raised in a loud voice that can be heard all over the land, and it is read by everybody and is talked about in every company, then surely it will turn out all right." The premise-author thinks that the outcry is like a wishing rod – and he has not observed that almost all have become outcriers. It quite escapes the attention of the premise-authors that it would after all be more reasonable in our age, the age of outcry, if a man were to think thus: The outcry will certainly be made anyway, therefore it would be better for me to abstain from it and collect myself for a more concrete reflection. One smiles at reading all the romantic tales of a bygone age about how knights fared forth into the forest and killed dragons and liberated princes from enchantment, etc. – the romantic notion that in the forests such monsters dwelt, along with enchanted princes. And yet it is quite as romantic that in a whole generation everyone believes in the power of outcry to summon such monstrous forces. The apparent modesty of wanting merely to make an outcry or to raise a discussion does not seem praiseworthy at all, seeing that experience again and again repeated must impress upon everyone the serious thought that he must look for real help in answer to his cry, or else refrain from doing anything to increase the confusion.

Premise-authors are the opposite of the essential authors, for the latter has his own perspective, he constantly comes behind himself in his individual productions; he strives forward indeed, but within the totality, not after it; he never raises more doubt than he can explain; his *A* is always greater than his *B*; he never makes a move on an uncertainty. For he has a definite world-view and life-view which he follows, and with this he is in advance of his individual literary productions, as the whole is always before the parts. Be it much or little he has hitherto understood by his world-view, he explains only what he has understood; he does not wait superstitiously for something from the outside to turn up suddenly and bring him to an understanding, instruct him suddenly what he really wills. In real life it may make a comic effect when a man pretends to be another whose name he doesn't know and only learns later what he is called. Scribe has used this situation wittily in a passage in one of his plays. A young man introduces himself to a family, claiming to be a cousin who has been away for many years. He doesn't himself know what the cousin's name was, till an overdue bill made out to this cousin was presented to him and helped him out of his embarrassment. He takes the bill, and in an aside which is fairly witty he says, "It may always be well to know what my name is." Thus the premise-author, too, produces a comical effect by pretending to be somebody other than he is, by pretending to be an author, and in the end he must wait for something from outside to enlighten him as to what he really is, that is, spiritually understood, what he really wills. The essential author on the other hand knows definitely what he is, what he wills; from first to last he is attentive to understand himself in his life-view; he does not fail to observe that the expectation of an extraordinary result from a discussion he has started is skepticism, that the supposed reliability of the result really nourishes doubt.

In so far as an essential author may be said to feel a need to communicate himself, this need is purely immanent, an enjoyment of his understanding raised to the second power, or else for him it would be an ethical task consciously assumed. The premise-author feels no need to communicate himself, for essentially he has nothing to communicate: he lacks precisely the essential thing, the conclusion, the meaning in relation to the premises. He does not feel the *need to communicate himself*, he is a *needy person*, and like other needy persons he is a burden to the state and to the poor fund – thus essentially are all premise-authors needy persons who become a burden to the race for the fact that they want to be supported, instead of laboring themselves and nourishing themselves with the understanding they themselves earn. There can be no reason in existence unless every man may be assumed to have as much understanding as he needs, if he will honestly labor. If he has great talents and can also raise many doubts, so also he must have powers in himself to gain understanding, if he seriously wills it. But everyone should keep silent in so far as he has no understanding to communicate. Merely to want to raise an outcry is a sort of glittering idleness. It is easy to do that, it is easy enough to make oneself seem important thereby; it is easy enough to get on the poor list, and then it is easy enough to cry out to the state, "Support me." And every premise-writer cries out to the state, "Support me." But divine governance answers, "Thou shalt support thyself, and so must every man." Then the apparent modesty of merely prompting a discussion is seen to be a hidden presumption; for if the person in question is not capable of being an essential author, it is presumptuous to pretend to be an author. The essential author is essentially a teacher; and, if he is not and essentially could not be a real author, he is essentially a learner. Instead of being *nourishing*, as every essential author is (the difference being only with respect to talents and compass), every premise-author is devouring. He is devouring precisely because, instead of keeping silence, he utters doubts and makes an outcry.

The art of all communication consists in coming as close as possible to reality, i.e. to contemporaries who are in the position of readers, and yet at the same time to have a viewpoint, to preserve the comforting and endless distance of ideality. Allow me to illustrate this by an example from an earlier literary production. In the psychological experiment "Guilty?/not guilty?" (in *Stages upon Life's Way*) there is depicted one who is taxed to the utmost, even to the point of despair, by the mortal danger threatening his spiritual life, and the whole thing is depicted as though it might have happened yesterday. In this respect the production is brought as close as possible to reality; but now comes the comforting reflection that the whole thing is an experiment, spiritually understood, he is what in civil life would be called a very dangerous person; such a person as ordinarily is not allowed to go out alone and is usually accompanied by a couple of policemen for the sake of public security. So it is too in this production that to assure public safety there is included an experimenter (he calls himself a policeman) who very quietly shows how the whole thing hangs together, theoretically develops a life-view, which he completes and rounds out, while he illustrates it by pointing to the subject, in order to indicate the movements he makes in proportion as the noose is tightened. If this were not a mere experiment, if there were no experimenter at hand, no life-view developed – then such a literary production, whether or no it displayed talent, would be simply consuming. It would be agonizing to come in contact with it, because it merely made the impression of a real man who presumably the next instant might go mad. It is one thing to depict a passionate man when with him is depicted a *Gewaltiger* and a life-view which can control him, and it is quite a different thing when a passionate man with the highest degree of personal reality becomes an author, runs amuck, and by the help of a book assaults us as it were with his doubts and torments.

If one would depict a man who thought he had had a revelation but later became insecure about it, and if one did this as an experiment, and if there was at hand an experimenter who understood his business thoroughly, and if a whole life-view was developed which made use of the subject of the experiment as a physicist might do – then that would be all right, perhaps much might be learned from the report of it. Perhaps the experimenter had assured himself by observation that such a thing might happen in his generation, and hence brought the experiment as close as possible to this age – but *nota bene* that he himself was in possession of the explanation which would be communicated. When on the contrary a real man in the perplexed condition of the subject of this experiment precipitates himself upon the public

– then he is consuming in the highest degree. The abnormal man may be instructive when he is controlled and forced to take his place in a total life-view; but when he bluntly claims the authority of a teacher without being able to teach anything else but abnormality and its pain, one is painfully affected by the importunate reality of such an ex-author, who personally is in mortal danger and quite personally wants to claim our aid, or by the fact that he knows no way of escape, wants to make us uneasy, to make us suffer as he does. It is one thing to be a physician who knows all about cures and healing, upon which he lectures in his clinic where he recounts the history of a disease – it is one thing to be a physician beside a sickbed, and another thing to be a sick man who leaps out of his bed by becoming an author, communicating bluntly the symptoms of his disease. Perhaps he may be able to express and expound the symptoms of his illness in far more glowing colors than does the physician when he describes them; for the fact that he knows no resource, no salvation, gives him a peculiar passionate elasticity in comparison with the consoling talk of the physician who knows what expedients to use. But in spite of that there remains the decisive qualitative difference between a sick man and a physician. And this difference is precisely the same decisive *qualitative difference* between being a premise-author and an essential author.

What here is said about premise-authors in a way so general that it may apply to perfectly insignificant pates and to superior talents as well, if they lack a definite life-view and lack a conclusion, has an application also to Magister Adler, an author against whom I am not conscious of any animosity, since in all honesty I even owe him thanks for the service he has rendered the pseudonymous authors whose natural protector I am, for the fact that he has hardly made any reference to them – at least he has not showed it in such a way that in quoting them and other such writers he has brought them into any intimate and annoying relationship with himself. And not only for this do I owe him thanks, but also in many ways as a reader. For it is certain that in his books there are many passages which one who is well-disposed cannot read without edification, that sometimes he is moving, not rarely entertaining by his liveliness, and does not altogether lack profundity, though he entirely lacks consistency in his thought. Magister Adler is equipped with many happy gifts, with many desirable presuppositions with respect to learning, and along with these he has one premise more which distinguishes him absolutely from all other premise-authors: he has a fact of revelation to which he can appeal. Far from me truly is every foolish jest. I shall certainly think of this claim with every possible concession and reserve; I do not presume to deny it or to affirm it. I regard myself simply as a learner. This at least is certain, that had he held fast to this fact of revelation as an unshakable fact, though others might consider him mad or else bow to his authority – had he done that, had he not indecisively, waveringly, higgled about it and privately interpreted it away, I would not have been justified in calling him a premise-author. But to press such a fact upon the attention of the public, and then in the end not to know himself what is what, what he himself means by it – that is to characterize himself as a premise-author, for that is to bluster in the most frightfully loud tones – and then to wait for the world to come to his assistance with the explanation that he had had a revelation, or had not had it. Such a phenomenon may have profound significance as a bitter epigram upon our age. In a wavering, doubtful and unstable age, where the individual is accustomed to seek outside himself (in the world about him, in common opinion, in town gossip) what essentially is only to be found in the decision of the individual himself – in such an age a man steps forward and appeals to a revelation, or rather he bolts out like a terrified man, with fright and fear depicted upon his countenance, still trembling from the impression of that moment, and announces that he has been favored by a revelation. *Pro dii immortales*, here then at last there must be help, here at last there must be firm ground to stand upon! Alas, he resembles this age only too thoroughly – the next instant he does not himself know definitely what is what, he leaves that unresolved – and meanwhile he writes big and (perhaps) clever books. Lo, in those remote times when a man was honored by high revelations he retired for three years, so that he might not be taken by surprise, so that he might comprehend himself in this incomprehensible experience before teaching others. Nowadays one takes for a revelation any sort of strong impression, and the same evening puts it in the newspaper. Any strong impression – indeed, to all eternity I should not regard myself as justified in saying that about the lowliest man who appealed to a revelation, if he himself stood firmly by what he had said; but Adler's conduct has justified me in saying what he himself says in his latest works. Nevertheless, Magister Adler stands or falls with his fact of revelation, he may write folios, and even though they were richer in ideas and happy thoughts and many a profound hint than are the last books, an answer is nevertheless due as to what is what, whether the whole thing was a prank – or whether in that case he will say that he repents it, since at one time he obtruded upon us its reality – or whether it was a fact of revelation, whether he then will assume that role, while other men with becoming reverence for the person so eminently favored come forward as inquirers, each one particularly in proportion to the talents bestowed upon him, but only as a learner.

What has been briefly touched upon here and will be treated more fully in a subsequent investigation sufficiently shows that it is not my intention to appraise aesthetically or critically particular passages in Magister Adler's books, or in general to deal with his writings as a critic usually does. Usually one deals with the writings and leaves the author out. Here this cannot be done. My whole criticism and whatever ability I may have as a critic is all within the assumption that I am an insignificant individual. It is Magister Adler who has put himself forward with his fact of revelation, and for me at least this is so decisive that I cannot forget it for an instant, nor for an instant can I regard myself as justified in using my measuring rod, and I cannot criticize revealed scriptures in the same way as I would books by men. Magister Adler is not simply an author, by reason of his revelation he is a phenomenon, in the midst of everyday life he is a dramatic person, and there can be no question of forgetting him while dealing with his writings, which commonly would be a duty. No, in dealing with his works it is necessary to be attentive to him, to him who by his fact of revelation is placed in a position so extreme that he must either be a charlatan – or an apostle. It will not do to carry the game so far as when one speaks of Denmark's Aristotle, though God knows he does not resemble him at all, but here in Denmark he resembles him more than others do – so that at last one plays the game that one was very near having a revelation, that in this country he came nearest to being an apostle. Since he has no other legitimation, the concept veers about, and it is he that is farthest precisely because he would obtrude himself.

As a phenomenon in our age (so that as much attention is paid to our age as to Adler) shall Magister Adler be the subject of discourse in this little book. His books should not be appraised aesthetically and critically as if they were by an ordinary author; no, he shall be treated by the lowly serviceable critic with the respect due to his claim, and his writings shall be used only to see whether he understands himself in being what he gives himself out to be, and which *in any serious sense* he has not given any sign of wishing to revoke. Neither shall anything be said about the doctrine he expounds, as to whether it is heretical or not. All such questions must be regarded as unimportant in comparison with the qualitative decisive factor. On the contrary, the ethical accent of seriousness shall be laid if possible upon that which must either give him divine authority (and in that case he must be required to make use of this authority instead of being ambiguously clever in big books), or else it must be penitently revoked, since once he thrust himself forward by claiming it. It shall if possible be emphasized with the accent of seriousness that he has appealed to a fact of revelation.

Should anyone ask who am I who do this, here is my reply: I am a serviceable critic, a lowly person, who has only ethical justification, as every man has over against an author. In case the whole episode of Magister Adler is not to be treated as an insignificance which had best be ignored, then it is disquieting that an author presses upon us as a riddle, not what we are to understand by the fact that he had a revelation (for that he has a right to do), but the riddle whether he himself thinks it was a revelation, or that it was just another sort of Hurrah boys. I am firmly convinced that the Apostle Paul, as can easily be seen from his writings, would not have taken it ill if anyone in a serious conversation had asked him whether he really had had a revelation; and I know that Paul with the brevity of seriousness would have expressed himself briefly and replied, "Yes." But in case Paul (may he forgive me for what I am about to say – it must be done to illustrate something), instead of answering briefly, were it yes or no, had entered upon a long and prolix discourse to this effect: "I see well enough now, in fact I already have said it, but perhaps after all revelation is too strong an expression, but something it was, something like genius it was . . ." Well, then the question would have been a different one. With geniuses I can hold my own fairly well. God preserve me – if it is in truth the greatest genius, then with aesthetic propriety I gladly express my reverence for the superior mind from whom I am learning; but that I show him religious subjection, that I should submit my judgment to his divine authority – no, that I do not do, neither does any genius require it of me. But when a man coolly wishes to explain away what was intended to be an apostolic existence into being a genius, without revoking the first claim – then he confounds the situation terribly.

To this a critic must hold fast, as I shall do in this little discussion. Without praising my own wares I also venture to promise that he who reads attentively will find in this book illumination; for I am not unacquainted with my age and with what is fermenting in it, I follow along with it, though like one who sails in the same ship and yet has a separate cabin, not in the quality of anything extraordinary, as though I had authority, no, in the quality of an eccentric who has anything but authority.*

Here this introduction should properly end. However, I still wish to add a word. It is not without sorrow, not without sadness, I write this review; I would rather leave it unwritten, if I had no need to fear that Magister Adler's works, which recently have been highly (and stupidly) praised in the *Northern Church Times*, might yet attract attention, and in such a case he must necessarily occasion great confusion in the religious field, precisely because he possesses a certain cleverness, and most men have not enough ability to distinguish *inter et inter*. The sad and

*The passage omitted here in 1847 referred to the "trousers" which had been made a subject of ridicule by *The Corsair*. This vulgar attack was made in 1846 and still rankled when S.K. wrote the first draft of this book. Later he proposed to abbreviate it as follows: Authority – well, yes, this might have been by the help of my trousers, for by my writings I have not attracted the attention of anybody, and, God knows it, my old gray trousers are entirely innocent of the fact that public opinion has paid so much attention to them.

sorrowful aspect of this, according to my conception, is due to the proportions of this land. In a little land like Denmark there naturally can be only a few who have time and opportunity to occupy themselves with the things of the intellect, and of this small number there naturally can be only some individuals who really have talents and also comprehend decisively that to them is appointed occupation with the things of the intellect as their only task. But all the more important it is that such an individual, precisely because the small proportions of our land hardly have room for a quick corrective, should check himself by the strictest discipline not to grasp at a glittering confusion instead of the truth. Magister Adler is such an individual, it is not impossible that he might attract to himself the admiration of one or another less informed person, but by this nothing is gained; just because in a little land there are so few who can judge with competence and insight, either with superior or at least with equal justification, just for this reason everyone who by talents or favor is advantageously placed ought to keep watch on himself. But even if Adler with his last works has augmented the capital fund of cleverness which in our age is in so many ways accumulating with the contribution of so many clever sayings, this is of not much avail in comparison with the confusion of all the most important concepts upon which Christianity depends. There is also in the intellectual world a glowing sensuality, a dangerous temptation to cleverness, which precisely by the play of multiplicity conceals a total lack of clearness. And although every author has a responsibility, yet it seems that an author in a great literature like the German or the French has less responsibility because he occasions less harm by swiftly vanishing in the multitude. It seems to me that Magister Adler should take this into account. I at least have sought to make this clear to myself in the consciousness of being such an individual. It is certain that in a small literature, precisely for the reason that it is small, one can realize tasks of a special sort which could not succeed in a great one where one author supplants the other; but it is also certain that the responsibility is all the more serious. When there are many springs it is not so dangerous that one of them is muddied, but in a little land, where in every direction there is hardly more than one spring, anyone who muddies it assumes a high degree of responsibility. And little as I love adherents and imitators, coteries and cliques, things that again thrive best in a little land but also do irreparable harm, all the more would I be glad if there were several other individuals who, on their own account and perhaps from entirely different points of view, were laboring for the cultivation of this field. But hitherto Adler has been of no profit; there is no concept he has explained, no new categorical definition he has supplied, no old and established one he has refreshed by new dialectical sharpness. Thus in no decisive sense has he been profitable, and to me in a way he has been a hindrance; for since he belongs to the religious field, and since he confuses *pro virili*, and since the proportions of this land are small, I have regarded it as my duty to interrupt my customary activity in order to correct a little bit the thinker whom I would have been more than willing to regard as my superior or as a fellow-worker – but *nota bene* one who was working on his own account. – Moreover, I myself understand very well how strange the whole thing looks. About an author who till now has not had many readers I write a book which presumably will not be read. As it is related of two princely personages who were very fat that they took their exercise by walking around one another, so in a little land the exercise of authors consists in walking around one another. However, I have chosen my problem in such a way, as I am accustomed to do, that in spite of the fact that it is an instant of time about which the investigation revolves, the treatment because of its more universal and ideal character will be fit to be read at all times. I have no talent nor competence to write for the instant.

CHAPTER I

THE HISTORICAL SITUATION

Magister Adler's collision with the universal as teacher in the State-Church; a special individual who has a fact of revelation.

It was in the year 1843 that Magister Adler published his *Sermons*, in the preface to which he announced with the utmost solemnity that he had experienced a revelation, that by this a new doctrine was communicated to him, and in the sermons themselves he distinguished (and thereby made everything definitely clear) between the discourses which were by him and those which were by the direct assistance of the Spirit.* He instructed us in the preface that the Spirit commanded him to burn everything he had formerly written. Thus he stood, or so he presented himself in the preface, as a picture of a new point of departure in the most decisive sense: behind him the conflagration, and himself saved from it with the new doctrine.

At that time, strange as it may seem now, afterwards, he was a teacher in the State-Church, he had, if one will so say, happily and well become a priest, only then occurred the event which must put him in the position of the special individual *extra ordinem* by having a new point of departure from God. Dear as it may be to the State, and in the religious field to the State-Church, to see, if it were so, a new generation of functionaries all equipped with talents and other abilities quite different from those of the former ones, dear as it may be to the State, and in the religious field to the State-Church, to see the most distinguished and superior talents consecrate themselves to the service of the State and the State-Church, it follows as a matter of course that this joy has one condition, namely, that they really wish to serve the State, that within its presuppositions and

*In a sense this is confusing, inasmuch as the qualitatively heterogeneous sermons ought not to have been published together; in any case there is lacking here a dialectic middle term of comparison as to how he understands himself in the qualitative decisive difference: of being assisted by the Spirit or being without it.

recognizing them they will *ex animi sententia* use their glorious gifts; otherwise joy must be transformed into anxiety and disquietude for its own security, in any case into anxious sympathy for the individual or the individuals who are making their lives a failure. For the State, including the State-Church, is not selfish, not tyrannical (as the evil-minded or dissatisfied wish to think and to make others believe), it is, according to its idea, benevolent; when it accepts the service of the individual it means to do him a service by indicating to him the appropriate place for the expedient and advantageous exercise of his powers.

By the fact of his revelation, by his new doctrine,* by standing under the direct outpouring of the Spirit, Magister Adler might easily become aware of being placed as a particular or peculiar individual altogether outside the universal, altogether *extra ordinem* as *extraordinarius*. Under such circumstances to wish to be in the service of the Establishment is a self-contradiction, and to expect of the Establishment that it shall keep him in its service is

*That Magister Adler has said later in a way that there is nothing new in his doctrine does not alter the case. By his course of action he has confirmed it in the strongest and loftiest terms. It is a fact, as I learn from the printer, that he had the type remain undistributed at the press, presumably with the expectation that his *Sermons* might soon have a new edition. The fact that he says later irresponsibly that there is nothing new, as well as the fact that he, who by his course of action evidently aimed at a sensation, later tried to give as it were a certain humoristic turn to the matter – such behavior surely might give a newspaper writer who was disposed to advocate his cause occasion for total confusion. To my notion there is nothing more pernicious than these slovenly transitions and alterations. A man should know what he wills and stand by it: if he alters his position, he must do so officially. Otherwise all is confusion. By the help of an anachronism a newspaper writer shows up a man to his advantage by the help of the fact that he had blundered. One lets it seem as though it were not at a different time he had said this, one treats the latter saying as though it were the contemporaneous interpretation; and lo, the man who precisely by his duplicity characterizes himself as unstable becomes a hero and perfectly consistent – the State and the State-Church on the other hand are put to embarrassment. But Magister Adler has never solemnly (which by reason of the relation of the spheres calls for repentance) revoked what he most solemnly had said. On the contrary, he has let the first affirmation stand, and then in a gossipy way said this or that as it were about it not being something new, that neither was it quite a revelation, but something in some way remarkable, and such like. (But about this later in its proper place.) But in respect to ambiguous phenomena one cannot too often oppose the ambiguity, which precisely when it is not held together is calculated to confuse.

really to wish to make a fool of the Establishment, as though it were something so abstract that it was not able to concentrate itself in an energetic consciousness of what it is and what it wills. To wish to be in the service of the Establishment, and then to wish to perform a service which aims precisely at the life of the Establishment, is just as unreasonable as if one were to wish to be in the service of a man, and yet to admit openly that his labor and zeal were to serve this man's enemy. This no man would put up with, and the reason why one thinks that the Establishment might put up with it is that one has a fantastic abstract conception of the impersonal character of the public and a fantastic notion of the public as a means of livelihood, in consequence of which the public is supposed to take care of every theological candidate. When the army stands drawn up with its front facing the Establishment, then to wish to be in the ranks and a *stipendiarius*, but to wish to take the inverse position, is a thing that cannot be done. The moment the march is to begin (as soon as life begins to stir) it will be evident that one is marching in the opposite direction. The *extraordinarius* has therefore to step out of the ranks. This is required as well for his high importance as for the seriousness of the universal; for an extraordinary man is too important to take his place in the ranks, and the seriousness of the universal requires unanimity and unity in the ranks, it needs to see who the extraordinary is, or to see that he is the extraordinary. In this *discrimen* precisely shall the extraordinary acquire his competence: on the one hand the lowly one, a man all but lost, due to the fact of being pointed out as the individual in the peculiar sense, of being pointed out as a poor Peer Eriksen in comparison with the universal, so that no shrewd man dare be his friend or even walk with him in the street, so that his friend, if he were shrewd, would swear that he did not know the man, so that "they that passed by wagged their heads" (Matt. 27:39) – and yet to be the man from whom something new shall issue. This is the painful crisis, but it never will be easy to become an *extraordinarius*.*

*The long passage which follows, containing 13 paragraphs, is found in *Papirer* VIII B, pp. 61ff. S.K. wrote it as a "supplement" to this book. The translator can find no place for it more appropriate than this.

So Magister Adler's collision with the universal is that of the special individual, with a revelation. Without wishing to deny straightway the possibility that this extraordinary experience might also occur to a man in our age, it certainly would be a very suspicious sign. But, if there is nothing new under the sun, neither is there any direct and monotonous repetition, there is constantly something newish or a new modification. Our age is the age of reflection and intelligence, hence it may very well be assumed that he who in our age is thus called of God would be *en rapport* with his age. He would then have at his disposition as a serviceable factor an eminent power of reflection. So this would be the difference: in olden times the man thus called would be the immediate instrument; in our age he would have as a serviceable factor this eminent reflection before which this lowly serviceable critic is obliged to bow. The man chosen in our age will be not merely an instrument in the immediate sense but will consciously undertake his calling in a sense different from that which has always characterized a divine calling: he will think of himself and understand himself in the fact that this extraordinary thing has happened to him.

How far it may be possible to conceive of a divine call within a human reflection, as a coefficient of it, I as a lowly serviceable critic am not bold enough to say; the answer would first be contained in the life of the extraordinary man, if such a one were to come. But to a certain point I can carry out the thought dialectically until reflection runs aground.

In case everything was in order about a man being called of God by a revelation, but he has as a serviceable factor an eminent reflection, he would then understand that to this call and to the fact of having a revelation there corresponds ethically a prodigious responsibility in all directions, not only inwardly (that he was sure within himself and understood himself in the fact that something extraordinary had happened to him, for that we can assume), but outwardly, in relation to the established order, because the extraordinary has in reflection the dialectic of being the highest salvation, but also of being able to be the greatest corruption. His responsibility in reflection would then be that he might not become the greatest misfortune to the established order, but might make everything as easy as possible for it, and that with fear and trembling he might watch out that no one, so far as lay in his power, should suffer harm by a direct relationship to his extraordinarity. In case he now let the serviceable reflection follow its own counsel alone, the ultimate consequence would be that he completely annihilated himself, annihilated the impression of himself, humanly understood, made himself as lowly, as insignificant as possible, almost odious, because in reflection, where every definition is dialectic, he rightly understood that the extraordinary, except at the point where it is and is in truth the extraordinary, is and may be the cause of the most frightful corruption. In the ultimate consequence of reflection he would then transform the fact of revelation into his life's deepest secret, which in the silence of the grave remained the law of his existence, but which he never communicated directly. – But, behold, just this would be to fail entirely to accomplish his task, it would be indeed disobedience to God. For he who is called by a revelation is called precisely to appeal to his revelation, he must precisely exert authority in the strength of the fact that he was called by a revelation. In a revival it is not assumed that the man awakened in an extraordinary way should go out and proclaim this to men; on the contrary, this may remain precisely the secret of the awakened man with God, it may precisely be humble to keep silence about this in a womanly way. But he who is called by a revelation and to communicate a revelation, or the fact that he had a revelation (for the principal thing is precisely that he has had a revelation, not always so much its contents – as with regard to a letter from heaven, if you will imagine such a thing, precisely the most important point is the fact that it has fallen from heaven, not always so much what is in it), he should proclaim this, appeal to it, exert authority.

So it is to be seen that when the fact of having had a revelation is transposed completely into reflection, this fact of having had a revelation must in one way or another come to be altogether impenetrable, or else work itself into a contradiction. For if the idea of the serviceable reflection conquers, a man will keep the very fact of revelation isolated and hidden, watching out with fear and trembling for the ruinous consequences which the direct communication might have, and shuddering at the responsibility. But therewith at the same time he gives up *authority*; he makes himself presumptuously into a genius, whereas God had called him to be an apostle. That is to say: in the idea of reflection a genius is the highest, an apostle is an impossibility; for the idea of an apostle is precisely the divine authority.

So reflection is brought to a standstill before the problem whether it is possible that human reflection is capable of understanding a call by revelation, whether one revelation does not imply continuous revelation. But on the other hand, since our age is the age of reflection and the human race may be assumed to be more and more developing in reflection, it seems after all self-evident that, if in such an age a man is called by a revelation, he must have in him an element of reflection more than the man thus called in an earlier age, who belonged to an earlier formation. In earlier times the reflection required of a man that was called signified only reflection within himself, understanding himself in the experience of the extraordinary thing that had happened to him; now it must signify reflection upon his whole relation to the environment, so that at the moment of undertaking his calling he must be able consciously to take account of his responsibility and also to take account of what would befall him as it befell the elect of an earlier time. He who in our age is called by a revelation must unite in his own person the fact of being the greatest maieutic of his age and the fact of being called, the fact of being called and the fact of being devoted (in the Latin sense of the word); in addition to the divine authority granted to him (which is the qualitatively decisive point) he must have an eminent wisdom to survey the circumstances of his life.

Farther human dialectic cannot go than up to the admission that it cannot think this thing, but also up to the admission that from this there follows nothing more than that it cannot be thought. But human dialectic, if it will understand itself and so be humble, never forgets that man's thoughts are not God's thoughts, that all the talk about genius and culture and reflection has nothing to do with the case, but that the divine authority is the decisive thing, that the man God has called, be he fisherman or shoemaker, is an apostle – for nowadays it is perhaps all too easy to understand that Peter was an apostle, but in those days people found it far easier to understand that he was a fisherman.

The divine authority is the category, and here quite rightly the sign of it is: *the possibility of offense*. For a genius may very well at one time or another in the course of 50 or 100 years cause *aesthetically* a shock, but never *ethically* can he cause an offense, for the offense is that a man possesses divine authority.

But with respect to this determining factor of being called by a revelation, as indeed with respect to everything Christian, indolence and custom and dullness and thoughtlessness have taken the liberty of loosening the "springs" [i.e. the primal forces]. Now it was an hysterical woman who got a revelation, now it was a sedentary professionist, now it was a professor who became so profound that he almost could say that he had had a revelation, now it was a squinting genius who squinted so deeply that he almost was near to having, and so good as had had, a revelation. This afterwards became pretty much what one understood by being called by a revelation, and so in a sense Paul too had a revelation, only that in addition he had an unusually good head.

No, the divine authority is the category. Here there is little or nothing at all for a *Privatdocent* or a licentiate or a paragraph-swallower to do – as little as a young girl needs the barber to remove her beard, and as little as a bald man needs the *friseur* to "accommodate" his hair, just so little is the assistance of these gentlemen needed. The question is quite simple: Will you obey? or will you not obey? Will you bow in faith before his divine authority? Or will you be offended? Or will you perhaps take no side? Beware! this also is offense.

But, as has been said, people have loosened the springs, or have weakened their tension in and through the parenthetical. Exegesis was the first parenthesis. Exegesis was busy about determining how this revelation was to be conceived, whether it was an inward factor, perhaps a sort of *Dichtung und Wahrheit*, etc., etc. Strangely enough, Paul, whom this question concerned most closely, seems not to have spent a single instant in wanting to conceive in this sense; but we others – well, we are not Paul, and so we must do something, for to obey him is not doing anything. Now, as a matter of course, from generation to generation, in every university, in every semester, there is a course about *how*, etc., etc. Yea, that is an excellent means of diversion. In that way we are diverted farther and farther from the task of obeying Paul.

Philosophy, and with that the theology which caricatures philosophy, was the second parenthesis. It said, as becomes a noble, high-born human science, "In no way shall I enter pettily into the question, with which I shall not allow myself to be disturbed, who was the author of a particular book of Scripture, whether he was only a fisherman or a lowly person of some sort. No, away with all pettiness! The content of the doctrine is the main thing, I inquire only about that. As little as an aesthetic critic inquires who was the author of a play but only *how* it is, just as indifferent is it to me who the author was" – just as indifferent also whether it was "the Apostle," a man with divine authority, which precisely is the knot. In this way one can easily be done with Paul without even beginning with him, or beginning with the fact that he possessed divine authority. People treat the Scriptures so scientifically that they might quite as well be anonymous writings.

Behold, from the moment the parenthetical got going there naturally was plenty to do for *Privatdocents* and licentiates and paragraph-swallowers and squinters; afterwards, as more and more work was done in this direction, things went more and more backward for the category of being called by a revelation; it became an insignificance, a matter of indifference, with which finally every man could compete; and then it went so entirely out of fashion that in the last resort it became a great rarity to see anybody in the "equipage."

So Magister Adler proclaimed that he had had a revelation, and thus came into collision with the State-Church. Since our age is an age of movement which would bring something new to birth, it must often experience this collision between the universal and the individual, a collision which may always have difficulty enough in itself but sometimes has a difficulty which does not lie in the collision itself but in the colliding parties. In case, for example, the individual in the peculiar sense loves the universal, thinks lowly of himself in comparison with the universal, shudders with fear and trembling at the thought of being in error, then he will make everything as good and easy as possible for the universal. And this conduct is a sign that it might be possible after all that he was a real *extraordinarius*. But in case the individual does not love the universal, does not honor the established order (as one may well do in spite of the fact that he has something new to contribute), in case he is not perhaps in his inward man agreed within himself as to what he is, but only dabbles at being the extraordinary, is only experimenting to see whether it pays well to be that – then will he, partly knowingly (chicanery), make everything as difficult as possible for the established order; partly he does it, without being quite conscious of what he does, because at bottom he cannot do without the established order, and therefore clings to it, seeks to shift the burden of responsibility from himself upon the established order, seeks like a clever advocate to get the public to do what he himself ought to do. When an individual gets the idea that he must separate himself from another man with whom he is living in the closest relationship, in case he himself is certainly and decisively resolved, in this case the painful operation of separation becomes easier. But in case he is uncertain, unresolved, so that he wishes it indeed but has not quite the courage to venture it, in case he is a cunning chap who wishes to shift the responsibility from himself but to steal the reward of the extraordinary – then the separation becomes a tiresome story, and for a long time remains a painful, grievous, vexatious relationship.

Let us suppose that a theological candidate in our time had adopted the notion that the oath of office is unjustifiable. Well then, he can say this freely and openly, if he thinks it expedient. "But by this he will close the road to advancement, and perhaps not accomplish anything, not even arouse a sensation, for a candidate is far too small an entity, and moreover he has no monopoly on the State-Church, since he has no official position." So (now I will think of a selfish man who not only does not love the Establishment but at bottom is an enemy of it) what can he do? He keeps silent for the time being; then he seeks a position as teacher in the State-Church; he gets it; he takes the oath. So now he is an office-bearer in the State-Church. Thereupon he publishes a book wherein he sets forth a revolutionary view. The whole situation is now changed. It would have been easy for the State-Church to bounce a theological candidate, easy to say to him, Very well then, having these views, you cannot become an office-bearer – and the State-Church would not have had to take any action at all with regard to this case, at the very most it would have to take a preventive measure against him quite particularly by not promoting him. But the theological candidate was shrewd and shrewdly understood how to make himself far more important. The responsibility which he as a candidate would have to assume for his peculiar view and would have bought dearly by sacrificing his future in the service of a higher call, while seeking to make the affair as easy as possible for the Establishment – this responsibility is now devolved upon the State-Church, which is required to take positive action to *deprive* of his office a man who by having become an office-bearer has at the same time made an attempt to interest the whole body of office-bearers in his fate. In this way such a revolutionary who is an enemy of the established order (which one need not be to be a reformer, and which a true reformer never is) seeks in cowardly fashion to give the universal as much trouble as he can.

For however conscious the State or the State-Church may be that it is in the truth and has the right on its side, and also that it is sound enough in health to excise such an individual without fearing that many might be harmed by it, yet it never can be expedient for the State-Church to have its first principles too frequently made the subject of discussion. Every living being, every existence, has its hidden life in the root from which the life-force proceeds and produces growth. It is well enough known to physiologists that nothing is more injurious to digestion than constant reflection upon digestion. And so it is also with relation to the spiritual life the most injurious thing when reflection, as it too often does, goes amiss and instead of being used to advantage brings the concealed labor of the hidden life out into the open and attacks the fundamental principles themselves. In case a marriage were to reflect upon the reality of marriage, it would become *eo ipso* a pretty poor marriage; for the powers that ought to be employed for the realization of the tasks of married life are employed by reflection to eat away the foundation. In case a man who has chosen a definite position in life were to reflect constantly whether this position were the right one, he would become *eo ipso* a sorry partner in business. Therefore, even though the State or the State-Church is sound enough in health to separate from it the revolutionary member, it is nevertheless deleterious that this gives rise to reflection. To everything hidden and concealed applies the saying of the ballad: "Merely one word thou hast uttered." It is easy enough to utter such a fateful word, but it is incalculable what harm may be occasioned by it, and a giant will be needed to stop the injurious effect of one word such as Peer Ruus let out in his sleep. And if the State or the State-Church must often suspend many such individuals, then at last an appearance is conjured up as though the State itself is *in suspenso*. The appearance of being in suspense always results when one does not rest upon the foundation but the foundation itself is made dialectical.

Such a situation may easily become dangerous for the State, principally because this sort of discussion is especially tempting to all insignificant pates, to all gossipy persons, to all empty blown-up bladders, and so more especially to the public. For the more concrete a subject is about which one is to think and express an opinion, the quicker and the more clearly will it be shown whether the speaker has the qualifications to take part in the discussion or not. But the prodigious problems – that really is something ... for the most insignificant twaddlers!* It is perhaps not beside the point to remind people of this, for our age, the age of movement, tends to bring fundamental assumptions under discussion, so that the consequence is that a marvelous number of men in the mass get on their feet and open their mouths all at once in the game of discussion, along with the public which understands absolutely nothing about it, whereas the prodigious size of the problem advantageously hides the ignorance of the discussers and the speakers respectively. In case a teacher wants to favor a know-nothing of a pupil, he can do it

*The prodigious problems from which the most eminent thinkers will shrink beckon to all insignificant pates as the task for them, and so foolish men make use of such opportunity to come forward and take part in the discussion. There even comes about a certain equality, for he who perhaps is eminently equipped by nature and has spent the best years of his life thinking over such matters admits that he dare not decide anything, and the most insignificant chatterer "expresses himself" in about the same way – so both are equally knowing.

in various ways, but among others he can do it by assigning to him such a prodigious problem that the examiners can infer nothing whatever from the triviality of his reply, because the immense magnitude of the subject deprives them of any standard of judgment. Perhaps I can illuminate this by an example from the world of learning. A learned twaddler who at bottom knows nothing can seldom be got to deal with anything concrete; he does not talk of a particular dialogue of Plato, that is too little for him – also it might become apparent that he had not read it. No, he talks about Plato as a whole, or even perhaps of Greek philosophy as a whole, but especially about the wisdom of the Indians and the Chinese. This Greek philosophy as a whole, the profundity of Oriental philosophy as a whole, is the prodigiously great, the boundless, which advantageously hides his ignorance. So also it is much easier to talk about an alteration in the form of government than to discuss a very little concrete problem like sewing a pair of shoes; and the injustice towards the few capable men lies in the fact that by reason of the prodigious greatness of the problem they are apparently on a par with every Peer, who "also speaks out." So it is much easier for a dunce to criticize our Lord than to judge the handiwork of an apprentice in a shop, yea, than to judge a sulphur match. For if only the problem is concrete, he will, it is to be hoped, soon betray how stupid he is. But our Lord and His governance of the world is something so prodigiously great that in a certain giddy abstract sense the most foolish man takes part in gossiping about it as well as the wisest man, because no one understands it.

Perhaps the sophistical is all too characteristic of our age, for the fact that we bring into discussion the greatest problems in order to encourage men who are the most insignificant and devoid of any thought to take part in the discussion. Let us not forget that noble reformer, that simple wise man of Greece, who had in fact to deal with Sophists, let us not forget that his strength lay in chasing the Sophists out of their roguish game with the abstract and the all-embracing, that his strength lay in making conversation so concrete that everyone who talked with him and who wanted to talk about some prodigious subject (the government of the State in general, about educational theory in general, etc.) before he knew how to put in a word was led to talk about himself – revealing whether he knew something, or didn't know anything.

But, back again to the theological candidate. Perhaps one might say, "But it is hard on a man to require him to shut the door upon his future prospects, so that he has no hope left, which he yet might have had if after he had been inducted he had been deposed – the hope of getting his pension." Yes, certainly it is hard, but it also will be hard to be an *extraordinarius*. Yes, it will be so hard that no one, if he understands it, could wish to be such a one; although he who is that in truth will surely in his relationship with God find comfort and satisfaction and blessedness. For the true *extraordinarius* will not be comforted nor seek relief nor find relief in the public, but only in God; and therein consists the dialectical, which is anguish and crisis but at the same time blessedness.

On the other hand, when an age becomes characterless it is possible that one or another individual may show symptoms of wishing to be an extraordinary; but he has no natural disposition for it, and therefore he wants the public to help him to it, he wants the public, the established order, to join forces with him to let him become an *extraordinarius*. How preposterous! It is precisely the extraordinary who is to introduce the new point of departure, in relation to the established order he is as one whose feet stand outside and will carry the old away – and then it is the established order itself that should be helpful to him! No, the universal precisely must hold him up tight; and if the established order does not do this, then there is developed here again something sophistical like that of the discussion of prodigious problems, so that it becomes the easiest thing in the world to become an *extraordinarius*, something every botcher aspires to, something for all those who otherwise are not capable of anything. There are epigrams enough in our age which the age itself produces without understanding them or heeding them. Let us not forget that nowadays a martyr, a reformer, is a man who smells of perfume, a man who sits at table with garlands in his hair, and perhaps with guests, a man who has all his goods in gilt-edged securities, a man who really never risks anything and yet wins all, even the title of reformer, his glorious title. But when the established order does not hold the reins tight, then finally every man who will not obey becomes a reformer. When the father becomes weak, when the family life is stirred by a rebellious reflection, then the naughty children easily confuse themselves with a sort of reformer. When the schoolmaster loses the reins, then it is very easy for a pert pupil to regard himself as a kind of reformer. In our age therefore it has indeed gone so far that it really requires no courage to defy the King, to vex and disturb the government of the State; but indeed it requires no little courage to say a word to the opposition, even down to the triumphators of the mob, courage ... to talk *against the reformers*.

So he was a clergyman – and then for the first time occurred the event which might put him in the position of the special individual *extra ordinem*. There is the collision. For it is easy to see that Adler was so situated; and only for the sake of greater clarity shall I indicate very briefly the dialectical relationship between (a) the *universal*, (b) the *individual*, and (c) the *special individual*, that is, the extraordinary. When the individual merely reproduces in his life the established order (of course with variations in accordance with the powers and faculties he possesses and his capacity), then he stands related to the established order as the normal individual, as the regular individual; he displays the life of the universal in his existence; the established order is for him the basis which educationally permeates and develops his faculties in likeness with itself; he is related as the individual whose life is inflected in accordance with the established order as its paradigm. However, let us not forget (for discontented and evil-minded men are ready to spread false rumors) that his life is not for this cause spiritless and insipid. He is not just one of the patter of words in the glossary which follow the paradigm. No, he is free and essentially independent, and to be such a regular individual is as a rule the highest, but also the qualitatively significant, task which therefore is assigned to every man. On the other hand, so soon as the individual lets his reflection grasp so deep that he wants to reflect upon the fundamental presuppositions of the established order – then he is by way of intending to want to be a special individual, and so long as he thus reflects he refuses to follow the *impressa vestigia* of the established order, he is *extra ordinem*, on his own responsibility and at his own risk. And when the individual continues in such a path and goes so far that he no longer is the regular individual *reproductively renewing* in himself *the life of the established order* though willing, under eternal responsibility, to take his place therein, but wills to renew *the life of the established order* by *introducing a new point of departure* for it, *a point of departure which is new in comparison with the fundamental presuppositions of the established order*, then by classifying himself immediately under God he must relate himself to the established order as refashioning it – then he is the *extraordinarius*, that is to say, this place is to be assigned to him whether he has a right to it or no. Here he must conquer and face his judgment – but the universal must decisively exclude him.

It is important here especially, as indeed everywhere it is, that the qualitative dialectic be respected with ethical seriousness. For in an age which lacks character the sophistical situation may arise where one who intends to be an extraordinary wants this intention to be profitable to him in the service of the universal, so that because of this he may become an uncommon figure among ordinary men. Unhappy confusion which has its ground in the thoughtless and frivolous tendency to judge quantitatively! A man must either wish to serve the universal, the established order, expressing this in his life, and in this case his merit will be measured by the faithfulness and punctuality with which he knows how to subordinate himself to the universal, knows how to make his life a beautiful and rich and faithful reproduction of the established order by forming himself to be a type of it – or else he must be seriously the extraordinary, and so, as *extra ordinem*, he must get out of the files, the ranks, where he does not belong. But in our age everything is confused. A discontented office-bearer, for example, wants to be something extraordinary – and at the same time discontented. A sorry, immoral confusion! If he is discontented, if he has something new from God to bring us – then, out of the ranks! "with a halter about his neck"; and then let him speak out, for then the situation is such as a true *extraordinarius* needs and must demand in order to be able to gesticulate and start up the music. But if he hasn't anything new from God to bring us, it shall by no means be to his advantage that he is discontented – and at the same time an office-bearer. But the characterlessness and pert indolence of this age comes at last to regard it as a kind of disgraceful narrow-mindedness to be anything out and out: either an office-bearer faithful in body and soul; or a reformer with the sword hanging over his head, in mortal danger, in self-denial.

What makes this difference between the ordinary individual and the special individual is *the starting-point*. Apart from this it may well be that an ordinary individual is, humanly speaking, greater than a real *extraordinarius*. The final measure according to which men are ranked is the ethical, in relation to which the differences are infinitesimal; but conversely the worldly mind lets the differences determine the rank. Let us take an example of what here is called the *ordinary individual*, and let us be right glad that we have an example to which we can point, let us mention *honoris causa*, but also to illuminate this situation, the much admired Bishop of Zeeland – and here everyone may well express admiration, for to admire him who expresses the universal is a glad privilege, for from him one can learn. Bishop Mynster does not possess in the very least the marks which characterize what one might call in the strictest sense the special individual. On the contrary, with lofty calm, reposing gladly in his convictions as the abundant content of an abundant life, with the admonishing emphasis, with the sober discretion of seriousness, though not without a noble little turn of expressions directed against confused pates, this man has always acknowledged that it was nothing new he had to bring, that on the contrary it was the old and well known; he never has shaken the pillars of the established order, on the contrary he has himself stood unshaken as a foundation pillar. And when he looks over the first edition of his earliest sermons he "finds nothing essential to change" (as though perhaps since that time he had been so fortunate as to run across one or another freshly arrived systematic novelty); and when the time comes that on his deathbed he reviews all his sermons, not for a new edition but as a testimony, he presumably will find "nothing essential to change." No, it was all the old and well known – which in him nevertheless found a spring so fresh and so refreshing, an expression so noble, so beautiful and so rich that during a long life he profoundly moved many and after his death he will continue to move many. Yea, verily, in case a doctrine once at its very beginning may wish for an apostle who in the strictest, in a paradoxical sense is an *extraordinarius*, standing outside the ranks – ah, but then will the same doctrine in a later time wish for such householders who will have nothing new to bring out of their treasures, who on the contrary seriously find pleasure only in themselves expressing the universal and find pleasure in marching together in the ranks and teaching the rest of us to mark time. But is it not insulting to the right reverend man to sit and write anything like this? In case what has been said here is true, Bishop Mynster is indeed no great man, he has never indeed followed with the times, he does not know indeed what the age requires, still less was he able to invent it. No, he has invented nothing. Whether perhaps he might have been able to do it (he who nevertheless as a sharp-sighted psychologist knows human folly thoroughly, and also is in possession of the key to the great storehouse where the requirements of the age are piled up) I shall not venture to decide, but certain it is that he has invented nothing.*

So the new starting-point was the difference between the true ordinary and the true extraordinary individual. They both have in common the essential human measuring-rod, the ethical. When, then, the individual is the true *extraordinarius* and really has a new starting-point, when he understands his life's pressing difficulty in the *discrimen* between the universal and the individually *extra ordinem*, he must be unconditionally recognized for the fact that he is willing to make *sacrifices*. And for this he must be willing *for his own sake* and *for the sake of the universal.*

*The translator remarks that S.K. gave no sign that he might wish to suppress this eloquent panegyric or to alter it in any important respect. Evidently he was glad to seize the opportunity of uttering it, and doubtless at the end of his life he was glad he had done so, he "found nothing essential to change." His youthful enthusiasm for his Bishop had long since grown cold, but here he says all he could truthfully say in his praise. But he emphatically excludes the notion that Mynster was what he called a "special individual," and still more that he was, as Martensen called him, "a witness to the truth," which in S.K.'s vocabulary meant a martyr, one who suffered or was ready to suffer for the truth. *That* Bishop Mynster certainly was not. This utterance of Martensen's in his funeral oration ignited the conflagration, that is, prompted S.K. to launch out upon his violent attack upon Mynster and the "established" Christianity which he represented. In the midst of that he died without regretting what he had said in praise of the deceased Bishop.

Precisely because the *extraordinarius*, if he is that in truth, must by his God-relationship be aware *summa summarum* that *κατα δύναμιν* he is stronger than the established order, he has nothing at all to do with the concern whether he will now barely be victorious. No, from this concern he is entirely exempted; but on the other hand he has the terrible responsibility of the special individual for every step he takes, whether he now is following his order accurately in the smallest details, whether definitely, alone, and obediently he has heard God's voice – the dreadful responsibility in case he heard or had heard amiss. Precisely for this reason must he wish for himself all possible opposition from without, wish that the established order might have power to make his life a *tentamen rigorosum*, for this trial and its pain is yet nothing compared with the terror of responsibility, if he were or had been in error! In case, for example, a son should feel called to introduce a new view of the domestic life (and as a son is bound by filial piety, so shall or ought every individual be bound by piety towards the universal) – would he not then, if there was truth in him, wish precisely that the father might be the strong one who could encounter him with the full power of parental authority? For the son would not so much fear to get the worst of it, if he was in the wrong, so that humbled but saved he must return to the old ways, as he would shudder at the horror of being victorious if he were in the wrong.

Thus it is with the true *extraordinarius*: he is the most carefree man in comparison with the worldly man's temporal anxiety as to whether what he has to proclaim will be triumphant in the world; on the other hand he is as much in anguish as a poor sinner with a contrite heart whenever he thinks of his responsibility, whether in any way he might be mistaken; yea, for him it is as though his breathing were obstructed, so heavily weighs the weight of his responsibility upon him. Precisely for this reason does he wish for opposition – he the weak man – he the strong one who though a lone man is in his weakness *κατα δύναμιν* stronger than all the united powers of the established order, which of course has power to scourge him and put him to death as nothing. When the berserker rage came over our northern forebears they let themselves be pressed between shields: so also does the true *extraordinarius* wish that the power of the established order would put up a suitable resistance. In this case Magister Adler, if in truth he were the *extraordinarius*, might honestly be very glad of the fact that as the highest clerical authority in the Danish Church there stands such a man as Bishop Mynster, a man who, without being cruel or narrow-minded, by his own obedience has sternly disciplined himself with the strong emphasis or gravity of seriousness to dare to require of others the universal, a man of whom it may be said with the seriousness of a Cato that he *ad majorum disciplinam institutus non ad huius seculi levitatem*; a man who very well can join in the game if only a true *extraordinarius* is there. In this case too Magister Adler did not need (as in other cases might be necessary) to lend the established order a bit of his power in order that it might be able to put up a suitable opposition to him. But in any event the cause of the *extraordinarius* owes much to the firmness of such a man. A weaker man in that official position, a man who himself had some symptoms of wanting to be something of an *extraordinarius* – then perhaps Adler might not have been deposed, the situation not consistently and efficiently regulated, thus the whole affair would have become a meaningless and "remarkable something." A confused *extraordinarius* introducing the new, and a weak-kneed man of government, are to be sure a perfect match for one another, but only as Punch and Judy are. And perhaps the time may soon come to exhibit such a relationship. For if our age lacks the true *extraordinarius*, it lacks also those serious figures, those individuals disciplined in the highest sense, who precisely by self-discipline know how to hold others in check, and hence to educate genuine extraordinary figures; for it is not loose concepts, and it is not indefinite and shifting relationships which create the true *extraordinarius*, they only coddle and spoil him. And possibly our age does not really need the true *extraordinarius*, but on the contrary those upright men who with God-fearing resignation conceive it as their task not to invent something new but with life and soul to be faithful to the established truth. But whether or no our age needs extraordinary figures, one thing is sure, that the extraordinary one is recognizable by the fact that he is willing to make sacrifices.

In our age the man of movement (the spurious *extraordinarius*) understands and takes the matter in hand differently. Perhaps it is after a thoroughly reasonable finite reflection upon the situation, the aim, etc., that a man reaches the *result* that he has a new proposal to make. From now on he is through with the inward direction of the mind in self-searching and with responsibility before God – he has indeed already a result. He now takes up a position opposed to the established order, and the *telos* of his effort is that this proposal, this plan of his, must triumph. It is certain and sure that his plan is the true one. The problem and the labor is only to insure that it may be brought to victory.

One sees plainly that the situation of the true *extraordinarius* is the converse of this. He is concerned only about his instructions and his relationship to God, occupied alone with his subterranean labor in the mine to dig up the treasure, or to hear God's voice; he jokes lightheartedly about the question of being victorious in the world, for he knows well enough that, if only all is as it should be in his relationship with God, his idea will surely triumph, even though he fall. The true *extraordinarius* in this relationship with God is conscious of his heterogeneity with the temporal, and therefore in this *spatium* of heterogeneity he has room in which he can move in venturing for his cause, venturing life and blood. The man of movement has no eternal conviction, therefore in an eternal sense he can never be sure, neither is he busy alone about gaining the assurance: precisely for this reason he has no room and no time to venture anything especial. His cause is altogether *homogeneous* with the temporal, therefore not only is the *telos* of his effort that he shall triumph, but *the fact that he triumphs* shall at bottom convince the man of movement that *he was in the right*, that his proposal was true. The same men who constitute the established order he not only will need again but he *has need of them*, if only they will don a new uniform in correspondence with his plan. One easily sees how the dialectic of his effort must shape itself: he would upset the established order, and does not dare to give it a shove for fear of falling himself, for this would not only be a fatal circumstance, but at the same time, according to his own conceptions, be proof that he was in the wrong. Everything depends, as has been said, upon victory, not only because his plan will then be true, but also because his plan by being victorious may become true. He has no certainty, but acquires it only when he has triumphed;

whereas the true *extraordinarius* possesses the heterogeneous certainty, the certainty of eternity, whether he falls or no.

To wish to move people in that way is essentially as if one were to offer to perform a trick – "if it succeeds" – and now for the sake of completeness would have his name included on the placard. He who would move anything must himself stand firm, but the man of movement has nothing firm about him, he is firm only when he is taken into custody [*blevet fast*] – i.e. afterwards. He might therefore wish that the established order were weak and decrepit, in order that he might the more easily conquer. If such is not the case, then he must resort to every expedient to conquer, to cunning and wiliness, to handshaking, to conciliation, exclaiming as his trump card "the devil take me," or a concessive "beg your pardon," the reformer's behavior must be like his who seeks a position and runs errands all over the town, or like a huckster selling his vegetables on a busy Thursday he must stop and chaffer about the very plan itself, get it cluttered up by the help of committees, and above all there must be sent out a message to the public, with an exceedingly obliging and flattering invitation that a highly revered and cultured public will do the huckster – but what am I saying? – I mean the reformer, the honor of standing as godfather to the baby ... and so at last this bungling triumphs.* Such a man of movement is

*In these times one is busy solely and only about being victorious, one seems to live in the vain conceit that if only one can manage barely to conquer, it makes no difference about the means – as if the means were of no importance, whereas when there is any question of the situation in the world of spirit they are the determinant factor, or, more precisely expressed, the means and the victory are one and the same. Of course, in relation to money, titles, horses and carriages, torchlight processions and Hurrah boys, and other such like indecencies, it is true that the means are of no account, that the means of acquisition are not the same as possession. So one can *really* come into possession of money – in many shabby ways; one can *really* get a torchlight procession in one's honor and have attained it in many shabby ways. But in relation to spirit there are no such outward, palpable, indecent realities. The profound and elegant thing in relation to spirit is the fact that the *mode of acquisition* and *the possession* are one. Hence he who is not aware of this fact in the spiritual sphere, but is blissful in the vain conceit of being victorious, in spite of the fact that the means were thoroughly paltry, does not notice with what elegance the profundity of the spirit makes sport of him for the fact that he has not really conquered but has written a satire upon himself. Let us refer to the most dread and highest example: in case Jesus Christ did not conquer unable – unable even to venture – to stand alone as an individual and thereby find room to venture life and all; on the contrary he has need of the majority to be certified if it is true, if what he wants is any good. He wishes to move others, and at bottom he wants the others to hold on to him in order that he may stand firm. But then indeed there is no movement, for he stands firm only when the case is decided and the majority has won. So long as this is not decided (and this in fact is the period in which the movement should go on) he does not stand firm.

When one has the view of existence characteristic of the man of movement it can easily be seen that the reflection must develop to the point where it is regarded as ludicrous madness or stupidity that one should *risk* himself; and it may be reasonably conceded that from this point of view it does look so. But in requital the man of movement betakes himself, comically enough, to another point of view; the man of movement who does not stand firm at the moment when he ought to (i.e. so long as the cause is in the minority) but first stands firm when he doesn't need to; the man of movement who, strangely enough, thinks that the whole thing is due to him. All movement presupposes (as anybody will be convinced who thinks the dialectic of this situation) a point, a firm point outside. And so the true *extraordinarius* is the point outside, he stands upon the Archimedean point outside the world – a firm point *extra ordinem – et terram movebit*. But he also has room to move when it comes to life and death and scourging and other such like, which surely

by being crucified, but had conquered in the modern style by business methods and a dreadful use of His talking gear, so that none of the balloters could refuse Him their vote, with a cunning that could make people believe anything – in case Christ had come in that way and was regarded as the Son of God, then He didn't come into the world at all, and Christ would not have been the Son of God. What would have triumphed would have been, not Christianity, but a parody of Christianity. To shrewd folks this may well seem a confounded *nota bene* that the spirit is not like money, that the scurvy fellow may shamelessly pride himself that he *really* came into possession of money ("the unrighteous mammon"), really was victorious; but for every optimate it is an indescribably blessed comfort that there is after all one place where eternal *righteousness* prevails. In relation to spirit nothing can conquer in an accidental and outward way, but only in the essential way; but the essential way is neither more nor less than the reduplication of victory, since in the spiritual world the form is the reduplication of the content.

are of no help if one resolves to enter the majority, and could not conceivably happen to one who is in the majority. Whether the true *extraordinarius* prevails today or tomorrow or in a thousand years is a matter of no concern, for he *has conquered*, his relationship to God is his victory; yea, though what he has to proclaim were never to prevail in the world, to this he might reply, "All the worse for the world."

Behold, this attitude is the attitude of movement; but the "man of movement" has nothing eternal, and therefore nothing firm, so as a consequence thereof he has not the courage to become the *recognizable* individual who wills something and will take risks for it. Essentially he does not act at all, in the outcry he makes a feigned sally, his activity culminates in shouting out something. As when children are at play and one of them suddenly shouts, "Why not play this game?" the man of movement shouts, "Why not do this now?" Thereupon when they have become many, when the majority is on their side and the cause is forced through – then the man of movement is for the first time really recognizable, for he goes about with New Year's congratulations and says, "It was really I who stood at the head of the Movement and the New Direction." Sometimes it comes to pass that men behold with wonder several men going about with congratulations, each one of them saying, "It was really I who stood at the head of the Movement, etc." So it appears that there was not merely one but several men at the head. This comical confusion contains a deep truth, namely, that no one at all stood at the head, and therefore the one is as much justified as the other in going about with congratulations. A true *extraordinarius* who stood alone, forsaken, pointed out in the pillory of the special individual, a true *extraordinarius* who was recognizable by the fact that he was executed – well, it is a matter of course that after this he cannot very well go about with congratulations – but neither can he be mistaken for another.

The man of movement might perhaps better be called a stirring-stick (muddler). Indeed this is the essential distinction between moving and stirring, that movement is in a forward direction, stirring is movement up and down or round about, like the rod in the butter-churn, like the foot of him who treads the peat, like rumor and gossip, like the stick in the hand of the kitchen-maid when she stirs in the muddling pot. Hence it is only an illusion when these men of movement scoff at the capable men, the unshakable, who do in truth stand still – meaning that they themselves are not standing still; for stirring is not movement, there is no muddling in a running river, but in still standing water, and neither is there in that when it lies still and deep. If what is said here is read by one or another, to some it will perhaps seem a horrible and inhuman demand upon the *extraordinarius*. Well, possibly; I can do nothing for it, that a modern age by becoming entirely earthly and worldly succeeds in forgetting what paganism understood.

In the dreadful responsibility which the true *extraordinarius* has to face (for he does not possess the result once for all, he has not become God's plenipotentiary once and for all)* is included also the concern lest his example when he assumes a position *extra ordinem* may beguile other men who are weak, lightminded, unsteadfast, inquisitive, to wish also to try their hand at something similar, so that his example may become a snare, a temptation for them. For with regard to the concern which torments busybodies and gadabouts to win several apes and several adherents who agree with him, to get a society founded which has his own seal – this concern the true *extraordinarius* does not know, in this respect he is entirely lighthearted and jocose. But the dreadful thought that he might damage another man, that he might occasion any other man to try his hand lightmindedly at what involves the heaviest responsibility of the individual – this dreadful danger he conceives profoundly. In an age of movement like ours, where symptoms of wishing to be a bit extraordinary are an epidemic disease, one must especially, with fear and trembling, be mindful of his dreadful responsibility. He will therefore here again make his position as deterrent as possible for others, as little alluring and tempting as possible. If only the lightminded see that a dose of seriousness is included in holding out for something, they soon fall away, yea, they even transform themselves into opposition to the *extraordinarius*. Light-

*This is also nonsense. A king may well nominate a highly trusted minister once for all, in consideration of the fact that the minister is perhaps a considerably shrewder pate than the king, but God does not find himself in such a position.

mindedness would fain accept the *extraordinarius* as a playmate; when it observes that this is not feasible it unites against him all its childish wrath. But every *extraordinarius* owes it unconditionally to the established order that by one or another deeply considered step he first contrive if possible to make his extraordinary call seem repugnant, so that his example may not do harm, become a snare. A true *extraordinarius* in our age (since reflection and intelligence are so prodigiously developed) must be thoroughly acquainted with all possible known forms of dangers and difficulties. That a man in our age might receive a revelation cannot be absolutely denied, but the whole phenomenal demeanor of such an elect individual will be essentially different from that of all earlier examples who never encountered anything of the sort.

The true *extraordinarius* must have the presuppositions of his age constantly at his service, in a highly eminent degree he must have at his disposition that which is the conspicuous mark of our age: reflection and intelligence. The essential phenomenal difference between a man in our age to whom a revelation has been imparted, and a man in a previous age, is that the former undertakes this extraordinary task with a discretion developed to a high degree. Ours is a reflective age – it is unthinkable that the divine governance has not itself taken note of this fact. Now though a revelation is a paradoxical immediacy, yet if it should happen to anyone in our age, it must also be recognizable in him by the serviceable reflection with which he accepts it. His reflection must not overwhelm the extraordinary man, but he must have reflection to introduce it into the age.

Now it is indeed true that the affair of Adler had a highly unfortunate outcome, so that his example was thoroughly deterrent; but this is no credit to him, for in this respect he has done nothing to help the universal, and presumably he had not expected that the outcome would be so unfortunate, having even made arrangements to have the second edition come out promptly. Supposing now that he had come off brilliantly with getting himself a revelation, suppose this had been what the age demands, suppose it had been a success; and then suppose that owing to Magister Adler's example the universal was encumbered with a small voluntary battalion of hysterical women, of students and virtuosi who wouldn't take their professional examinations, *item* of certain droll crotcheteers who sit and spin out whimsical notions in a parsonage – who all had sought to renew their credit by getting themselves a revelation.

Now, purely dialectically with the help of imagination, I shall essay a little sketch which may show if possible what Magister Adler might have done, or I shall lift him altogether into the sphere of reflection. If he had been the true *extraordinarius*, then what he would have found it necessary to do was of course far more profound than a lowly serviceable critic can imagine. It would have been something more profound, and properly speaking profundity is the deep *existential* realization of an idea which corresponds directly with God. Nowadays it is thought splendid when anyone is so fortunate as to get a fancy, to make a profound remark, to put together in writing *horis sucecivis* something profound which every other hour he disavows existentially. No, just as perseverance (in contrast with the flashy deception of the moment) is the true virtue, so profundity also is not exhibited in an utterance, a statement, but in a mode of existence. Profundity is the pictorial and metaphorical expression which indicates how many feet a man existentially draws, in the same sense in which this is said of a ship. But a ship is said to draw so and so many feet of water, not in the sense in which feet are measured by the lead which is cast anywhere for a moment, but it is the decisive description of the ship's whole and daily existence, that it draws so and so much depth of water. Or to describe this in another way: the greater extent the telescope can be extended, the better it is, and so also, the greater extension a man has when he reaches the secrecy of his inmost life, just so many more feet does he draw in depth. Depth of mind is therefore the opposite of externality. A man who lives only externally has naturally a tendency to anticipate his future with great words, vows, etc.: the profound man is precisely the opposite, concealing the principal machinery by which he moves. He looks perhaps in daily use as if he were moving with one horsepower, and really the machinery is working at the highest power.*

*The following 5 paragraphs are taken from *Papirer* VIII B 12, pp. 55f., omitting 4 footnotes (VII B 252, 2-4, 9).

In order to illustrate the whole situation, allow me to give an example, purely imaginary, and constructed with poetic license. For this I choose a genius raised to the power of reflection. But at the same time I shall make the situation as difficult as possible. He is a genius, but he did not know this from the beginning. Such a thing can very well be thought, and moreover it marks the difference between an immediate genius and a genius in reflection, for the latter needs a shock in order to become what was latent in him. So he has lived on without understanding himself, he has trained himself for the service of the state, he a clergyman.

Only now comes about the event which gives him the shock. At that very moment he understands himself as extraordinary, which, however, he views at the same time as his misery because henceforth he cannot take refuge in the universal. But, above all, with his eminent reflection he surveys the whole responsibility of his position.

Here then is his *discrimen*: either to take in vain his extraordinariness, regarding it as a glittering distinction, and so occasion irreparable confusion; or else, first and foremost, before he thinks of communicating the new view which has come into his mind, he sacrifices himself, and thus reconciles himself with the universal.

That he himself is willing to resign his office is the least part of this sacrifice, such an act of honesty will not satisfy him nor relieve his ethical anxiety.

Let us now begin. So it is assumed that something has happened to him which was extraordinary or by which he became extraordinary. From this moment his life has been sequestrated by a higher power. The question now is about the inwardness of the reflection with which he undertakes his task. Reflection is the mediator, the help of which he must use first and foremost to render himself harmless.

Dialectically he will at once perceive that the extraordinary has the dangerous *discrimen* that what he is in truth may for the others become the greatest ruin. He will therefore at the same moment shut himself up in impenetrable silence, shut himself up against every other, lest any undialectic imprudence should corrupt the whole thing into gossip, but that the extraordinary may have time to settle on the leas in the pause of silence. "One does not sew a new piece of cloth in an old garment, nor put new wine into old wine-skins, lest the rent become worse and the wine-skins burst" – and so it will come about when the absolutely new point of departure is by overhasty bustle bunglingly joined with the old, so that it only does harm. At the same moment reflection will also teach him silence, the silence in which he dedicates himself, as a mother consecrates herself to exist only for the sake of the child, the silence which prevents any communication with any other, in order not to communicate anything wrong or in a wrong way.

But, after all, this extraordinary thing must be communicated. Silence must not mean the abortion of truth. But no impatience! There is a neurasthenic trembling which because of shaking cannot hold anything nor pass anything on. Let us not be deceived by it. Everyone who knows what it is to be truly resolute, knows very well that one can hold out and hold fast to a resolution. A man may be so situated in life that he quietly said to himself before God, "The path I am following must lead me to the stake," and in spite of that he goes forward step by step. But impatience says, "The sooner the better"; and the neurasthenic impatience says, almost at the border of despair, "If only it does not pass away again, if only the impulse in me does not disappear, so that to me might be applied the dreadful words, 'The children are come to birth, and there is not strength to bring forth' " (Isaiah 37:3). But after all it is dreadful to be in travail and bring forth wind. In case one with a sacred resolution has resolved to sacrifice his life, and with neurasthenic impatience goes ahead and throws his life away and is executed "the sooner the better," has he gained anything, or has he really kept his resolution? The thing is that reflection and time be not allowed to shake his resolution. But on the other hand there is a remedy different from the foolish one of letting it occur at once, today; and this remedy is faith, humility, daily consecration.*

*The necessary slowness is also a cross which the elect man has to bear with faith and humility. Let us mention the highest instance, from which we believers ought to learn. When the angel had announced to Mary that by the Spirit she should give birth to a child – no, this whole thing was a miracle, why then did this child need nine months like other children? O what a test for faith and humility! That this is the divine will, to need the slowness of time! Behold, this was the cross. But Mary was the humble believer; by faith and humility she came to herself, although everything was miraculous. She remained the same quiet, humble woman – she believed.

So the extraordinary must be communicated, it must be introduced into the context of the established order; and the elect, the special individual, must receive the shock, the dreadful shock, by becoming the special individual, and therewith must pass the shock on. Dialectically we have here a duplex situation: that the shock be really a shock in the qualitatively dialectical sense; and on the other hand that the established order be spared as far as possible. As God is not a God of confusion, the elect is not called to make a confusion – and then run away from it. He must love the established order and therefore be willing to sacrifice himself. As one with the utmost caution deals with nitrate of silver [hellstone was the abhorrent name for it] (not in order to make no use of it but to use it rightly), as one wraps it up in something so that no one may come in direct contact with it, so must he take care to consecrate himself as a special individual in order that no one by a direct relationship to him may be harmed. The man who is called is at the same time the man who is "devoted." For what in him, the true *extraordinarius*, is eternal truth, a divine gift of grace, in every other man, who stands only in a direct relation to the *extraordinarius*, it is coquetry, untruth, perdition.

When we go farther along this path there must lie here at this point the profound task which has been spoken of, that the man who is called must first make himself almost repulsive. For the extraordinary character of the gift of grace is in one respect like hellstone, in spite of the fact that in another respect it is the blessing of heaven. The special individual is not in a direct sense the *extraordinarius*, he becomes such only when there intervenes the thought that he is paradoxical; and this dialectical situation may be expressed by the fact that the special individual first makes himself repulsive, so that no one could wish to be like him or to be as he is. In this pain consists, among other things, the sacrifice of himself and the atonement he makes with the established order out of love towards it. The fact that inquisitive men and fools and windbags prefer something different in order to have something to run after and to imitate, that confused extraordinary men who abhor discipline and constraint would rather break loose with others as *fratres et sorores liberi spiritus* – the fact that they disdain restraint has nothing whatever to do with the case. A truly competent spokesman for the established order will judge differently. He will not deny the possibility that there may be something new to contribute, but neither will he deny that the aforementioned precaution is pretty nearly the greatest possible.*

But, now, how make oneself repulsive? Let us first recapitulate. The elect man has had a revelation, that stands fast; he has shut himself up within himself with this fact; not one word has betrayed anything, not a gesture, and neither is his silence obvious, for then he would betray something; no, he is entirely like other men, talks like other men about what is happening – hence no one can see that he keeps silent. For one may keep silent in two ways: one may keep absolutely silent, but this silence is suspicious; or he may talk of every possible subject, thus it can occur to no one that he is keeping silent. And yet the extraordinary has come to pass, and there lives a man who with a life consecrated by a holy resolution is laboring in perfect silence. If God has graciously granted him his confidence (though he knows very well how hard it must be for God to have dealings with a lowly man, even though this lowly man is exerting himself with might and main), he will at least not insult God by treating his confidence as an idle tale and as town gossip, as something that must be bawled out. For there must be no impatience! But there is a neurasthenic cry, "Confess, confess!" The neurasthenic impatience may have its ground in the fact that the individual lacks the power to bear, that he is like a broken jar, or that the individual has been frightened by a despairing dread, or has a sort of compulsion to penitence which would make up for lost time by instant confession and would in self-mortification expose himself to all possible ridicule. For there are religiously awakened individuals so confused in their heads that they maltreat other men by getting them to ridicule them,

*The translator remarks that anyone who knows S.K. must recognize that this long passage about the right behavior for the true *extraordinarius* represents the author's profound reflection upon the role he was preparing to play as "the special individual" (without revelations and "without authority") in opposition to "the established order." He did not need to "step out of the ranks," for in many entries in the *Journal* he congratulated himself that he had not become a priest.

which is in intention just as tyrannous as when a tyrant maltreats men as slaves.

So how then is he to make himself repulsive? The *extraordinarius*, if he is the true one, must of course know in an eminent degree what I who am a lowly serviceable critic am not so badly informed of, namely, how thoroughly undermined our age is in a religious respect, while busy men hold general conventions about unimportant matters, and while the thunder of cannon call people together for amusement.* Since this is so, it must not be difficult to find in the demonic sphere the disreputable garment which might make him repulsive. And let us remember well the foregoing postulate: there is as yet in the whole world no man who knows any more what happened to the *extraordinarius* than does the pen I hold in my hand or the inkstand into which I dip it but without drawing my thoughts from it.

Adler might perfectly well have resigned his office, have said that the whole thing of being a priest was a fleeting fancy, something he wanted to try out, and he might have seen to it that this was accepted as the authentic interpretation. All this while the compass by which he steers must of course be unalterable, not varying a line with respect to his inward direction, but by holy consecration he must be renewed day by day in the same resolution. Of course when one suffers from neurasthenic impotence it is easier to let it out – the sooner the better.

Thereupon Adler (for his absolute silence up to this moment gave him up to this moment absolute control of the situation) might perhaps have furnished a poetical account wherein he would have described a demon who knew the lack of religiousness and of Christianity in our age, who was sent by the devil to show what Christianity was and to scorn it, he who in his heart was not merely a pagan but a Mephistopheles. He became a priest and attained the triumph of scorn over men. Thereupon he resigned his office. All the better sort in the established order would be disgusted with such a repulsive thing, and it is precisely the better sort that should be protected against harm. Were it some bandit who found this situation glorious – well, a bandit is lost anyhow.

*S.K. dwelt at this time near the great amusement park called Tivoli and could not but hear the goings on – especially the cannon.

Naturally this method is slow. It is easier to bawl it out at once.* On the other hand, it is so dreadful to work thus silently, and in a certain sense to work against oneself. Suppose one were to die in the meantime, and there was no one who knew a word about it. It is harrowing when Hamlet at the moment of death is almost in despair that the hidden life he had led with prodigious exertion in the service of the idea should be understood by no one, yea, that no one would know anything of it; but if Hamlet had become softened at death, he also would have talked in his lifetime, that is, let the whole thing go. There is a remedy for neurasthenic debility: it is faith, humility. The God who every day has been invoked with holy consecration, He indeed knows – and so all is well. For the result no one is responsible.

So if Adler had made himself repulsive in this way and thereby assured himself that none of the better sort might be tempted by his example – yea, then could he, humbly before God, have beaten his breast and said, "Now the first thing has been done, the sacrifice has been offered to the universal – now I can begin. Humanly speaking, I am weakened, I cannot become anything great in the eyes of men, now I can serve God."

Now let us recapitulate and see what Adler has done, and as a motto recall the words of Paul, "Let all things be done unto edification," whether one speaks in tongues or prophesies. These words contain an exhortation to reflection and ethical responsibility, that no one should think tumultuously that it is a man's

*It is true enough that in his later books Adler has gone over to the principle of silence, but without letting this quantitatively essential change make a decisive impression. Thereto add the fact that it comes rather late. God knows what he has to be silent about after having bawled out the highest thing he had, or rather more than he had, as he did from the beginning. There is something strangely feminine about Magister Adler. One can almost always count upon it that a girl when she is led into a great decision and at the decisive moment does the mad thing, then afterwards when she has changed and come at last into the right course, she will persuade herself that she has done that from the beginning. In general Magister Adler may be regarded as a good example of loquacity in a dialectical sense, which is so common in our age. One dabbles in one thing after another, gives up one system of philosophy and, as it is said, "goes farther," but at no point comes to a serious indication why one gave up the old and why one accepted the new, it never comes to a serious accounting with regard to the responsibility for thus changing oneself.

task, not to speak of the elect, to be like the darling of the fairy queen.

Did Adler resign his office, to satisfy in that way the established order? No, he remained in office and made out as if nothing had happened, until the State-Church took several steps – and then he tried to remain in office, though no one can blame him for all the chicanery which is usual in such circumstances. Has he done anything to hinder, if possible to remedy, all the unfortunate consequences his example has had for the established order? No, nothing whatsoever. Without having understood himself, without, as it seems, having given the least thought to the difficult problems he set in motion by his assertion of a revelation, he incontinently burst in upon the established order with his alarming fact. It is the business of the special individual to know everything down to the minutest details that stand related to his difficult position; instead he has left it to the established order to interpret all these difficulties. Perhaps he was like that toll-clerk who wrote so that nobody could read, and considered it his business to write and the business of the tariff commission to read – so he thought it was his business to cast a firebrand into the established order, and its business to take care of the consequences. In a vacillating age when unfortunately the growing generation almost from childhood is initiated into all sorts of doubts, in a vacillating age when the few competent men find it hard enough to hold out and to defend the pathos of the holy and the venerable – in such an age to break out impetuously with an immaturity which stands in the closest and most fatal relation to the highest interests . . . is, to put it in the mildest terms, the height of irresponsibility. That fortunately one can say of Adler that up to date he has done no special harm, is certainly no merit of his; it is due to the fact that he has been entirely ignored. And yet for all this he has done harm, for religiousness in our age is by no means so great and serious a thing that it is desirable for ridicule and lightmindedness to get hold of such a prize as Adler.

CHAPTER II

The so-called fact of revelation itself as a phenomenon coordinated with the whole modern development.

The very thing which seems to give to Christendom and to its learned or eloquent defenders such extraordinary success, this very thing it is which in many ways holds back and hinders individuals from making a qualitative and essential decision, this very thing it is which in the end must play into the hands of the free-thinkers, this very thing is the so-much-talked-about eighteen hundred years, whether by them the question is removed to such a prodigious distance that the impression of decision or the decisive impression vanishes in the twilight of imagination, or whether we have the paralogistic argument of the eighteen hundred years to the truth of Christianity, by which glittering and triumphant proof the trust of Christianity is unfortunately undermined, since in that case it is true only as an hypothesis, is by this triumphant argumentation transformed from eternal truth into an hypothesis. How could it ever occur to an eternal truth to sink to the point of proving its truth by the fact that it has endured for so and so many years, sink to a paltry comradeship with lies and deceits – which also have endured for many centuries and do still endure; an eternal truth which from first to last is equally true, in its last instant not more true than in its first, so that it did not come into the world shamefaced and embarrassed because it had not yet the centuries to which it could appeal, then was not foolishly puffed up for having endured for so long a time. True, an hypothesis which was embarrassed at the beginning becomes pompous with the years, but in requital it may any instant be discarded. This paradoxical fact (the offence of the understanding, the object of faith) does not become more true after eighteen hundred years than it was the day it happened. The fact that the eternal once came into existence in time is not a something which has to be tested in time, not something which *men are to test*, but is the paradox by which *men are to be tested*; and the eternal proudly despises every pert and impudent argumentation from the many years. And the paradox itself did not last throughout many years: it existed when Christ lived, and since then it has existed only whenever someone was offended and someone did in truth believe. If the paradoxical had existed for a thousand years or only for half an hour makes no difference; it becomes not more probable because it existed a thousand years, nor less probable because it only lasted half an hour.

If the thing of being or becoming a Christian is to have its decisive qualitative reality, it is necessary above all to get rid of the whole delusion of after-history, so that he who in the year 1846 becomes a Christian becomes that by being contemporaneous with the coming of Christianity into the world, in the same sense as those who were contemporaneous before the eighteen hundred years.* To this end it is important above all that there be fixed an unshakable qualitative difference between *the historical element in Christianity* (the paradox that the eternal came into existence once in time) and *the history of Christianity*, the history of its followers, etc. The fact that God came into existence in human form under the Emperor Augustus: that is the historical element in Christianity, the historical in a paradoxical composition. It is with this paradox that everyone, in whatever country he may be living, must become contemporary, if he is to become a believing Christian. With the history of Christianity he has in this respect nothing whatever to do. But the baleful fact in our age is, among others, that it is almost impossible to find a man who has time and patience and seriousness and the passion of thought to be well brought up to respect the qualitative dialectic.

*About all the dialectical problems which belong here (the paradox, the instant, the dialectic of contemporaneousness, etc.) I must refer to a pseudonym, Johannes Climacus, and his two works: *Philosophical Fragments* [pp. 78–93] and *The Concluding Postscript to the Philosophical Fragments* [pp. 45–47]. With regard to what is so dialectically composed one cannot in a few lines give a résumé; a reference, if it is to be reliable, must be just as elaborate and just as difficult as the original production, for if there be left out one single little subordinate definition, the whole dialectical construction suffers. Whether such is the case, as it is said to be, in the organic realm, that when one member suffers the whole suffers, I do not know; but in the dialectical construction the case is precisely this.

When the requirement of becoming contemporary with the coming of Christianity into the world in the same sense in which the contemporaries were is rightly understood, then it is *a truly religious requirement* and *precisely in the interest of Christianity*. However, the same requirement may be made by *the enemies*, by persons *offended* at Christianity, with the intent of *doing harm*. It is strange that, so far as I know, this has not been done, since after all in our times attacks upon Christianity have ventured the utmost with renewed power and not without talent.

But instead of insisting upon this concept of contemporaneousness, orthodoxy has taken another path – by the help of the eighteen hundred years. If one were to describe the whole orthodox apologetic effort in one single sentence, but also with categorical precision, one might say that it has the intent to make *Christianity plausible*. To this one might add that, if this were to succeed, then would this effort have the ironical fate that precisely upon the day of its triumph it would have lost everything and entirely quashed Christianity. It is well therefore that the apologists who know not what they do, troubled as they are with bustling, have not quite succeeded, it is well that they see a book written against them which shall, etc. To make Christianity plausible is the same as to misinterpret it. And after all, what is it the free-thinkers want? Why, they want to make Christianity plausible. For they know very well that if they can get Christianity's qualitative over-intensity fooled into the bustling busyness of plausibility – it's all over with Christianity. But the orthodox-apologetic effort also wants to make Christianity plausible, so it works hand in hand with heterodoxy. And yet it has worked thus in all simplicity, and its whole tactic, along with the relationship between orthodoxy and heterodoxy, may be regarded as an amazing example of what lack of character and lack of a qualitative dialectic may lead to: that one attacks what the other defends, that orthodoxy and heterodoxy continue to be enemies who would extirpate one another, in spite of the fact that they want one and the same thing – to make Christianity plausible.

Every defense of Christianity which understands what it would accomplish must behave exactly conversely, maintaining with might and main by qualitative dialectic that Christianity is *implausible*. For I should like to ask where a trace can be found of the qualitatively altered method. Under various names, right down to the last name, Speculation, people have labored to make Christianity plausible, conceivable, to get it out of the God-given language of paradox and translated into the Plattdeutsch of Speculation or Enlightenment. And yet, in order to have something to despair of, they have despaired whether it would succeed (what irony!) or they have rejoiced that it has succeeded and let Christianity receive congratulations on this occasion (what irony!). The man who journeyed from Jerusalem to Jericho and fell among thieves was not so badly off as Christianity; for the orthodox apologetic which had compassion upon it and took care of it treated it quite as badly as the thieves.

The Christian fact has no history, for it is the paradox that God once came into existence in time. This is the offense, but also it is the point of departure; and whether this was eighteen hundred years ago or yesterday, one can just as well be contemporary with it. Like the polar star this paradox never changes its position and therefore has no history, so this paradox stands immovable and unchanged; and though Christianity were to last for another ten thousand years, one would get no farther from this paradox than the contemporaries were. For the distance is not to be measured by the quantitative scale of time and space, for it is qualitatively decisive by the fact that it is a paradox.

On the other hand, so soon as one confuses Christianity with the Christian fact, so soon as one begins to count the years, one begins to change the implausible into the plausible. And one says, Now that Christianity has lasted (the Christian fact indeed occurred eighteen hundred years ago) for three hundred, now for seven hundred, now for eighteen hundred years – so it certainly must be true. By such a procedure one accomplishes the feat of confusing everything. The decision (that of becoming a Christian) easily becomes for the individual a mere trifle, already it seems to him easy enough to follow the use and wont of the town in which he lives, because the majority do so, it might well seem to him a matter of course to join in being a Christian – when Christianity has lasted eighteen hundred years! On the other hand the Christian fact is weakened, made a mere trifle by the help of the distance, by the help of the eighteen hundred years. That which if it happened contemporaneously either would be an offense to him which he would hate and persecute and try if possible to eradicate, or would appropriate by faith; that now one regards as something one can accept in a way and believe (i.e. regard it with indifference) since it was eighteen hundred years ago.

So now throughout a long course of years a disoriented orthodoxy which knew not what it did, and a revolutionary heterodoxy which knows demoniacally what it does, and only to that extent does not know what it does, have united with the help of the eighteen hundred years to confuse everything, to be guilty of delusions each one madder than the other, of paralogisms each one worse than the other, of *μετάβασις εἰς ἄλλο γέγος* each time more confusing than the other – so that the principal concern now is to be able to clear the ground, get rid of the eighteen hundred years, so that the Christian fact takes place now, as if it happened today. That which has blown up the attack upon Christianity and the defense of it to the size of folios are the eighteen hundred years. That which has stupefied the defenders and helped the attackers are the sixteen, the seventeen, and the eighteen hundred years. That which has held the lives of countless multitudes in a vain conceit are the eighteen hundred years. By the help of the eighteen hundred years the defenders, going backwards, have made Christianity into an hypothesis, and the attackers have made it into nothing.

What Johannes Climacus, by no means the least busy person, has done to scent out every delusion, to detect every paralogism, to apprehend every deceitful turn of phrase, cannot be repeated here. It has been so done by him that every man of culture, if he has a certain amount of learning and will seriously spend a little time to initiate himself into dialectics, will easily understand it. Otherwise, indeed, it was not done, nor could it have been done in any other wise. Such a thing cannot be propounded in a newspaper and read by a man who "is having his beard taken off." Climacus' presentation is fatiguing, as the case required. His merit is to have "drawn" (as it said of a telescope) the unshakable Christian fact so near to the eye that the reader is prevented from looking askant at the eighteen hundred years.

His merit is by the help of dialectic to have created a view, a perspective. To direct one's eye towards a star is not so difficult, because the air is like an empty space, and hence there is nothing in the way to stop or divert the glance. It is different, on the other hand, when the direction the eye must follow is straight ahead, as along a path, and at the same time there is a crowding and thronging and tumult and noise and bustle through which the eye must pierce to get the view, whereas every sidelong glance, yea, every blinking of the eye, produces absolutely a qualitative disturbance; and it becomes even more difficult when at the same time one has to stand in an environment which labors *pro virili* to prevent one from getting the view. – And to be contemporary with the decisive Christian fact is the decisive thing. This contemporaneousness, however, is to be understood as having the same significance that it had for people who lived at the same time that Christ was living.

What is needed first of all is to have the prodigious libraries and writings of every sort and the eighteen hundred years thrust to one side in order to get the view. And this is by no means the impudent suggestion of an ambitious dialectician, it is the modest and genuine religious requirement which every man may make, not for the sake of learning or for the public but for his own sake, quite personally for his own sake, if he is serious about becoming a Christian, and this is what Christianity itself must demand. For Christianity wishes precisely to stand immovable like the polar star, and hence would get rid of all the twaddle which takes the life out of it.

However, the contemporaneousness here in question is not the *contemporaneousness of an apostle*, but is *merely the contemporaneousness which everyone who lived in Christ's time had*, the possibility in *the tension of contemporaneousness* of *being offended*, or of *grasping faith*. And to this end precisely it is necessary to let in air so that it may be possible, as once it was, for a man seriously to be offended, or to appropriate Christianity, so that with the Christian faith it may not become as in a law case which has gone on so long that one does not know his way in nor out by reason of so much knowledge. The situation of contemporaneousness is that of tension which gives the categories qualitative elasticity; and one must be a great dunce not to know what an infinite difference it makes when one for his own sake in the situation of contemporaneousness reflects about something, and when one thinks in a way about something in the vain conceit that it was eighteen hundred years ago – in the conceit, yes, in the conceit, for since the Christian fact is the qualitative paradox it is a conceit that eighteen hundred years is longer ago than yesterday.

Since then the situation in Christendom is such that it is precisely necessary to put an end to the tough-lived indolence which appeals to the eighteen hundred years, it cannot be denied that a desirable incitement might be given if suddenly there were to appear a man who appealed to a revelation, for then there would be created an analogous situation of contemporaneousness. Yes, I am sure, all the profound and speculative and learned and sweaty praters who can well understand that eighteen hundred years ago someone received a revelation – they would fall into embarrassment. He who understands in general that a man might receive a revelation, must after all understand it quite as well whether it happened six thousand years ago, or will happen six thousand years hence, or has happened today. But perhaps the prater has been living off the eighteen hundred years, has prated himself into the belief that he could understand it – because it was eighteen hundred years ago. If the case were not so serious, I could not deny that it is the most precious comedy that ever could have been written in the world: to let modern exegesis and dogmatics go through their curriculum in the situation of contemporaneousness. All these deceitful psychological inventions, all this about "up to a certain point," all this *bravura profunda*, and above all the eloquent meditation which explains – since this was eighteen hundred years ago, as has been explained. All this would make a splendid effect in contemporaneousness with the matter which was explained. It is quite certain that far better than all learned attacks, one single comedy in the style of Aristophanes would clear up the confusion of modern learning.

Hence when I, without having seen the *Sermons* or the preface to them, heard that Adler had stepped forward and had appealed to a revelation, I cannot deny that I was astonished. When I heard this I thought: Either, thought I, this is the man we need, the elect who in divine originality possesses the spring for refreshing the parched ground of Christendom; or he is a man offended at Christianity, but an accomplished knave who to demolish everything, even the dignity of an apostle, to topple everything over, brings such a Christendom as we now have to the painful and laborious test of having to go through its course of dogmatics in the situation of contemporaneousness.

On the latter supposition it would indeed have surprised me that an offended man had really been so shrewd. For though it cannot be denied that the "offended" have talents and demoniacal inspiration, yet for the most part they are generally rather stupid in a total sense, that is to say, they do not quite know how to take hold of a thing in order to do harm, they attack Christianity, but they take a position outside of it, and precisely for this reason they do no harm. No, the offended man must try to get a different hold on Christianity, try to work his way up like a mole into the midst of Christianity. Suppose Feuerbach, instead of attacking Christianity, had gone to work more slyly, suppose that with demoniac silence he had laid his plan, and thereupon had stepped forward and announced that he had had a revelation, and suppose now that, just as a criminal is able to maintain a lie, he had unshakably maintained this claim, while at the same time he had been shrewdly watching out for all the weaker sides of orthodoxy, which however he was far from attacking, but only in a simple-hearted sort of way knew how to hold up before the light; suppose now that he had done this so well that no one was able to discover his stratagem – he would have put orthodoxy in the greatest embarrassment. Orthodoxy fights in the interest of the established order, to preserve the appearance that we are all Christians of a sort, that the land is a Christian land, and that the congregations are Christian. Now when one attacks Christianity and takes a position outside it, orthodoxy defends it with the help of the eighteen hundred years; it talks in lofty tones of God's great works performed in his time, i.e. eighteen hundred years ago. And now it may be said of the extraordinary and of God's extraordinary works that they go easier into people the farther they are away. So then the offended man attacks Christianity and the orthodox defend it by the help of the distance, and the congregation thinks thus: Since it was eighteen hundred years ago one may well understand that something extraordinary happened – and so again the offended man accomplished nothing. On the other hand, it would have been different if he himself had slyly come forward with a revelation, and thereupon read nothing but orthodox works and then transferred all this to himself, and then forced orthodoxy in the situation of contemporaneousness to speak out.

It is often said that in case Christ were now to come forward in Christendom, if in a stricter sense than in time gone by "He came unto his own," He would again be crucified – and especially by the orthodox. That is quite true, for contemporaneousness gives the necessary qualitative pressure; on the other hand, it helps both to make something nothing, and to make something extraordinary, almost in the same sense as nothing. Why was it that most everyone was offended in Christ while He lived, unless it was that the extraordinary occurred before their eyes, so that he who would talk about it might say, the miracle occurred yesterday. But when a miracle happened eighteen hundred years ago – well, yes, one can surely understand that it happened and that it was a miracle. Among the many precious and priceless syllogisms of thoughtless clerical eloquence this must be regarded as the most precious, that what one cannot understand if it were to happen today, one can understand when it happened eighteen hundred years ago – when this, be it noted, is the miraculous, which at every time of day, at 4 o'clock or at 5, surpasses man's understanding. For if one were only to say that such and such a man eighteen hundred years ago believed it was a miracle, then he may declare bluntly that he himself does not believe it. However, one prefers to help himself out with deceitful phrases, as with this which appears so believing yet precisely denies the miracle, as when one says of such and such a man that he believed it, i.e. he thought so, i.e. after all there was no miracle.

As has been said, in trying to interpret the extraordinary event that a man appeals to a fact of revelation I proposed to myself a dilemma: that he either was the elect; or an offended man demoniacally shrewd. And this dilemma was what, according to my view, a revelation in our time in the situation of contemporaneousness might help us to. And (even if this should not come to pass, what Christianity absolutely needs, if it is not to perish and be brought to naught) is a little air, an either/or with respect to becoming and being a Christian. Adler's appearance has, however, convinced me that there must be a third term, for he is neither of the two. That he is not the elect, that the whole thing about his revelation is a misunderstanding, I shall later show and prove directly, not by the force of any view or theory of mine, no, but from Adler's later attitude and from his later works it can be sufficiently made out that he himself essentially does not believe it, though he has not found himself moved by this to revoke penitently his first claim. Still less, if possible, is he the offended man of demoniacal shrewdness. Of that there is not the least trace or symptom. But he is not for this reason without significance, and I know of no other man in my time who in a stricter sense may be called a phenomenon. The powers of existence have got hold of him, and as a phenomenon he is an anticipation of the dialectic which is fermenting in our age. But the phenomenon itself knows nothing about the explanation, i.e. one must oneself be a teacher to learn anything from Adler. At the same time he tumbles into the old heresies, and all this pell-mell. Thus Adler is quite properly a sign. He is a very serious proof that Christianity is a power which is not to be jested with. But, on the other hand, rather than being an elect, he is a soul whirled about, flung aloft as a warning of dread, like the terrified bird which with anxious beating of its wings rushes out ahead of the storm which is about to follow, though as yet one hears only the hissing of it; and his thoughts are like the confused flocks of birds which flee helter-skelter before the storm. That for this reason one might be justified in giving him up or of thinking meanly of his possibilities is by no means my opinion. Undoubtedly as a theological candidate he lived on in the vain conceit that the meager theological knowledge required of a candidate in the official examination is Christianity. So when the Christian experience came over him he fell into the strange situation of knowing all about it in a certain sense, but by the aid of an (unfamiliar) nomenclature. In his haste he grasped at the strongest expression to indicate what he had experienced – and so we have his fact of revelation.

CHAPTER III

Alteration of Adler's essential standpoint, or documentation of the fact that he did not himself believe he had experienced a revelation. This is elucidated by his four latest books and a brochure containing the documents having to do with his deposition.

I

DOCUMENTS CONCERNING HIS DEPOSITION

This brochure, apart from a lot of correspondence regarding a dispute about a chaplain's wages, contains chiefly the questions put to Adler by the clerical authority requiring an explanation about himself and about his teaching, along with Adler's answers and his subsequent answers.

In order that all this may be precise and vivid to the reader, it will be best to recall that preface to his *Sermons*. Here Magister Adler reports how he was at work on a book which would have been called "Popular Lectures on Subjective Logic," a work in which "with a superficial knowledge of the Bible he had assumed to explain creation and Christianity." Thereupon he continues, "One evening I had just developed the origin of evil, when I saw, illuminated as by a flash of lightning, that everything depends, not upon the thought, but upon the Spirit. That night a hateful sound went through our chamber. The *Saviour* bade me stand up and go in and write down the words." Thereupon follow the words,* which in stereotype form recur again and again in verse and prose.

* The words are as follows: "The first men might have had an eternal life; for when the thought unites God's Spirit with body, then the life is eternal; when man unites God's Spirit with the body, then man is God's child; so Adam would have been God's son. But they sinned. The thought is absorbed in itself. It separated the soul from the body, the Spirit from the world, then must man die, and the world and the body become evil. And what does the spirit become? The spirit goes out of the body. But God does not take it back. And it becomes His enemy. And where does it go? Back into the world. Why? It is angry with the world which gave it up. It is the evil spirit. And this world itself created the evil spirit."

We shall not deal directly, either pro or contra, with the factual question involved in this quotation, nor with the remarkable fact that Christ talks almost like a *Privatdocent*; we argue only *e concessis*; but this at least is perfectly clear, that he declares in the most solemn way that he has had a revelation in which the Saviour imparted to him a doctrine. It may indeed seem striking that already, even before he had received the revelation, he was on the point of discovering the same thought which was imparted to him by the revelation; for it was in the evening "he saw as in a flash of lightning that everything depended, not upon the thought, but upon the Spirit." But again we shall not dwell directly upon this either, but only remark that the expression, "as by a flash of lightning," should not be regarded after all as more or less than a metaphorical expression for the suddenness of the insight, or for the suddenness of the transition from not having perceived to having perceived. Moreover, the content of the doctrine communicated by the revelation is concentrated in the statement that "man's thought is absorbed in itself." But this also seems to have been fathomed before the revelation was imparted to him; for in the preface he says about his work ("Popular Lectures on Subjective Logic"): "It was my thought which was absorbed in itself." Hence there is not much left over which was imparted to him by a revelation; but all the more definitely the accent falls precisely upon the fact that this was imparted to him *by a revelation*, that "the *Saviour* at night bade him stand up and go in and write down the following words." In so far as Adler, unshakable, holds to this fact, I have no yea and no nay: I am engaged merely in arguing *e concessis*. But, on the other hand, if he does not hold it fast, he must put up with it if out of his own mouth one concludes that he does not himself believe he has had a revelation, or in any case that he is in such confusion regarding the categories that he does not himself know what he says, because he associates no sharp thought with the words.

In the preface it is further related, "Thereupon Jesus bade me burn my own [works] and for the future hold to the Bible. Of the *Sermons* and addresses from No. VI to the end I know that they were written with Jesus' cooperative grace, so that I have been only an instrument." In case Adler did not know this of the other addresses, or in case he knew of the other addresses that they were not that, it is certainly strange that he published them, especially in one volume, which like Noah's Ark seems to contain species qualitatively very various. This, however, is Adler's business. The principal point for me is that he said in the most solemn way that he knew the discourses from No. VI to the end were written with Jesus' cooperative grace, so that he was only an instrument.* So we have here with Adler's call by a revelation the analogy with the call of an apostle; in his writing with the cooperation of Jesus' grace we have the analogy with the situation of a man who was inspired. Adler had both a doctrine which was communicated to him by a revelation, and a development of this doctrine which was inspired. So reliably is hardly the New Testament guaranteed. If only he had left out the first five sermons, this book would have been *instar omnium*.

Now we pass on to the questions which the clerical authority found itself obliged to put to him.

THE QUESTION OF THE ECCLESIASTICAL AUTHORITY

(1) Whether you (Mag. Adler) recognize that you were in an exalted and confused state of mind when you wrote and published your printed "Sermons" and so-called "Studies"?†

*The solemnity of this assertion suffers, however, from a little defect due to a couple of notes in the same book, of which I, were the matter not so serious, might be tempted to say that they surely were written with the cooperative assistance of distraction. From the preface one learns indeed that the discourses from No. VI to the end were written with the cooperation of Jesus' grace; but on page 20 (in a note to sermon No. IV, Maundy Thursday, April 13, 1843) one reads: "Here for the first time Jesus' cooperative grace came to my aid." Good Friday, as everyone knows, comes after Maundy Thursday, sermon No. V after sermon No. IV, and yet one learns in the note to No. V that Jesus' cooperative grace came then for the *first* time to Adler's aid – after one has read the note to No. IV, and after one has read in the preface that he *knows* of sermons No. VI to the end that they were written with Jesus' cooperative grace, this seems to indicate that he was doubtful about the notes to IV and V, unless in distraction he had written the notes, and again in distraction had forgotten that he had written them.

†The question itself has moreover a curious difficulty with respect to the answer which might be expected. When one challenges a person for an explanation whether in a previous moment of time he was in a confused state of mind, it seems to be implied that if he is willing to explain this, willing to admit it, then all is well again, and the person is no longer in a confused state of mind.

The letter of the authority was dated April 29, 1845. Magister Adler's reply under date of May 11, 1845 is as follows:

"Since I can point out meaning and connection in what I have written in my *Sermons* and *Studies*, I do not recognize that I was in an exalted and confused state of mind when I wrote them."

Strictly considered, this is not an answer to the question. By "meaning and connection" one may think rather only of the grammatical consistency one may require of a speech. But, supposing that there was such meaning and connection in what was written, the author might very well have been in an exalted and confused state of mind. Moreover the act of publishing what was written is something for itself, and one might, e.g., write something quite calmly, but betray an exalted state of mind by publishing it. Hence Adler's reply is in no sense an answer to the question; neither is it veracious, for not only is there one but there are many passages in the *Sermons* which are plainly wanting in meaning and connection. So the answer may be regarded as evasive, and also one cannot yet say that by this answer he has altered in the least what he originally said about himself. In this he is still consistent. This I reckon to his credit, for I argue only *e concessis*.

But some time later there followed a further answer. We shall suppress nothing which might seem to speak in Adler's favor, and therefore we recall that in speaking of his last reply he himself says, "In order to reach a point of agreement with the authorities, I made, after a conversation with Bishop Mynster, as great a step towards approach as was possible by sending on July 5th the following confession:

"I recognize that the unusual, the strange, the objectionable, aprioristic and abrupt form may with reason have aroused the suspicion of the authority."

Now it is coming. It is true that A. does not say that the

However, it is possible to think that the person precisely by his willingness to make further admissions proves that he is in a confused state of mind. Suppose he answered, Well, if nothing more is required, then I shall not make them wait for me, but with the greatest pleasure will explain, etc. In such a case the questioner is brought again into the same embarrassment. In general it is very difficult to check the dialectic which develops when one begins to assume that a man has been in a confused state of mind, and especially difficult to check it by an explanation made by the man himself.

authority was right in concluding that he was in an exalted and confused state of mind, but he says it is right in affirming that the ideas in many places in his *Sermons* and *Studies* are presented in an unusual, strange, offensive, aprioristic and abrupt form; he says moreover that the authority has reason to be suspicious. So A. admits the premises but lets the conclusions remain doubtful. In his first answer he had denied the premises, in his second letter he admits the premises and says nothing to oppose the conclusion. Precisely because A. admits the premises (unless he would give support to the assumption of the authority, and in that case he might say it straightforwardly) he must defend himself with all his might against the conclusion, he must say in perfectly definite words: But in spite of this (and precisely because I have admitted the premises I have to hold to this all the more firmly), in spite of all this I can by no means admit that I have been in an exalted and confused state of mind. It is a well-known method of advocates to admit the premises in this way, and then by drawing no conclusion make it seem as if the conclusion was something quite different, something that comes from an entirely different hemisphere, something over which the person in question arbitrarily disposes whether he will admit it or not, something which by a qualitative definition is separated from the premises. But when a premise pregnant with the conclusion inclines threateningly over a man; when he himself knows that by admitting the justice of the premises he makes the angle of inclination all the greater; then he must with the utmost definiteness defend himself against the conclusion, or it falls upon him, and he has himself admitted it. Of course, even if he had defended himself against the conclusion with a definite statement, he might not have parried the conclusion, for sometimes the conclusion may be a pure formality which makes no difference one way or the other, but he may be regarded as having lost this point. The cunning or the thoughtlessness which further proves his confusion is the fact that he lets this answer serve as an explanation, that he does not understand the simple consistency which requires him to revoke officially his first position, his first answer, acknowledging that the *Sermons* along with the *Studies* were written in an exalted and confused state of mind.

In the last letter there remains a third point which, regarded as an answer, may well be referred to question No. 1 of the authority, to which we here hold fast. No. 3 in the last letter reads as follows:

"That with a longer time to labor and quietly develop the ideas for the future* I will find myself able to let the Christian content unfold itself in a form more appropriate and more consonant with the express words of Holy Scripture."

In connection with Adler's hope for the future one is tempted involuntarily to raise the question: But was there need of such haste in getting said (in an inappropriate and less Biblical way) that which with a longer time to labor and to develop the ideas will be able to unfold itself in a form more appropriate and more consonant with the express words of Holy Scripture? Is there any, or can there have been any reasonable ground for haste in doing in an inappropriate form that which with the employment of a longer time may be done in a more appropriate form? And when did Magister Adler begin with the longer time which is needed for quiet work? He has already written four books since then, but it does not seem as if he had got any nearer to the appropriate!

And in case it is so (as will be shown in the following where Adler's answer to No. 2 of the authority will be dealt with) that Adler himself authentically explains (i.e. alters his first statement to this effect) that he has nothing new to contribute† – in case

*This hope ... has not been exactly fulfilled, but it is talked about again in one of Adler's four last books. So since that hopeful word in the letter of July 5, 1845, Adler has written four new books, but the hope still finds its place as a repeated hope in the preface of one of them. In this way Adler may be able to remain for a long time a hopeful and promising author; yea, in all probability this hope will become a standing article in his prefaces – a sort of fixed idea, which sometimes is found in authors who never give it up, not even with death. So it is said that we have an example in an author who in the preface to each little book he published regularly wrote that in the future he meant to collect himself for a great work which he soon meant to publish – even in the last preface to a fragment of a little book this hope still found its customary place.

†That again in the preface to one of his last four books he fantasticates on the theme that "he who has something new to contribute must not permit any amalgamation with the old" may be regarded as a new confusion Adler has to contribute. One is justified in assuming that in this preface Adler is referring to himself, and so one may conclude further that he still regards that first

this is so, then precisely it is important that one take care that the form be as appropriate as possible, that one uses time and patience for the work to make it as appropriate as possible, since there is no reason at all for haste. Even if a man contributes something new, it is yet unpardonable to do it in a tumultuous way, but when one admits that he has nothing new to contribute it is doubly unpardonable.

That now Adler himself authentically admits (as an *explanation* of the assertion that he had a revelation by which a new doctrine was imparted to him by the Saviour) that he has nothing new to contribute, we go on to show by illuminating Adler's answer to question No. 2 by the authority. This No. 2 contains the principal point, for here the question is asked whether he has actually had a revelation, whether he himself thought so, etc. Question No. 1 is of far less significance, and actually I have dwelt upon Adler's answer to No. 1 only to give a foretaste of his confusions.

THE QUESTION OF THE AUTHORITY

Whether you perceive that it is fanatical and wrong to expect and to follow such supposed revelations as, for example, that which you have described in the preface to your "Sermons"?

Adler's two answers, though they pretend to be explanations, are not explanations but alterations, which alter his first assertion, without requiring him to revoke it decisively. Yet between his two answers there is a difference. In the first the fact of having had a revelation by which a new doctrine was imparted to him is transformed into an awakening by which he is rescued. In the last answer the fact of having had a revelation by which a new doctrine was imparted to him is transformed into the beginning of an enthusiasm, into an expression as vague and indefinite as enthusiasm. Instead of one called by a revelation to whom a new doctrine was entrusted, we get in the first case a religiously awakened man in the ordinary sense; in the second case, an enthusiast. Educated as Adler is with some Hegelian dialectic, it

declaration (which in the most solemn way gave itself out to be a revelation, and thereafter was authentically explained as not being anything new) – that he nevertheless regards it as something new.

is not strange if he himself lives in the notion that these three determinants (an apostle, an awakened man, and an enthusiast) signify pretty much the same thing, or that the one term can be used to explain the others. But in case there exists something called qualitative dialectic, one of these terms annuls the other, and the dilemma must constantly be posed: if Adler acquiesces in the explanation, then he must revoke the first claim; for the explanation is not a further predicate of the first claim but is a new position. So one may be very willing to concede to Adler that he is a sort of enthusiast so called, but cannot truly be willing to regard this notion as an explanation of what in the preface to his *Sermons* he gives himself out to be.

His first answer of May 10, 1845, is as follows:

"By having written in the preface to my *Sermons* that Jesus bade me in the future to hold to the Bible, by having preached Him, by having quoted the words of Scripture as proof-texts, it must be evident to what Gospel and to what revelations* I hold and have taught others to hold. But that one may be rescued in a miraculous way is – as I have described it in the preface – a fact which I cannot deny. Even if one regards my *Sermons* and *Studies* as a babe's first babbling, tender, imperfect voice, I believe nevertheless that an occurrence took place by which I was seized by faith."

Now the volatilization is in full course, and I would beg for the reader's patience so that I may set to work quite slowly to show in every line the uncertainty and confusion – it serves to illuminate very well a part of modern philosophy and dogmatics. According to my conception it is not uninteresting to go to work for once with exactitude, and in our times of dialectical confusion there might be someone who would find profit in reading it, even if he had no interest at all in the case.

So then: "By having written in the preface to my *Sermons* that Jesus bade me in the future to hold to the Bible, by having preached Him, by having quoted words of the Scripture as proof-texts, it must be evident to what Gospel and to what

*There is moreover something rather confused in the plural which Adler here uses in a different connection than the authority does, for the authority spoke in the plural of the fanatical revelations, Adler speaks in the plural of the Christian revelation.

revelations I hold and have taught others to hold." But this is by no means evident. Even if one will make the greatest possible concessions to Adler, there remains the decisive consideration, the very point, which he leaves out, while by his answer he seeks to *identify himself with every Christian in general.* For even though Adler holds to the Christian revelation and the Christian Gospels, there still remains the difficulty about which the question was asked, that he *by a revelation* was directed to hold to the revelation. A believing Christian in general holds to the Christian revelation, but Adler is directed by a revelation to hold to it. Therefore it is not by any means evident to which revelation he holds, for he holds first and foremost to the revelation which has fallen especially to his lot, by which he has been directed to hold to the Christian revelation. Besides, he says himself that Jesus bade him in the future; but the question is not what Jesus bade him do and bade him do in the future, but about the assertion that *Jesus appeared to him and bade him do something.* Even though Adler in the future remained like every believing Christian in general, there still remains always the decisive qualitative difference about which the question was asked, that through a revelation by Jesus Himself he was directed to be like the others.* To this may be added, and it is really the principal point, that Adler in his answer has left out what was chiefly emphasized in the preface. For according to this Jesus did not call him at night to bid him in the future to hold to the Bible; no, the Saviour bade him "stand up and go in and write down these words," i.e. the whole passage which contains the new doctrine. When this was done, then "Jesus bade him thereupon to burn his own [works] and in the future to hold to the Bible."

When moreover A. in the first sentence of this answer appeals to the fact that "he had preached Jesus," in order thereby to make

*The fact should not be overlooked that Adler involves himself in a new difficulty. For dialectically a new contradiction is contained in the notion that by a paradoxically extraordinary measure (a new revelation) one should be called to be like all others. By the paradoxically extraordinary call a man can be called only to be the paradoxically extraordinary man. By a revelation with which one is entrusted with a doctrine a man cannot be called to become what all others are or could be, nor to become a faithful adherent of this doctrine, but he is called to become the extraordinary, to become the apostle of it.

it "evident to which Gospel and to which revelations he holds and has taught others to hold" – this again is not evident from what he says. He again leaves out the decisive thing (about which the question was asked) and, volatilizing the whole thing, seeks in his answer *to identify himself with every believing priest in general*. The believing Christian priest preaches Christ and thereby shows to which revelations he holds, but the believing priest in general is *not called by any revelation* to preach Jesus. Inasmuch then as Adler preaches Jesus, it is by no means evident to which revelations he holds. It would only be evident in case that preface to his *Sermons* did not exist; but that preface and the revelation described in it is precisely what the authority asked about. The authority did not ask Adler whether he like every believing priest preached Jesus; no, it asked whether he recognized that it is fanatical to hold to such revelations as are described in the preface to his *Sermons*. Adler answers: I preach Jesus. But thus he does not answer the question – or else the answer implied the concession: I have never had a special revelation, and such being the case the whole preface to the *Sermons* must be officially revoked.

Moreover, in his answer he again leaves out something, and something very important, which stood in the preface. For in the preface there stood: "About the Sermons and Addresses from No. VI to the end I know that they were written by Jesus' cooperative grace, so that I have been only an instrument." But no believing priest in general preaches in this way. For example, I assume that had another preached literally the same sermon as Adler, there would yet have been between the two a decisive qualitative difference, for the fact that Adler's was in the capacity of "being only an instrument."

The first sentence in his first answer to authority's No. 2 thus shows itself to be sophistical and thoughtless. If there is to be any seriousness in calling this an explanation, he must repentantly revoke the preface to his *Sermons*, for the answer is no more an explanation of what was said in the preface to the *Sermons* than it was enlightening information a messenger once brought back that he had found what he was sent to seek but it was not a widow but a bricklayer.

The next sentence in his first answer to authority's No. 2 is as follows: "But that one may be rescued in a miraculous way – as I have described in the preface to the *Sermons* – is for me a fact which I cannot deny." It is not required of him at all that he should deny a fact; I for my humble part am as far as possible from requiring that, I require only that he shall either stand firm decisively by what he himself has said he was, or else solemnly revoke that which by him in the most solemn way was affirmed. He does not hold fast his first decisive declaration, he alters it, and yet he would give that alteration the appearance of being an explanation. That he does not stand fast by what he said of himself in the preface to the *Sermons* (the point of the authority's question) it is not difficult to see; for after all there is a decisive qualitative difference between *receiving from the Saviour by a revelation a doctrine entrusted to him*, and *being rescued in a miraculous way*. In case A. when he wrote the preface and later the answer had been in possession of the necessary Christian knowledge, he naturally would have known this; but one who has no other presuppositions with which to make Christianity secure except some Hegelian dialectic can readily go astray.

Let us now define a little more precisely the difference between the two statements. When a man is said to be rescued in a miraculous way it is assumed that what he has been rescued into or to is in existence, perhaps has long been in existence, but he, alas, has frittered away his years in lightmindedness and dissipations, or wasted them in confused studies, or turned his back upon the well known, or reaped the sorry consequences of a weak and spoiled bringing up, etc. He is now rescued in a miraculous way, it may be in various ways which, and according to the psychological knowledge one has of such stories of religious awakening, it may be told in a longer or shorter form. It is assumed that Christianity is that into which one is rescued, but he is rescued in a miraculous way. Suppose, for example, it happened this year, and with that Christianity has been in existence eighteen hundred years, in it there certainly comes about no alteration for the sake of the rescued man; ah, no, but the wayward one is rescued in a miraculous way into that which has been in existence unchanged for eighteen hundred years and in which all others are assumed to have their life. On the other hand, it is something quite other and qualitatively different when one by a revelation is entrusted with a doctrine. This doctrine indeed was not in existence before, there has therefore come about an alteration in that in which rescue is to be found. The man thus called may not, humanly speaking, have been in the way of perdition. No, there comes about an alteration of an objective sort, and this it is which the man called must communicate as it was communicated to him. He who is called by a revelation and entrusted with a doctrine may be called to be a teacher; he is called indeed for his own sake, but principally for the sake of others (the teleological), that he may preach the new doctrine. On the other hand, he who is rescued in a miraculous way is entrusted with no new doctrine, he is not appointed to be a teacher in an extraordinary sense or to communicate something new; he has to be quiet and subordinate himself humbly to the old order; the consciousness of being *rescued* in a miraculous way cannot tempt him to regard himself as something extraordinary, since this consciousness rather reminds him constantly, to his humiliation, that he was so far out on the way of perdition that a miraculous way was needed to rescue him.

Thus I think I have defined the difference. Let us now look at Adler. In the preface to the *Sermons* there is no hint that he was saved, "rescued"; no, in the preface Adler was the one called by a revelation, to whom a new doctrine was entrusted. For the first time in the answer (which, be it noted, is in reply to the question about the meaning of the preface to the *Sermons*) this explanation comes out. Naturally, it is no explanation of the preface, it is an entirely new view, a new character in which Adler appears upon the stage, as though he were just now beginning, as though he had no antecedent history – he who precisely had antecedents about which the question was asked. In case one had given himself out to be king, and then the authority put to him the question what he meant by saying such a thing about himself, and he then explained that thereby he had meant that he was a councilor of chancery – this answer is no explanation, it is a new assertion: first he gives himself out to be king, then councilor of chancery. The dialectical cunning or thoughtlessness consists in not revoking the first claim but treating the last claim as though it were an explanation of the first.

The last sentence in Adler's first answer to authority's No. 2 is as follows: "Even though one may regard my *Sermons* and *Studies* as a babe's first babbling, tender, imperfect voice, I believe nevertheless that the words witness to the fact that an event has taken place whereby I was grasped by faith." Now this last is a very vague determinant: that an event has taken place whereby I was grasped by faith. The event moreover is exactly described in the preface to the *Sermons*: "that there was heard a hateful sound which went through the chamber, and then the Saviour bade him stand up and write down the words." The authority indeed had not asked A. whether an event had taken place, but about the event described in detail in the preface to the *Sermons*. This statement of Adler about himself, that an event had taken place by which he was grasped by faith, is something entirely different from what is related in the preface. Thus there have been many examples of men who have been grasped by faith by falling into mortal danger. It is well known, and it made an extraordinarily deep impression and had a decisive influence upon Pascal's life, that at one time the horses ran away with him. But this again is something quite other and qualitatively different from having by a revelation received a doctrine.

As for the *first* statement in the last sentence of the answer, it might seem indeed a praiseworthy modesty on the part of an author, a compliment to others, to refer thus in relation to his first effort to "a babe's first babbling, tender, imperfect voice" and "a highly educated and cultured public" who, lacking any categories, has a fond predilection for complimentary twaddle, would surely like it – if there was nothing to hinder. But here there is no call for modesty, there up and here down, but for a categorical definition in a highly serious case. When a man begins an effort in a confused and exalted state it may be quite right for him to hope for perfectibility, that he will succeed later when he has attained calmness and reflection in doing it better. But a man who begins with a revelation and with the Saviour's dictation has only in an unessential sense to hope for perfectibility – so this is blasphemy. It is true that Adler does not say expressly that he thus regards these words in the preface and in the *Sermons*, but how does he dare (in case what stands in the preface is truly true) to engage in any such accommodation by saying, "even though one might regard my *Sermons* and *Studies* as a babe's first tender, imperfect voice," and engage in it in such a way that he "believes nevertheless that the words witness to the fact that an event has taken place." So then, when his solemn assertion that Jesus bade him write down the words does not avail to make his voice heard, he hopes then that an insignificance will do it. Just think how almost detestable it is merely to be obliged to write such a thing; imagine that Paul as an explanation of the words: "I have received of the Lord that which also I deliver unto you, that our Lord Jesus Christ, etc.," were to have added: even though some were to regard this as a babe's first babbling, tender, imperfect voice, etc.! Where in all the world did Adler come upon this about a babe's tender, imperfect voice! So may a man speak in relation to a production which in a perfectly common human sense is his own – but in the preface to the *Sermons* it is indeed not Adler's voice, it is in fact Jesus who dictates it and so through Adler speaks to us . . . and His voice surely is not that of a tender babe, and surely it has not occurred to any one, or occurred to the authority, to raise the dilemma, but surely it meant to ask Adler what he means by thus making Jesus dictate something to his pen. On the other hand, in case this whole preface is poetry and vanity and confusion of mind – then it is quite right, and yet, no, it is not right to talk about a babe's tender voice . . . for then the whole thing must be penitently revoked.

But then what was it the authority had asked him about? Whether he had been in an exalted and confused state of mind when he wrote the preface and the *Sermons*. And when one has begun in an exalted condition it may be quite right to hope for a certain perfectibility,* to hope that, as Adler himself said, "with a longer time to labor and quietly develop the ideas I will find myself able to let the Christian content unfold itself in a more appropriate form and more consonant with the express words of the Holy Scripture." Yes, when one has begun in an exalted and confused state – but it is precisely not right when one has begun with the plainest and clearest of all, with the fact that Jesus

*The whole affair about Adler's perfectibility is one of those unblessed reminiscences of the theological seminary. If only Adler had been a layman! For his misfortune among other things is that his inwardness stands in no proportion to his wretched theological learning. Christianity is a revelation – seventeen hundred years later men began indeed to develop it so that it might be perfectible. Now that is something to be said for the many centuries. But in one's own lifetime to go through this exegetical curriculum with regard to what he himself has experienced, is really comical.

Himself dictates to one what he shall write down. Even with regard to a purely human effort it is true for all competent men that the first is the best; the first of enthusiasm, of resolution, of love is the best, as is the dialectical first judgment of a situation. It is true only of confused men that the first comes stumbling into the door like a drunken man – and so it may sometimes be true enough that afterwards, when reflection enters little by little, something quite good may come out of it. But then is the first not something one may leave as it was, but, on the contrary, something one must revoke.

So it has been shown that Adler's first answer to authority's No. 2, either sophistically or thoughtlessly, contains an alteration of his whole first standpoint: instead of being called by a revelation and entrusted with a new doctrine he substitutes the statement that he was rescued in a miraculous way. According to his own authentic view (from which we are of course justified in drawing an argument, since we protested against it only when it pretended to be an explanation of the first, as it is not an explanation but an essential alteration, and as an essential alteration demands its recognizable expression in a decisive form, which can only be the revocation of the first). He holds to the Bible, preaches Jesus, appeals to Scriptural words as proof-texts, in short, he is quite like every other Christian, only he was rescued in a miraculous way. *But ergo, he has in conformity with his own authentic view nothing new, no new doctrine to communicate, nor ever has had.* The confusion then consists merely in the fact that he allows the first to stand. If there is to be the least ethical meaning and seriousness in Adler's whole effort, he must revoke his first claim, saying: "Neither did Jesus appear to me, nor did He have me write down those words – but I was in a confused and overstrained condition. For me, however, that moment has had a decisive significance, so that I may say of myself that I was rescued in a miraculous way." Yes, then the case is different. Honor to him who humbly but frankly acknowledges of himself that he had to be rescued in a miraculous way. But in Adler's first and decisive statement (in the preface to the *Sermons*) there was not a word said about being saved or rescued – there he was the one called by a revelation to whom a new doctrine was entrusted. Now, to let the first stand, and to give the answer the appearance of being an explanation, is a total confusion. The answer is no explanation but a qualitatively new statement, the explanation does not explain the first, it explains the first to be something different. In case one were to explain a circle and explain that it was a square, that is no explanation, it is a new assertion. When I explain something I make of course no alteration in the nature of what I explain; what is to be explained must remain unaltered, but by the explanation it becomes plain what it is. When one says that by a revelation there was communicated to him a doctrine according to Jesus' own dictation, and one asks him what he means by this and requires an explanation, and he then explains that by this he means that he was rescued in a miraculous way, with this he does not explain the question asked but produces a new story.

This was the first alteration, but it did not stop with that. With the first alteration we still remain after all in the religious sphere, though there is a decisive qualitative difference between being rescued in a miraculous way, and being entrusted by a revelation with a new doctrine.

We pass on to Adler's last letter and the answer it contains to that question No. 2 of the authority. In order to do everything that can be done in favor of Adler we will again call attention to the fact that he himself regards this letter "as the greatest possible step towards approachment."

His second answer is as follows:

"I do not insist upon regarding my *Sermons* (or *Studies*) as revelations alongside of or over against Christianity, but I regard the words written down in the preface to the *Sermons* and my frequently recurring dogmatic categories as points of reference which were necessary to me at the beginning of the enthusiasm to hold fast the Christian matter in a form."

Now the game is in full swing. Ah, what was the use of burning those Hegelian manuscripts when one remains so much of a Hegelian that he is able to accomplish so much by mediation! First Adler says that he cannot insist* that these are revelations –

*The reader will perhaps remark how droll it is that in his first answer he had said less than this, for then he altered the claim that he had had a revelation by which a new doctrine was entrusted to him, into the statement that he had been rescued in a miraculous way; but in the last answer, in which he yet makes the that is; he says both yes and no; that is, he freshens up the old claim: *A* is surely *B*; but on the other hand it is after all not *B*. They are revelations; but he does not insist upon it, for after all to a certain degree they are not revelations. Ah, what was the use of burning the Hegelian manuscripts? *Naturam forca pellas*, but it comes back again at once.

To go further – he says, "I do not insist in regarding my *Sermons* (or *Studies*) as revelations." Here Adler in his answer goes beyond the question of the authority, for the authority had asked him only about the revelation in the preface to the *Sermons*. How could it occur to the authority to ask Adler whether he regarded the whole collection of sermons and studies as revelations, since he had not said that they were?

Now comes the principal point: he regards the words written down in the preface to the *Sermons* and his frequently recurring dogmatic categories as points of reference which were necessary to him at the beginning of the enthusiasm to hold fast the Christian matter in a form. So these words he regards as points of reference. But the authority had not asked him *how* he regarded these words, but how he regarded the statement that *Jesus bade him write down these words*. So the principal thing is altogether omitted. – Adler speaks of "those words *written down* in the preface ...": by this careless phrase he beguiles everyone into believing that the question is about words which Adler himself had written down, in the same sense as I am now writing these words down. But according to the preface it was in fact when the *Saviour* at night bade him stand up and he (Adler) wrote down these words as they were dictated. This is surely the qualitative decisive point. – Adler "regards those words written down *and* his frequently recurring dogmatic categories as points of reference." So for Adler himself there is no essential difference between those words and his dogmatic categories, both of them stand as authorities on the same plane – and yet those words in the preface were dictated by the Saviour, whereas the dogmatic categories are Adler's invention, so that he may quite rightly use the possessive pronoun and say "my dogmatic categories." If then the dogmatic categories and the words in the preface are in Adler's view qualitatively

---

greatest possible step towards approach, he begins again about having had after all to a certain degree a revelation.

on the same plane with one another, it follows quite simply that he may say, *my* words written down in the preface. And yet those words were dictated to Adler by the Saviour Himself. – Adler regards those words in the preface and the dogmatic categories (both of them alike) as "points of reference." A point of reference, according to linguistic usage, indicates the provisional. It may well happen that a point of reference does not turn out later to be altogether true; but in danger, in a moment of haste, one grasps it to have something to hold on to.* When two men are arguing with one another and confusion begins to set in, one grasps something as a point of reference which one establishes provisionally in order to have something to hold on to. When one has not had time to make his thoughts thoroughly clear and yet would communicate them, one grasps a particular definition and fixes it provisionally as a point of reference. Afterwards when one gets more time one investigates whether the particular definition which had served as a point of reference is quite right or no. As for Adler's categories, it may be permissible then and justifiable to call them points of reference, though later they may have to be subjected to a sharp test, for there is nothing to prevent one from hoping for this perfectibility – their perfection at least is not a hindrance. But as for those words in the preface which were written down by Adler at the Saviour's dictation, it is blasphemous to call *them* points of reference which for him (Adler) "were necessary in the beginning of the enthusiasm." So Adler has been in a state of enthusiasm. Yes, that is something different. In case Adler in the preface to his *Sermons*, instead of what stands there now, had written: "In a moment of enthusiasm at night a light appeared to me, whereupon I stood up and lit a lamp and wrote down the following words" – then perhaps it hardly would have occurred to the authority to call him to account with questions. Then Adler's hope for perfectibility would have been fitting, for those words give indeed the impression (assuming that they are Adler's own words – for ordinarily I argue only *e concessis*) of not being so perfect that they could not be made more perfect. On the other hand, it seems either inconceivably thoughtless and confused or else impudent to present to the authority such an answer,

*The Danish word is *Holdningspunkt* (point of holding) – in German *Verhältnispunkt*, in French *point d'appui*.

as though the question were about a determinant so infinitely vague as enthusiasm, and in what degree Adler was enthusiastic, since the question after all is about the fact that he said that he had had a revelation and had had a doctrine dictated to him by the Saviour. – Adler himself regards those words in the preface as something imperfect. He says indeed that the points of reference were "necessary" *for him* (the purely subjective determinant) *in the beginning of the enthusiasm* (that is, when he was still a little confused) in order to be able to hold fast the Christian matter *in a form* (this careless expression, "in a form," points clearly to the hope for a more appropriate and more perfect form, in comparison with which the Saviour's form was inappropriate). Who in all the world, merely reading Adler's answer, would think that he was talking about words which, according to his own declaration, were written down at the Saviour's own dictation? If then the words in the preface, as indeed Adler has said, are the words of the Saviour, his answer is nonsense; but if they are Adler's own words, then the preface must be most solemnly revoked. That Adler himself could not perceive this is precisely the best proof that he is confused.

When then these words in the preface, according to Adler's authentic view (against which I protest only when it pretends to be an explanation of his first claim), are to him only what his dogmatic categories are, when to him these words are points of reference, when to him, Adler (the subjective determinant), these points of reference were necessary only at the beginning of the enthusiasm, and then only necessary in order to hold fast another thing, and this other thing is and was the Christian matter, *then in Adler's own authentic explanation it is implied that he has had nothing new, no new doctrine* to contribute, that he has had no revelation.*

*Already I have in a note referred to the fact – and will do so here again to give the reader at the proper place an impression of contemporaneousness – that Adler, as was indeed to be expected, begins all over again like Jeppe. In the preface to one of his four last books he dwells especially upon the fact that "he who has something new to contribute must prevent any amalgamation with the old." Ah, if Adler has not been amalgamated with the old, he has chiefly Bishop Mynster to thank for it that by the help of his most compliant concessions he did not remain in his office. So, after all, Adler has something new to contribute. However, he has, as it seems, in the last books chosen the least embarrassing of all categories, namely, that he is something of a genius or such like.

The other points in the letter of the authority are less important – but now we come to the end of the story. Adler's deprivation followed on September 13, 1845. It might seem strange and uncalled for, coming immediately after concessions so compliant and so important on the part of Adler. So it might appear, but if one will give himself due time, one will see more properly that it was called for by the concessions, for the importance of the concessions is that when they do not contain a formal and solemn revocation of his first claim they make his deprivation inevitable. The fact that he, in spite of such concessions, still fancies that he holds fast his first claim makes it perfectly evident that he is confused, that he knows neither the in nor the out of what he says about himself. Had Adler laconically, without budging a hair's breadth, maintained stubbornly his fact of revelation, the case would have been far more difficult for the State-Church, which would have come fairly near to judging how far a man in our age may be justified in asserting that he has had a revelation. But herein precisely consists the profundity of Bishop Mynster's conduct of this case, that he has helped Adler by some concessions to prove further that he is confused, and thereby to necessitate his deprivation, when, as Hegel says, the concept veers and the concessions precisely prove that he is confused.

For the State-Church the total result of the case of Adler is null. No believers will thereby be thrown into an intense state of anxiety at the thought that a teacher has been declared to be in a confused state of mind and has been deprived of his living because he said he had a revelation. No, because he said this he was suspended in order that the case might be looked into more thoroughly, but by the help of concessions he slew himself. In case one does not think that profundity consists in profound and clever sayings, in case one assumes, as I do, that profundity stands in an essential relation to action, one cannot deny that Bishop Mynster, precisely by his profundity, has conducted excellently a difficult case. It was important above all that the blow fell at the right place (precisely after the concessions) and that the thing had no disastrous consequences, which now it cannot possibly have. For something might well have resulted from Adler's assertion that he had had a revelation, his deprivation being connected with that; but from his concessions nothing results for other men. Of course, the State would be right in depriving a man who quietly and coolly appealed to a revelation, for the *extraordinarius* must leave the ranks. It is true that Christianity is built upon a revelation, but also it is limited by the definite revelation it has received. It must not be built upon the revelations which John Doe and James Roe may get – and in any case John Doe and James Roe must venture out into the same danger which those men faced who once built the Church upon a revelation. But I am thinking only of the impression such a necessary step might have made upon the weaker brethren, and I rejoice therefore that this was not the case with Adler. Moreover I am convinced that the true *extraordinarius* would of his own accord resign his official post.

2
ADLER'S FOUR LAST BOOKS*

Adler seems now to wish to be promoted to the position of a genius, or to be content with that; that nevertheless he treats this difference as nothing and thinks he is in identity with his first claim (according to which he was a man called by a revelation and entrusted with a doctrine). – The qualitative difference between an apostle and a genius. – Even if A. Adler had not from the first wished it, regarded as the author of the four last works he must be characterized as a confused genius, a judgment which is suggested already by the form of the books.

The last words of a man at the moment of departure [the same word as deprivation] have always a special value, are always impressed more strongly upon the memory. A.'s last words (the last in his last publication of July 5, 1845) contain, as the reader will remember, a hope, a beautiful hope, or anyway a hope confidently expressed, that he "with a longer time to labor over and quietly develop the ideas will be able for the future, etc." – a hope which does not seem to have made much impression upon the ecclesiastical authority, for there followed what does not

***Studies and Examples; An Attempt at a Brief Systematic Presentation of Christianity in its Logic; Theological Studies; Several Poems.*

seem to imply any hope for the future, his deposition with grace and with a pension, depriving him for the future of his parish. And from this what does one learn for the future? In a little land where not much is done to encourage arts and learning, where an author or an artist only after the accomplishments of considerable importance, and then after many laborious and miserable journeys of supplication from Herod to Pilate, after having been obliged to make his bow before the Head of the State (which is and ought to be a delight to any subject), not only before the high officials of the government (which itself is a satisfaction), but almost before each of the clerks in the bureau, between whom he is sent to and fro and fro and to – he obtains a little pinch of public support. In this land one may also take another way. One may undergo an official examination, or an examination which qualifies one for an official position. So one seeks it – it turns out that he is not competent for it, and the State thanks God it can get rid of him. One need not go to a single man, one may sit quite quietly in one's room – it comes to one: deprivation and pension. One has only to give utterance to slightly revolutionary principles – then by deprivation and grace one is relieved of the tiresome official duties which really prevent one from becoming an author, which one would like to be, one gets a pension – and now has leisure and sometimes a considerable pension from the State, in order without disturbance and with favor to write against the State. Alas, a faithful subject who cannot make himself interesting by attacking the government will with great difficulty obtain some support for an undertaking which is both permissible and distinguished.

Favored by leisure and a pension, Adler kept still for one year, yet presumably, as we read of Ulysses, *βυσσοδομεῦον* [brooding] – for in the early summer of 1846 he came forward quite unexpectedly with four books at once. Four books at once! If this custom is more generally introduced, the standard for being an author will thereby be raised to an extraordinarily high pitch. When in the future there is talk of somebody being an author, one must ask at once if of one book or four – thus pashas are classified according as they wear one horse-tail or three, and barbers as having one or three basins. To publish three or four books at once is something so striking that an essential author, even if he had them ready, would surely wish to avoid what easily might draw a wrong sort of attention to him, and what, regarded as a whim, would at the most have a little charm the first time it was done, not the first time for the individual, but the first time in the little world to which as an author he belongs; and anyhow, every real author must have a special reason for doing such a thing. Subjectively he must be conscious of a youthful force which will permit him to realize in due measure a task which will challenge in so high a degree the envy of the critics; perhaps his impetus is strengthened by an accidental circumstance, by the sad consciousness that the externally favorable conditions will permit him only for a short time to labor on a scale almost too great for him. But principally the four books must have objectively a deeper aim – for example, as I think of it, to compass, if possible maieutically, a certain field from various sides at once. It must be important for the author of the four books, a half-poetical artistic task for him, that each book, which *in itself is* essentially different from the others, may be *characteristically* kept apart from the others; the author must know how to express poetically the illusion which is essentially confirmed by the special point of departure of each book, he may himself try in the notice of the books to separate them, so that the impression of the four books at once is really the product of the reader's self-activity, so that no one is obliged to know that they are four books at once, so that the literary specialist, if he happened to learn that there is one author, may feel a certain pleasure in entertaining the illusion that they are not four books by one author but by four authors, and that the one and the same does not appear even in the newspaper advertisements as presenting himself and offering his wares as an author of four books at once. In such an artistic way the thing was done not long ago in Danish literature.* I at least had not expected to find

*Here S.K. obviously refers to his own pseudonymous works. In 1843 (only three years before Adler's four books) S.K. had published on the same day, October 16, *Fear and Trembling* and *Repetition*, each ascribed to a different pseudonym, and *Three Edifying Discourses* in his own name and, like one of Adler's books, dedicated to his father. But his method illustrates what he says here in criticism of Adler, and shows how Adler's four books might have been produced maieutically, poetically, and artistically, dealing with the same subject, but characteristically separated.

the memory of this so quickly refreshed – and so much by way of parody. Four books at once, one dedicated to his father, all bearing Adler's full name, all essentially in the same form, dealing essentially, sometimes word for word, with the same subject, in short, four yards in one piece, but each yard for itself bearing Adler's full name! There seems to be no trace of any reasonable ground for making four books. If any such a writing, such a merry-go-round, is to be published, it may just as well be run together in one volume; and if in the publication it is divided, it may just as well be twelve books as four. Neither is there any reasonable ground for the one and only variation A. has attempted on the title-page of a book by calling it "An attempt at a *short* presentation," for essentially all his books are equally long and short, inasmuch as they all come under the rubric of *fortuitous length*. In case A., to make the variation quite obvious, on the title-page of the voluminous *Studies and Examples* had modestly added, "An Attempt at a Long Book," in spite of the modesty and the unmistakable effort to write a long book (which we leave to other critics to encourage by their praise), one would be justified in saying that, in spite of its length regarded as a book, it is essentially short. What gives itself out to be a book cannot without more ado, like stuff sold by the yard, be comprised under the categories of the long and the short, it must first prove itself to be a book. With regard to a book we must judge as with the grammatical concept of a period. Two lines of premises without a conclusion is not a short period, and a whole page of premises without a conclusion is not a long period: regarded as a period, both the one and the other have only fortuitous length, and are therefore equally long and equally short. In order that something may be called "a short presentation" it must have essentially the character of completeness and precisely prove its shortness by the fact that within so small a space it reproduces nevertheless the whole matter on a shortened and diminished scale. On the other hand, three pages may very well be a long twaddle, and thirty pages may quite rightly be called a short book. With regard to the first production the author in question may say with Lessing that, "it was so long because he had not time to write it shorter"; and with regard to the last the author in question could say that "it was such a short brochure because he had not a longer time to write, as he had to publish." And Adler's books are a singular sort of production. Had he had a longer time, the book might have become . . . well, here we are at a standstill, not knowing whether it would have become longer or have become shorter. And now Adler! His hope indeed is "with a longer time to labor and quietly develop the ideas for the future, etc." But, whatever the future (to which Adler can always hold) may bring forth, he who critically holds to the completed whole which lies before him must admit that A.'s books are a singular sort of production, an almost anguishing sort of production. When a clergyman has luckily reached the third point of his sermon and already is so far along in it that one who knows the proportions of clerical elocution ventures with a good deal of security to assume that he is about to hum and say Amen – then it may be anguishing when he, instead of pronouncing the significant Amen, becomes gossipy and adds one period after another, while the knowing hearer may say that essentially the sermon is over and essentially the Amen has been said. This is an example of fortuitous length, recognizable by the fact that it begins where, essentially viewed, the Amen should have been said. One knows instances of people who, embarrassed and embarrassing, may remain sitting in one's home a whole hour merely because they are embarrassed to leave: so perhaps it is the case with such a clergyman, that he, after having been embarrassed to mount up to the solemn place, is now embarrassed to say Amen and go down again. But in any case, the sermon which really begins where the Amen should be said, like the visit which begins when the moment has come when it properly should end, are both examples of fortuitous length, the sign of which is the negative category, *beginning when one should stop*. But essentially the same negative category is expressed by *beginning before the beginning*, that is, before the tug of the ideal resolution has indicated: Now thou canst begin. In case a man in this way, before he had gained enough clarity and ripeness to write a book (which he could not yet write), began to write the preface to the book, then would the preface come under the rubric fortuitous length. And this is precisely Adler's case as an author, that he began before the beginning. That "longer time," so often and for so long a time talked about, by the right use of which Adler "in the future" hopes (this is the present tense in the historical style) "in order to let the ideas unfold themselves in a more appropriate form, etc.," must either not yet have come about, or not have been long enough, or not have been rightly used. A. has begun before the beginning, and therefore his productions come under the rubric fortuitous length. All three of the new books (for the fourth contains verse) are an aggregate of tumultuous aphorisms, the beginning of them fortuitous, the factual range without *telos*, and the possible prolongation endless.

To indicate the content of the books is clearly impossible, but one may characterize them by referring to a verse of Horace interpreted in a special way: *Dum meum canto Lalage et ultra terminum vagos curis expeditis.** For often indeed it is outside the ploughed land, on the further side (*ultra terminum*) that A., free from all cares of authorship (*curis expeditis*), carelessly dawdles about (*vagatur*), humming about his Lalage, in whose honor he strews epigrams along his path and sprinkles it with fancies. As one who in a rural spot, left entirely to himself, now in love with one impression, now with another, now making a spring for gladness, now a long leap for sheer pleasure, now again stands still and ponders, now is really profound, and then again is rather insipid and without flavor – thus does Adler dawdle as a reader of the Bible. When a Biblical text attracts him he writes something about it, and then he goes along another street; sometimes he makes a note of something for the sake of using it another time, but this too will be given up. If Adler as a private reader lives in this way, I have no objection to make; but he lives thus as an author. For all this he does not forget his Lalage. By Lalage many different things may be understood, according to who interprets the ode. I remember from my school days that the Rector understood thereby life's innocent pleasures. Adler's Lalage may be understood to be that doctrine communicated to him by a revelation, which now he interprets, now cites; for he does not seem *to have quite forgotten that the doctrine was communicated to him by a revelation*, neither has he forgotten the doctrine, the

*A line from the well-known ode which begins with *Integer vitae*: While I sing of my Lalage and wander freely beyond the border [in the Sabine forest] free of care.

words, which rather have fixed themselves fast in his head. – In case being called by a revelation must make a man serious in the highest and deepest sense – then it is certainly strange to see such a one who in distraction must have forgotten the revelation, just as one may forget his hat, and as people very much *distrait* may forget their heads – to see him now carrying on like an adventurer in the religious style, a mystical knight errant, an itinerant, or like one who without aim or object makes motions in the Bible for the sake of motion, one essentially without occupation who seeks and finds and seeks and gossips – and that man was called by a revelation! In case being called by a revelation must in the highest and deepest sense make a man a zealous and active servant who takes part actively in life as one called in an eminent sense to be a laborer – then it is certainly strange to see a man thus called (who acts as if it were nothing and as if it were all right with the identities) transformed into an *otiosus*, who now has some womanish work to putter over, now with a humorous swing of the hat à la one or another of the Pseudonyms reflects upon this and that or upon himself, and upon the staggering sight of the pale countenance of fearful Jonah,* and then again lets himself be heard melodiously on the erotic pipe of reeds.

Now what is of special importance for an understanding of Adler is that in these last books *absolutely nothing more is said about that fact of revelation, or of continuous revelation, or that this thing and the other was written by direct inspiration*. But even if we assume that this last is as it should be, inasmuch as Adler had no later revelation and later found no occasion to distinguish what is of the Spirit and what is his own, yet surely that fact of revelation in the preface to his *Sermons* cannot be laid to one side as a girl lays aside her decorations for the ball. He indeed often returns to the doctrine communicated to him, but nothing at all is said about its being communicated to him by a revelation, from it he draws no inference to his divine authority, he does not appeal to this as a proof of the truth of the doctrine, on the strength of it he does not defend himself as one who has divine authority. And yet, as was shown in the introduction, the fact that a doctrine was

*Alluding to a passage in Adler's *Studies and Examples*.

imparted to him by a revelation is the decisive point, that which categorically transposes the whole matter and the whole relationship into an entirely different sphere from that in which Adler with all his learning belongs. But then it is wonderful that the very thing which one who has a revealed doctrine to communicate reminds people of again and again, namely, the fact that it was revealed – that this very thing with respect to his revealed doctrine Adler himself seems to have forgotten, and I must constantly remind him that it was indeed, according to his own statement, a revealed doctrine.

Perhaps, however, Adler (the Hegelian, later the Apostle) finds himself along with his revealed doctrine in a new stadium, and now from the "immediate" (which in Hegel's veiled language means revelation) has entered the stadium of "reflection" and now understands the revelation, and then too, in the Hegelian way, he "goes farther" and does not stop with the revelation – with the revelation he himself has had. At the time Christianity came into the world it proclaimed itself to be a revelation and has persisted in that claim. But then time went on, by degrees we all became Christians as by accident, and then many centuries after that there lives a generation (in geographical Christendom) which likes to think that one can understand and comprehend the revelation. The same revealed doctrine is then dealt with in many different ways by a generation which is separated by many centuries from the first. But the one and identical man who has announced that he has had a revelation must surely know precisely what is what with regard to the revelation imparted to him: he must either stand fast by the fact that it was a revelation, and in that case he must speak and act and write in accordance with it; or he must say that now he has understood and comprehended it. But here a little caution. What may it be after all that he has understood? Has he understood that there was no revelation? Then he must revoke the first claim. Or has he understood, what surely he must have understood originally, since he said it, that it was indeed a revelation? Then he must stand by it, argue from it, act in accordance with it, transform his whole existence in relation to it. One cannot deny that there is some excuse for the confusion of Christian truth in modern speculation at the distance of eighteen hundred years from its beginning; but that one and the same man in the course of a few years should strike up this music before us is, if the thing were not so serious, exceedingly comic, and is surely a good proof that he is confused. But above all, one who is supposed to be called by a revelation must with the utmost conscientiousness strive to act honestly. He must not cast a revelation from him as a thief casts away stolen goods when the police are after him – for then he is an intentional deceiver, which Adler certainly is not – but neither must he let the revelation go unexplained while he, treating it as nothing, takes another path ... for then he is confused.

In the four last books, while again and again there is talk about the doctrine, *absolutely nothing more is said about that fact of revelation whereby it was imparted, or about the fact that the doctrine was imparted by a revelation*; on the other hand, almost to one's disgust, there is talk about *genius – genius here and genius there, that genius is something inexplicable, that genius is something nobody can understand, that "the autodidactical foal"** etc.

We will stop here and look carefully before us, for it seems clear enough that the upshot of Adler's whole story is that he is a genius. *Quel bruit pour une omelette!* All honor to genius. In case Adler is a genius, in God's name! I certainly shall not envy him for that. But he began by having had a revelation – though *summa summarum* by this we are to understand that he is a genius. This surely is confusion doubly confounded. The first claim may perhaps be a sort of hasty expression for being a genius. This is a hitherto unheard-of confusion! After all, the category of genius is surely something other and qualitatively different from that of having by a revelation from the Saviour received a new doctrine! To have, if you will, by virtue of being a genius a new doctrine to contribute is surely after all (since it lies within the sphere of immanence, so that newness can only indicate the originality of the reproduction) – it surely is something other and qualitatively different from having by a revelation from the Saviour received a new doctrine! We speak of the primitivity of genius, its originality; but these categories, or this category, surely is not

*Adler's quaint characterization of that "colt the foal of an ass" upon which Jesus rode into Jerusalem.

identical with having had a revelation by which the Saviour communicated to the elect man a new doctrine!

An erring exegesis and dogmatic has certainly played on Christianity the trick of going on and *understanding* the revelation, or going on and *comprehending* it, pretty much in these terms: a revelation, that is, immediateness, that is, the quality of genius, something in the way of genius, the new, newness, originality, primitivity, etc. A. does about the same, but then he does a little more, whereby, ironically enough, he wins the credit of making indirectly evident how this behavior hostile to Christianity proceeds. A. begins by saying that he himself has had a revelation, and thereupon exegeticizes in the modern style upon the concept of revelation, that is to say, he exegeticizes in *action* by letting go his first claim and then becoming a genius, pretending that there was good sense in this connection, or sense in the fact that there was no connection. – What is it the erring exegesis and speculation have done to confuse Christian truth? And how has it been done? Quite briefly and with categorical precision they have done as follows: they have thrust back the sphere of paradox into the aesthetic sphere and thereby have gained the result that every Christian term, which remaining in its own sphere is a qualitative category, now, in reduced circumstances, can do service as a clever expression which may signify pretty much everything. But the erring exegete and dogmatician have not said at the same time of themselves that they have had a revelation; this is reserved for Adler. He can ... well, that is how the nursery rhyme goes: "Who can do it best? Surely our priest."

All the many explanations of Adler about genius are quite right aesthetically, and some of it would be quite right, if he had not had the first: being called by a revelation. In his explanations of the genius there is not to be found a trace, categorically understood, that he has any sort of conception of the qualitative and specific peculiarity of Christianity, and that in spite of the fact that he uses Christ's name perpetually, yea, in spite of the fact that he claims to have had a revelation from the Saviour. When* the sphere of paradoxical religion is abolished or

*Here begins the passage about "The Difference between a Genius and an Apostle" which S.K. salvaged from his "big book on Adler" and published in

explained back into the ethical, then an apostle becomes nothing more nor less than a genius – and then good-night Christianity. *Esprit* and spirit, revelation and originality, a calling from God and ingeniousness, an apostle and a genius, all coalesce in one and the same thing.

Thus can an erring* *Wissenschaft* confuse Christianity, and from the sphere of *Wissenschaft* the confusion has sneaked into religious eloquence, so that one not infrequently hears clergymen, bona fide, in all learned simplicity, prostitute Christianity. They talk in lofty tones of the cleverness and profundity of St. Paul, of his beautiful similes, etc. – sheer aesthetics. If Paul is to be regarded as a genius, it looks very bad for him. Only to clerical ignorance could it occur to praise Paul aesthetically, because clerical ignorance has no standard but thinks in this wise: If only one says something good about Paul, it's all to the good. Such good-humored and well-intentioned thoughtlessness is to be referred to the fact that the person in question has not been disciplined by qualitative dialectics, which would have taught him that an apostle is not served by saying something good about him when it is crazy, so that he is recognized and admired for being what in an apostle is a matter of indifference

---

1849 as one of the *Two Minor Ethico-Religious Treatises*. He felt free to publish it because it makes no mention of Adler. It reproduces almost exactly the text of the first draft of 1846, without taking into account any of the alterations he had proposed, and making only a few which occurred to him when he was transcribing it. At the time when he began the second systematic revision of *The Book on Adler*, about the middle of 1848, he wrote (*Papirer* IX A 498): "My health daily deteriorates, soon I shall be decrepit; but I do not fear death, I have learned like the Roman soldiers that there is something worse." He lived in fact five years longer and during that time wrote some of his most striking works; but in his decrepitude such a task of revision as I have undertaken here was likely too much for him. As a translator I must (or at least may) follow the text which S.K. thought fit to publish, without introducing any of the changes he had previously proposed.

This "minor treatise" was translated by Alexander Dru and was published in a volume entitled *The Present Age* which Charles Williams put together and to which I contributed the other "minor treatise." Though I of course kept Alic Dru's translation before me and relished his style, I was not tempted to imitate his translations – if only for fear of incurring the charge of plagiarism.

*The errors moreover are not merely those of heterodoxy but also those of hyper-orthodoxy and, principally, those of thoughtlessness.

and what essentially he is not, while with that what he is is forgotten. It might just as well occur to such thoughtless eloquence to laud Paul as a stylist and for his artistic use of language, or still better, since it is well known that Paul practiced a manual trade, to maintain that his work as an upholsterer must have been so perfect that no upholsterer either before or since has been able to equal it – for, if only one says something good about Paul, then all is well. As a genius Paul can sustain no comparison with Plato or with Shakespeare, as an author of beautiful similes he ranks rather low, as stylist his is an obscure name, and as an upholsterer – well, I may admit that in this respect I don't know where to place him. One always does well to transform stupid seriousness into a jest – and then comes the really serious thing, the serious fact that Paul was an apostle, and as an apostle has no affinity either with Plato or Shakespeare or a stylist or an upholsterer, who are all of them (Plato as well as the upholsterer Hansen) beneath any comparison with him.

*A *genius* and an *apostle* are qualitatively distinct, they are categories which belong each of them to their own qualitative spheres: that of *immanence* and that of *transcendence*. (1) The genius may well have something new to contribute, but this newness vanishes again in its gradual assimilation by the race, just as the distinction "genius" vanishes when one thinks of eternity. The apostle has paradoxically something new to contribute, the newness of which, precisely because it is paradoxical and not an anticipation of what may eventually be developed in the race, remains constant, just as an apostle remains an apostle to all eternity, and no immanence of eternity puts him essentially on the same plane with other men, since essentially he is paradoxically different. (2) The genius is what he is by reason of himself, i.e. by what he is in himself: an apostle is what he is by reason of his divine authority. (3) The genius has only immanent teleology: the apostle's position is that of absolute paradoxical teleology.

1. All thinking breathes in immanence, whereas the paradox and faith constitute a qualitative sphere of their own. Immanent

*S.K. here copies the first draft, but the correction of this paragraph made a year later (VII B 261, 8) omits the tiresome insistence of 15 lines of italics (spaced type), and here I have preferred that simplification.

(in the relationship between man and man *qua* man) means that every difference is, for essential and eternal thinking, a vanishing point, a moment which has indeed momentarily its importance but essentially vanishes in the essential indifference of eternity. Genius is again, as the word itself says (*ingenium*, what is inborn, original from *origo*, primitivity and pristine from *primus* etc.), immediateness, a natural characteristic – the genius is *born*. Already long before there can be any question to what extent the genius will devote his unusual gifts to God, or will not do it, he is a genius, he is a genius even though he doesn't do it. In the case of the genius there may come about the change that he develops himself to be what κατὰ δύναμιν he is, that he attains conscious possession of himself. In so far as one uses the expression "paradox" to indicate the new which a genius may have to contribute, it is used only in an unessential sense of the transitory paradox of anticipation which is compressed into something paradoxical and in turn disappears. A genius in his first effort at communication may be paradoxical, but the more he comes to himself the more the paradox disappears. A genius may perhaps be a century ahead of his age and hence stands there as a paradox, but in the end the race will assimilate what was once a paradox, so that it is no longer paradoxical.

Quite otherwise with the apostle. The word itself indicates the difference. An apostle is not born, an apostle is a man called and sent by God, sent by Him upon a mission. An apostle does not develop in such wise that he successively becomes what κατὰ δύναμιν he is. For previously to becoming an apostle he possessed no potential possibility. Every man is equally near to being an apostle. An apostle can never in such wise come to himself that he becomes conscious of his apostolic calling as a stage in his life's development. The apostolic call is a paradoxical fact which in the first as well as the last moment of his life stands paradoxically outside his personal identity with himself as the definite person he is. A man has long before perhaps reached mental maturity and the age of discretion – then he is called to be an apostle. By reason of this call he does not become a better head, acquire more imagination, greater acumen, etc. By no means. He remains himself, but with the paradoxical fact of being sent by God upon a definite mission. By this paradoxical fact the apostle is for all eternity made paradoxically different from all other men. The new which he may have to proclaim is the essential paradox. However long a time it may be preached in the world, essentially it remains equally new, equally paradoxical, no immanence can assimilate it. The apostle did not behave like a man distinguished for natural gifts who was born before his time, he was perhaps what we call a simple man, but by a paradoxical fact he was called to proclaim this new thing. Even if thought might think that it could assimilate the doctrine, yet the way in which it came into the world it cannot assimilate, for the essential paradox is precisely the protest against immanence. But the way such a doctrine came into the world is precisely the qualitatively decisive point, which only by deceit or thoughtlessness can be overlooked.

2. A genius is appraised on purely aesthetic grounds, according to the content and specific gravity his productions are found to have; an apostle is what he is by reason of the divine authority he has. *The divine authority is the qualitatively* decisive factor. It is not by appraising aesthetically or philosophically the doctrine that I must and can reach the conclusion that *ergo* he who has taught this doctrine was called by a revelation, *ergo* he is an apostle. The order of sequence is exactly the reverse: the man called by a revelation, to whom was entrusted a doctrine, argues from the fact that this was a revelation, from the fact that he has authority. I am not obliged to obey Paul because he is clever or exceptionally clever, but I must submit to Paul because he has divine authority; in any case it is Paul's responsibility to take care to produce this impression, whether anybody will submit to his authority or no. Paul must not appeal to his cleverness, for then he is a fool; he must not enter into a purely aesthetic or philosophic discussion about the content of his doctrine, for then he is *distrait*. No, he must appeal to his divine authority, and precisely by that, while he is willing to sacrifice life and all, he must *prevent* all aesthetic and philosophically direct objections against the content or form of the doctrine. Paul must not recommend himself and his doctrine by the help of the beautiful metaphors; conversely, he should say to the individual: "Whether the simile is beautiful or not, or whether it is tattered and threadbare, that is of no account, thou shalt reflect that

what I say was entrusted to me by a revelation, so that it is God Himself or our Lord Jesus Christ who speaks, and thou shalt not engage presumptuously in criticizing the form. I cannot, I dare not compel thee to obey, but by thy conscientious relationship to God I make thee eternally responsible to God for thy relationship to the doctrine for the fact that I have proclaimed it as revealed to me by a revelation and therefore proclaimed it with divine authority."

Authority is the qualitatively decisive point. Or is there not, even within the relativity of human life, though it disappears in immanence, a difference between the king's command and the word of a poet or a thinker? And what difference is there except that the king's command has authority and therefore prohibits all critical and aesthetical impertinence with regard to form and content? On the other hand, the poet or the thinker, even within this relativity, has no authority, his saying is appraised purely aesthetically and philosophically by appraising the content and form. But what is it that has fundamentally confused Christianity, unless it is that people have at first in doubt become so nearly uncertain whether there is a God that in rebellion against all authority they have forgotten what authority is and the dialectic of it? A king is sensibly present in such a way that one can sensibly convince oneself of it, and, if it should be necessary, the king can quite sensibly convince one that he exists. But God does not exist in such a sense. Doubt has taken advantage of this to put God on the same plane as all those who have no authority, geniuses, poets, thinkers, whose utterances are appraised precisely by aesthetic and philosophical criteria; and in case a thing is well said, then the man is a genius, and in case a thing is unusually and especially well said, then it is God who has said it!!!

By that trick God is really conjured away. What is He to do? If God stops a man on the street, calls him by a revelation and sends him out to the other men armed with divine authority – then they say to him, "From whom art thou?" He answers, "From God." But, lo, God cannot help His ambassador as a king can who gives him an accompaniment of soldiers or policemen, or his ring, or a letter in his handwriting which everybody recognizes – in short, God cannot be at men's service by providing them with a sensible certitude of the fact that an apostle is an apostle – this too would be nonsense. Even the miracle, if the apostle has this gift, gives no sensible certitude, for the miracle is an object of faith. And moreover it is nonsense to get *sensible* certitude that an apostle is an apostle (the paradoxical determinant of a spiritual connection), just as it is nonsense to get *sensible* certitude of the fact that God exists, since God indeed is spirit. So then the apostle says he is from God. The others answer, "Well then, let us see whether the content of the doctrine is divine, for in that case we will accept it along with the claim that it was revealed to thee." In that way both God and the apostle are mocked. The divine authority of the man thus called should be the surest defense which secures the doctrine and keeps from it at the majestic distance of the divine all impertinences; instead of which the content and form of the doctrine must allow itself to be criticized and sniffed at – before one is able in this way to reach the conclusion that it was a revelation or no. And meanwhile the apostle and God must presumably wait at the door or in the porter's lodge until the case has been decided by the wise men in the *bel étage*. The elect man should according to God's ordinance assert his divine authority to chase away all impertinent people who will not obey him but argue. And instead of obeying, men transform an apostle into an examinee who comes as it were to the marketplace with a new doctrine.

What then is authority? Is authority the profundity of the doctrine, its superiority, its cleverness? Not at all. If authority thus predicated is merely profundity, raised to a higher power, or reduplicated, then precisely there is no authority; for if a pupil by his understanding of it appropriated the doctrine totally and fully, there would in fact be no difference left between the teacher and the pupil. Authority, on the contrary, is something which remains unchanged, which one cannot acquire by having understood the doctrine in the fullest sense. *Authority is a specific quality which comes from another place and makes itself felt precisely when the content of the saying or of the action is assumed to be indifferent.* Let us take an example, as simple as possible, where nevertheless the situation is plain. When the man who has the authority to say it says, "Go!" and when he who has not authority says, "Go!" –

then indeed the saying "Go" along with its content is identical; appraised aesthetically, if you will, they are both equally well said, but the authority makes the difference. In case authority is not "the other" [το ἕτερον], in case it might in any way indicate a higher power within the identity, then precisely there is no authority. In case a teacher is thus enthusiastically conscious that he himself in his existence is expressing and has expressed by the sacrifice of everything the doctrine he preaches, this consciousness may well give him a sure and firm spirit, but it does not give him authority. His life as a proof of the rightness of the doctrine is not "the other" [το ἕτερον] but a simple reduplication of the doctrine. The fact that he lives in accordance with the doctrine does not prove that it is right; but because he is convinced of the rightness of the doctrine he lives in accordance with it. On the other hand, whether a policeman be a rogue or an honest man, being on duty, he has authority.

In order to illuminate more clearly this concept which is so important for the paradox-religious sphere, I shall pursue the dialectic of authority. *In the sphere of immanence authority cannot be thought, or it can be thought only as vanishing.** In so far as there may be question of authority or of the exercise of authority in political, social, civic, household, or disciplinary relationships, authority is only a transient, vanishing factor, which either vanishes later in temporal existence, or vanishes for the fact that earthly life itself is a transitory factor which vanishes with all its differences. At the bottom of all relationships between man and man *qua* man it is only possible to *think* that the differences lie within the identity of immanence, that is, within the essential equality. The one man cannot be *thought* to be different from all others by reason of a specific quality – otherwise all thinking ceases, as it quite consistently does in the paradox-religious sphere or the sphere of faith. All human differences between man

*Perhaps with one or another it may be as with me who recall with reference to the subject of "authority" Magister Kierkegaard's *Edifying Discourses* where it is so strongly accented and emphasized by the fact that every time the words are repeated in the preface: "These are not sermons because the author has not the authority to preach." Authority is either an apostolic call, or the specific quality of ordination. To preach is precisely to exercise authority, and that this is what preaching means is altogether forgotten in our age.

and man *qua* man vanish for thought as factors in the totality and quality of identity. In the moment I must be so good as to respect and take pleasure in the differences, but I am permitted to edify myself religiously with the certitude that the differences vanish in all eternity, both those which distinguish me and those which depress me. As a subject I must honor and obey the King with an undivided soul, but I am permitted to edify myself with the thought that essentially I am a citizen of heaven, and that, if once I should encounter there his deceased majesty, I shall not be bound to him by the obedience required of a subject.

Such is the relationship between man and man *qua* man. *But between God and man there is an eternal, essential, qualitative difference,* which no one without presumptuous thinking can allow to vanish in the blasphemous assertion that God and man are indeed differentiated in the transitory moment of temporal existence, so that man within this life ought to obey and worship God, but in eternity the difference must vanish in the essential equality, so that God and man would become equals, just like the king and his valet.

Thus between God and man there is and remains an eternal, essential, qualitative difference. *The paradox-religious situation* (which quite rightly cannot be thought but only believed) *comes to evidence when God appoints a particular man to have divine authority – nota bene* in relation to what was entrusted to him. The man thus called does not relate himself to [one must use here the literal translation of a phrase which idiomatically means "behave"] the relationship between man and man *qua* man, nor is he related to other men by a quantitative difference (like a genius, a man of distinguished gifts, etc.). No, he behaves paradoxically by reason of having a specific quality which no immanence can recall into the equality of eternity; for it is essentially paradoxical and after thinking (not before, in advance of thinking) – against thinking. If such an elect man has a doctrine to communicate according to a divine order, and another man (let us imagine it) has found out for himself the same doctrine, then are these two nevertheless not equal; for the first is by reason of his paradoxical specific quality (the divine authority) different from every other man and from the qualification of essential likeness and equality which immanently lies at the basis of all human differences. The qualification "an apostle" belongs in the sphere of transcendence, which, quite consistently, has a qualitatively different expression for the relation of other men to an apostle: they relate themselves to him [behave] believingly, whereas all thinking is and remains and breathes in immanence. But faith is not a transitory qualification, no more than the apostle's paradoxical qualification was transitory.

In the relationship between man and man *qua* man we found that no *established* and *lasting* differentium of authority was *thinkable*, that it was a vanishing factor. Meanwhile let us dwell for a moment upon some examples of such so-called relationships of authority between man and man *qua* man (which are true relationships under the conditions of temporal existence) in order to observe in them how authority is essentially to be regarded. A king is indeed assumed to have authority. Why is it then that one is almost offended at learning that a king is clever, is an artist, etc.? Surely it is because in his case one essentially accentuates the royal authority, and in comparison with this the commoner qualification of human difference is a vanishing factor, is unessential, a disturbing accident. A government board is assumed to have authority in a determinate sphere. Why is it then that one would be offended if such a board in its decrees, etc., were really clever, witty, profound? Because one quite rightly accentuates its authority. To ask whether the king is a genius, with the implication that in such case he is to be obeyed, is really *lèse majesté*, for the question contains a doubt concerning subjection to authority. To be willing to obey a board in case it is able to say witty things is at bottom to make a fool of the board. To honor one's father because he is a distinguished pate is impiety. However, as has been said, between man and man *qua* man authority, if there be any, is a vanishing factor, and eternity does away with all earthly authority. But now for the sphere of transcendence? Let us take an example as simple as possible but for that reason as obvious as possible. When Christ says, "There is an eternal life," and when Theological Candidate Petersen says, "There is an eternal life" – they both say the same thing; in the first statement there is contained no more deduction, development, profundity, thoughtfulness, than in the latter; both statements, aesthetically appraised, are equally good. And yet there is an eternal qualitative difference! Christ as the God-Man is in possession of the specific quality of authority which no eternity can mediate and put Christ on the same plane with the essential human equality. Christ therefore taught with authority. To ask whether Christ is profound is blasphemy and is an attempt (whether consciously or unconsciously) to annihilate Him; for in the question is contained a doubt about His authority and an attempt is made with impertinent simplicity to appraise and judge Him as though He were up for examination and should be catechized – whereas instead of that He is the one to whom is given all power in heaven and in earth.

Yet seldom nowadays, very seldom, do we hear a religious address which is perfectly correct. The better sort are fain to dabble a bit in what one might call unconscious and well-intentioned rioting, defending and upholding Christianity with might and main – in erroneous categories. Let us take an example, any one that comes to hand. I take it from a German. With that I know that nobody – not the stupidest and not the most ill-natured – will suppose that I write this concerning a matter which to my thinking is infinitely important in order to aim at some clergyman or another. Bishop Sailer of Regensburg, in a homily for the Fifth Sunday in Lent, preaches on John 7:47–51 as his text. He selects the verse: "He that is of God heareth God's word," and "If a man keepeth my saying he shall never see death." Then he says: "In these words of the Lord are solved three great riddles over which men in one way or another have racked their brains since the beginning of time." There we have it. The word "riddle," and especially "three great riddles," and then the next clause, "over which men ... have *racked their brains*," at once lead one's thought to the profound in the intellectual sense, to meditation, pondering, speculation. But after all how can a simple apodeictic statement be profound? – an apodeictic statement which is what it is only by the fact that this or that man said it, a statement which does not at all demand to be understood or fathomed but only to be believed. In the case of a simple statement, an assertion, how can it occur to a man that an enigma had to be solved by way of profound pondering and fathoming?* The question simply is, Is there an eternal life? The answer is, There is an eternal life. Where then in all the world is profundity to be found in this? In case Christ is not the one who said it, and in case Christ is not what He said He was, then, if the statement itself is profound, the profundity indeed has yet to be discovered. Let us take Mr. Petersen the theological candidate, who indeed also says, "There is an eternal life." Who in all the world would think of accusing him of profundity because of a plain statement? Thus the decisive point does not lie in the statement but in the fact that it is Christ who uttered it; but the confusing thing is that one, as though to entice men to believe, talks a lot about the profound and the profound. A Christian priest, if he would speak correctly, must say quite simply, "We have Christ's word for it that there is an eternal life – therewith the matter is decided. Here there is no question either about racking one's brains or about speculation, but about the fact that it is Christ who said it, not in the capacity of a profound thinker, but with His divine authority." Let us go further, let us assume that one believes that there is an eternal life because Christ has said it, so believingly he circumvents all the profundity and pondering and fathoming wherewith people rack their brains. On the other hand, let us take one who wants to rack his brains profoundly with the question about immortality – I wonder if he will have a right to deny that the simple assertion is a profound answer to the question? What Plato says about immortality is really profound, won by deep pondering – but poor Plato had no authority whatsoever.

Meanwhile this is the situation: Doubt and superstition, which make faith vain, have, among other things, made men embar-

*In 1847 (*Papirer* VII B 261, 13) S.K. proposed the following substitution for the remainder of this paragraph which has at least the advantage of being a notable abbreviation; but perhaps, according to an adage which S.K. adopted, "First thoughts are better than second thoughts." In this big book abbreviations are always welcome; yet perhaps I ought to have included S.K.'s first thoughts along with his second thoughts – if only it could be done without making this book look pedantic.

Instead of all this clerical twaddle about enigmas and racking the brain, Sailer ought to say: "We have Christ's word for it, and when He has said it the thing is decided. Here there is no question either of racking the brain or of enigmas, but of the one who has said that to Him is given all power in heaven and in earth."

rassed about obeying, about bowing to authority. This rebelliousness sneaks into the thinking even of the better sort of men, perhaps without their being conscious of it, and then begins all this extravagance, which at bottom is treachery, about the profound and the profound and the wondrously beauteous features which one can dimly descry, etc. If one were to describe with one single predicate the Christian religious eloquence which one now hears and reads, one would have to say that it is *affected*. Ordinarily when one talks about the affectation of a clergyman one thinks perhaps about how he dresses and gets himself up, talks in a sweet and languishing voice, rolls his R's like a Norwegian, wrinkles his brow, strains himself with forceful gestures and with leaps of religious enthusiasm, etc. All such things, however, are of minor importance, though it is always desirable that they should not be. But the pernicious thing is when the whole train of thought in his priestly eloquence is affected, when its orthodoxy is won by laying the accent entirely on the wrong place, when basically he requires people to believe in Christ and preaches faith in Him on grounds which cannot possibly be the object of faith. In case a son were to say, "I obey my father, not because he is my father, but because he is a genius or because his commands are always profound and clever" – then this filial obedience is affected. The son accentuates something which is entirely beside the point, he accentuates the cleverness and profundity in a *command*, whereas a command is precisely indifferent with regard to this qualification. The son is willing to obey by virtue of his father's profundity and cleverness, and by virtue of this it is precisely not possible to obey, for his critical attitude with regard to the decision whether the command is profound and clever undermines obedience. And this too is affectation when there is so much about accepting Christianity and believing in Christ on account of the profundity and profundity of the doctrine. One accepts orthodoxy by accentuating something which is entirely beside the point. The whole of modern Speculation is therefore "affected" by reason of having done away with *obedience* on the one hand and *authority* on the other, and by then wanting to be orthodox. A clergyman who is entirely correct in his eloquence must speak thus in introducing a word of Christ: "This word was spoken by Him to whom, according to His own statement, all power hath been given in heaven and in earth. Now, thou, my hearer, must consider by thyself whether thou wilt bow to this authority or no, receive it and believe it or no. But if thou wilt not do so, then for heaven's sake do not go off and accept the word because it is clever and profound or wondrously beautiful, for this is blasphemy, it is wanting to treat God like an aesthetic critic. For so soon as the dominant note of authority, of the specific paradoxical authority, is heard, then this sort of appropriation, which otherwise is permissible and desirable, is a crime and a presumption."

But now how can an apostle prove that he has authority? Could he prove it physically, he would be no apostle. He has no other proof but his own assertion. And thus precisely it ought to be, for otherwise the believer would come into a direct relation to him, not into a paradoxical relationship. In the transitory situation of authority between man and man *qua* man the authority will ordinarily be recognized physically by means of force. An apostle has no other proof but his own assertion, and at the most by his willingness to suffer everything for the sake of the doctrine. With regard to that his speech will be brief: "I am called by God; do with me now as you will, scourge me, persecute me; but my last word is my first: I am called by God, and I make you eternally responsible for what you do to me." In case it were true in real life (let us imagine it) that an apostle had power in a worldly sense, had great influence and powerful connections by the force of which he is victorious over the opinions and judgments of men – in case he employed this power he would *eo ipso* have lost his cause. For by employing force he would have defined his effort as essentially identical with that of other men, and yet an apostle is what he is only by reason of his paradoxical heterogeneity, by reason of having divine authority, which he can have, absolutely unaltered, even if by men he is regarded, according to Paul's saying, as worth no more than the filth on which they tread.*

* Here ends the passage which S.K. salvaged from *The Book on Adler* and published as a dissertation on "The Difference between a Genius and an Apostle"; but in the published work he added the four paragraphs which for the sake of completeness are here added between brackets.

[3. *The genius has only immanent teleology; the apostle is put paradoxically in an absolutely paradoxically teleological position.*

If any man can be said to be put in an absolutely paradoxically teleological position it is an apostle. The doctrine imparted to him is not given to him as a problem to ponder over, it is not given to him for his own sake; on the contrary he is on a mission and has to proclaim the doctrine and exercise authority. Just as one who is sent to town with a letter has nothing to do with the contents of the letter but only with the delivery of it; just as an ambassador who is sent to a foreign court has no responsibility for the content of the message but only for conveying it properly; so an apostle has principally the single duty of being faithful in his service, which is the performance of his mission. In this essentially consists the sacrificial character of the apostle's life, even if he were never to be persecuted, namely, in the fact that "as himself poor he makes many rich," that he never can give himself time or repose or freedom from care, in *otium*, in the enjoyment of "good days," to be enriched by that with which his preaching enriches others. Spiritually understood, he is like a busy housewife who herself hardly gets time to eat, so busy is she in preparing food for the many mouths. And though he at the beginning might venture to hope for a long life, yet his life until the last will remain unchanged, for there will always be new and newer people to whom the doctrine must be proclaimed. Although a revelation is the paradoxical fact which surpasses men's understanding, one can nevertheless understand this much, which has everywhere been manifested, that a man is called by a revelation to go forth into the world to proclaim the word, to act and to suffer, called to a life of ceaseless activity as the Lord's messenger.

It is very different with genius. Genius has only immanent teleology, and as it develops itself it projects this self-development as its work in the world. That acquires importance, perhaps great importance, but it is not itself related teleologically to the world or to other men, and without taking his gifts in vain the genius can live only humoristically, self-satisfied, in a place withdrawn from the world, where without concern whether or not others profit by it, he develops himself with seriousness and diligence. The genius is for this reason by no means inactive, he works within himself perhaps more than ten businessmen, accomplishes perhaps a great deal, but nothing that he accomplishes has any *telos* outside itself. This is at once the high humanity and the pride of genius: the humanity consists in the fact that it does not define itself teleologically in relation to any other man, as though there might be someone in need of it; the pride consists in the fact that it immanently relates itself to itself. It is modest of the nightingale that it does not require anyone to listen to it; it is proud of the nightingale that it doesn't care whether anybody listens to it or no. The dialectic of the genius will be especially offensive in our age when the multitude, the masses, the public, and other such abstractions, are bent in turning everything upside down. The "highly honored public" and the domineering multitude want the genius to express the fact that he exists for them and for their sake; the "highly honored public" and the domineering multitude are only one side of the dialectic of the genius, they are offended by his pride and do not notice that this same thing is also modesty and humility. The "highly honored public" and the domineering multitude would also take the existence of the apostle in vain. For it is true indeed that he exists absolutely for the sake of others, is sent forth for the sake of others, but it is not the multitude and not the masses and not the "highly honored public" and not even the "highly honored cultivated public" that are his lord or his lords – it is God, and the apostle is he who has *authority* to *command* both the multitude and the public.

The humoristic self-satisfaction of the genius is the unity of modest resignation in the world and proud elevation above the world, of being an unnecessary superfluity and a precious ointment. If the genius is an artist, then he produces his work of art, but neither he nor his work has any *telos* outside itself. Or he is an author who abolishes every teleological relationship with the world about him and defines himself as a lyric poet. Lyric art has quite rightly no *telos* outside itself; whether one writes a page of lyric or folios of lyric, that makes no difference with regard to determining the direction of his activity. The lyrical author is concerned only about his production, enjoys the delight of producing, perhaps through pain and effort, but he has nothing to do with others, does not write *in order to*, in order to enlighten men, in order to help them along in the right way, in order to put something over – in short he does not write *in order to*. And so it is with every genius. No genius has an "in order to." The apostle has absolutely paradoxically an "in order to."]

Now we return again to Adler and to his transmogrification already referred to, whereby from being one called by a revelation he became a genius, still thinking that he is identical with himself. For he who is called by a revelation must *eo ipso* assume a teleological attitude, being precisely God's instrument which is to be used to produce an effect. It is different with a genius, who may live humoristically withdrawn from the world in self-satisfaction. This is pretty much the attitude Adler assumes in his last works – but Adler began by being called by a revelation, and Adler now thinks that he is in identity with himself, that is to say, he fails to notice that there is a qualitative decisive difference between his first position and his last. Although a revelation is the paradoxical fact which surpasses men's understanding, yet one can understand this much, which is everywhere in evidence, that a man is called by a revelation to go out into the world to proclaim the word, to labor and to suffer, to lead an unremittingly active life as God's messenger. That on the contrary a man might be called to sit at ease in his own ample mansion employed in an active literary *far niente* in a quiet place, to be clever from time to time, and thereupon to be publisher as well as collector of the dubious proofs of his cleverness – is a thought almost blasphemous. Here again Adler's later attitude contains a proof against the reality and truth of his first claim, while the fact that he does not revoke his first is a proof that he is confused. At the beginning of his activity as an author he was also on another path when he shouted before all the people, "Confess! Confess!" Now in his last books he has adopted the principle of silence. "Silence is genius," says he. He does not develop this thesis more in detail, as in general he seems to have abandoned himself to the habit of touching tangentially upon the most various subjects and publishing his observations in a book – but, no, in four books at once. The significance of silence, moreover, is quite simple. For us simple men silence is a way for the expression of inwardness, and is the way by which originality is acquired, an originality which is more than a surrogate for the originality of the genius. (A revelation lies in an entirely different sphere, and therefore nothing is said about it here.) By holding fast a definite expression of one's life, a definite single thought, in absolutely silent inwardness, by not wishing to open the least communication with any other man (by which relative and comparative standards, the standards of mediocrity, are made accessible) every man will, if in the meantime he does not lose his reason (for this danger is inescapable), *acquire originality*. The converse and opposite of this situation of freedom, this slow acquisition, is the direct, immediate characteristic of genius (and hence again what lies within the paradoxical religious sphere, the fact of being called by a revelation). The idea of silence, the whole conception of silence as the way of inwardness, which for every man leads to the highest attainment, whether originally he was a genius or no, this conception has found an adequate expression in the writings of the Pseudonyms, to which therefore, so far as this subject is concerned, I refer everyone – only not Adler, who in his thesis, "Silence is genius," annihilates this idea of the Pseudonyms – which is comical enough and becomes still more so when one reflects that his four last books also annihilate his first position. Even though it be conceded that Adler is a genius, he wants, however, to be an immediate genius, and by the aid of silence it is impossible to become anything immediate, since after all it is nonsense to think of a method in relation to immediacy, which precisely is anterior to a method.*

*At this point S.K. proposed to suppress six pages of the first draft of this book and to substitute about two pages of a very different character. (VII B 256, 14–20) I have followed his proposal in the text, but the discarded pages contain something we ought to know about Adler and suggest a shrewd diagnosis of his derangement, so I have translated them in this footnote:

In the four last books A. is merely a genius, a pure and genuine genius – and yet, in this opinion, presumably he is in identity with his first position. He has forgotten that those words in the preface to his *Sermons* were imparted to him by a revelation dictated by the Saviour; he has forgotten that the *Sermons*, to which A. often refers, were written under the influence of Jesus' cooperative grace; A. as a genius has, so it seems, undertaken the whole management of affairs, presumably in distraction – in distraction, for, if it were done consciously, he must solemnly revoke his first claim. How far A. can go in distraction one can further ascertain by reading his four last books; for there one has an opportunity to observe with what levity (which only distraction can excuse) he deals with God and Christ, represents them as chatting with one another, and he chats with them. In the last

Instead of a man who was called by a revelation we get a genius, and one may say of Adler that by becoming a genius he is somewhat deranged, which in turn is precisely proved by the fact that he has not found himself obliged in the least degree to explain anything about the dreadful and topsy-turvy metamorphosis he has undergone, for he seems constantly to be blissful in the vain imagination that he is in identity with himself from first to last, which in fact he is as a deranged genius.

---

books he is poetically inventive, he represents God and Christ as talking with one another – and this surely is an invention! Thus Adler's *Attempt at a Short Exposition of Christianity* begins as follows: "Before God created the world He said to Jesus, 'I can do everything as perfectly as possible,'" etc. God and Jesus are introduced as speaking and conversing. But this surely was not communicated by a revelation! But what is it then? Well, it is a little poetical effort to enliven the presentation. But, lo, Adler later quotes the same conversation, he founds an argument upon it. He says in many passages, "as Jesus promised to let Himself be born"; that is, he talks of that conversation between God and Christ as something which actually occurred and to which one can make appeal as though these were the *ipsissima verba* of Jesus. Indeed in one place Adler even says: "For finally we must remember what Jesus said to God," etc., and thereupon he quotes several of the invented words. So first one ventures with frivolous inventions out into the sphere where one should rather leave inventions alone, and thereupon fixes his own invention so tightly in his head that he thinks it is reality. In that way a lightminded person can easily get a revelation. He needs only to fumble for some time as a crocheteer with the fantastic notion of a revelation until this notion that he has had a revelation at last fixes itself so fast in him that he poetically conceives he has had a revelation, and then this invention fixes itself fast as an actuality – until something new sets itself fast.

But, whereas Adler treats his own inventions as though they were realities, he treats the New Testament in an equally frivolous way, as though it were not a reality – he who undoubtedly has many a pretty word to say about the Bible, and precisely in view of this his behavior indicates that he is in a confused state of mind. With an arbitrariness which is perfectly fantastic he lays claim to words of the Bible as his own without using quotation marks. As between one author and another that would be called plagiarism; to plagiarize from God is blasphemy. Indeed there are passages where in his frivolity he actually reaches the point of identifying himself with Christ. A saying begins with the words of Christ in the first person: I say unto you. These words are not quoted, there is no indication that they are Bible words, which is important especially because they are in the first person. Immediately after these words in the first person comes the next sentence which likewise is in the first person but are the words of Adler. A reader generally must assume, as Adler leads everyone to assume, that it is he who utters the whole saying, that the "I" in the first sentence is the same as the "I" in the second and in the third sentence. And yet the first "I" is Christ and the other "I" is Adler.

He is a deranged genius of the instantaneous sort, and hence precisely has no conception of himself, is entirely without continuity. In the instant something grips him – then he is that. The next instant something else grips him – then he is that. His existence explains nothing, as though another might be directing his life and guiding him by a foreign will; and there is no aesthetic or religious concept he has developed in such a way that it has gained new clarity or is thought out with true originality. On the other hand, he touches upon the most diverse subjects and almost everywhere confuses them. It cannot be denied that he makes profound remarks, but he surely does not reach absolute profundity, if the explanation we gave at the very beginning of this book is right, that profundity is connection and continuity. And even in his profound remarks there is a certain uniformity, for in large part they are made on one last. Understanding a thought is something like being able to decline a paradigm: one can also decline all the words which come under that paradigm. If one has understood a thought, one can, by using it in many "examples," seem to make many profound remarks, and yet the many are really repetitions, and hence (to refer again to the simile of the last) one is not justified in saying that he has learned many declensions because he has learned the many words which come under the same declension. So it is too with having understood one thought: if the repetitions are not to be tedious, there must be added a poetical factor which makes the application of the examples aesthetically worthy. But for this Adler has no time – he has (according to his own authentic interpretation, cf. 1) nothing new to contribute – he who lives in a lyrical *otium*! With respect to form he is at a disadvantage. He who has not and never has had anything new to contribute by way of content must strive precisely by means of the form to accomplish something. The thought which Adler especially rides is the old Hegelian notion that the concept "veers about," only that it is used rather under the qualification of the ironical. This thought is thus expressed in my master's dissertation ("About Irony"): Irony makes the phenomenon evident; irony consists in the cunning that, while the opponent believes he is talking about another thing or even has grasped another thing, irony perceives that the individual has given himself away. Every idea consistently carried through has *eo ipso* the power to require the contrary to become manifest. How this is more particularly to be understood, how it proceeds, has often been explained and exhibited by the Pseudonyms. The ironical cunning consists in transforming oneself to nothing by negative-active consistency in order to help the phenomenon to become manifest. At the first glance and for stupid men it may seem as if the ironical man were the loser. The ironical cunning consists in keeping oneself negative, thus transforming the attack into self-revelation. The attacker raises a storm and makes a great fuss; in the eyes of foolish men it seems as though he were the stronger, and yet he accomplishes nothing more – and there sits irony so cunning and on the lookout – he accomplishes nothing more than to reveal his own nature, his own paltriness or his own insignificance. Thus, for example, one may employ irony against a shrew, and her shrewishness becomes more and more manifest. So too it is ironically correct when a man says something extraordinary about himself, for example, that he has had a revelation, then precisely to believe him (the negative attitude, not opposing him directly as foolish men do), in order in that way to help him to make it evident to himself that he has had no revelation. When a man really has ataraxia and self-mastery he will by negative consistency be able to make any kind of a dialectically complicated phenomenon plain; thus A. seems so awfully well pleased at the profound remark that "The law put its foot in it by condemning Christ, and thereby did away with itself." This whole thing is neither more nor less than Hegel's "veering about" of the concept carried out with a little ironic coloring. Hegel, it is well known, is nothing less than he is ironical; with him it is always a serious matter when the concept veers about. That irony owes its life to a dialectic of comparison is in 1846 not much of a discovery. Hegel believes that the concept veers about by an immanent necessity; nevertheless irony notices the transition inasmuch as it notices its drollery or its ingenuity. The qualitative dialectic is in the first place really in essential understanding with the category of the leap, a category which Adler also bungles.

Among Adler's profound remarks there are sometimes reminiscences of other writers to be found, and in view of this it may be quite natural that Adler frequently recurs to the thesis and defends the thesis that stealing in the world of spirit is entirely permissible. Well, about that every man has his own opinion. I don't deny that I hold the opposite opinion. But the strange thing is again that it is Adler (one who has a revelation to which he can appeal) who adopts this thesis; for after all a revealed doctrine cannot have been borrowed from others, and there is surely no one up to date that has stolen anything from Adler. On the other hand, in case Adler thinks himself guilty of a theft, or innocent of it, inasmuch as this theft according to his opinion is permissible, there results this strange and preposterous situation that he who is placed above other men by reason of a revelation should pilfer a little from poor folks. However, perhaps Adler after all does himself an injustice in suspecting himself of stealing; for in the world of spirit theft is so far from being permissible that it is impossible. For in the world of spirit, and only in the world of spirit, the security of property rights is absolute. If one leaves a manuscript lying about, another may steal it, he may publish it, but he cannot steal its thoughts, nor can he propound the thoughts contained in the stolen manuscript, in one way or another he will alter them, so that they do not remain the same thoughts.

If one regards Adler as a deranged genius (who neither as thinker nor as artist is in control of himself, who in the rapture of production touches tangentially upon the most diverse subjects) and if one would define totally and essentially the character of his genius, one may say that it is dizziness. With this it is not denied that individual utterances and remarks may even be profound. A drunken man may well utter good sayings, but the essential character of his genius is drunkenness. I shall now illustrate this dizziness by several examples from Adler's last works, while begging the reader not to forget that the principal characteristic which further illustrates his dizziness is the fact that he propounds dizzy aesthetic views which remind one strongly of paganism and the worldly view of life, though he gives himself out to be not only a believing Christian but claims even that he has had a revelation from the Saviour. It is simple dizziness to adopt a dizzy, aesthetic view, but it is dizziness raised to a higher power to wish at the same time to be a Christian in an eminent sense and to wish to help the understanding of Christian doctrine by means of aesthetics.

In a physiological sense attention has quite rightly been called to the fact that dizziness results when the eye has no fixed point on which to rest. Hence one becomes dizzy on looking down from a tower, for the glance plunging down finds no limit, no bound. For a similar reason one becomes dizzy at sea, because everything is constantly changing and so again there is no limit or bound. A physician has explained somewhere that it was *seasickness* the French soldiers died of in Russia, produced by the fact that there was nothing before the eye in the endless breadth of the plain. When therefore one notices that one is becoming dizzy one may stop it by catching upon something with the eye. In case a man who becomes thus dizzy in driving down a steep hill will himself undertake to be coachman he will hardly become dizzy. As a coachman, the definite way he is obliged to watch the reins will prevent dizziness. So it is with physical dizziness. The dizzy is the wide, the endless, the unlimited, the boundless; and dizziness itself is the boundlessness of the senses. The indefinite is the ground of dizziness, but it is also a temptation to abandon oneself to it. For surely indefiniteness is contrary to man's nature, and it is not merely science which, according to Aristotle's saying, abhors the boundlessness of vacuity, not merely ethics which abhors ambiguity, but precisely because indefiniteness is against nature it is at the same time tempting. The dialectic of dizziness has thus in itself the contradiction of willing what one does not will, what one shudders at, whereas this shudder nevertheless frightens only . . . temptingly. The remedy for dizziness is therefore limitation; and, spiritually understood, all discipline is limitation. So then he who, physiologically, has a tendency to become dizzy does well to avoid open places for the time being and feel his way along the walls of buildings, in order that the manifold may be of help as a relative scale. So also must he who, spiritually understood, suffers from dizziness try to limit himself. The limit is not only in the Greek sense the beautiful, but in the ethical sense it is a saving power.

Spiritually understood, dizziness may have a double character. It may be occasioned by the fact that a man has so wandered astray in the infinite that nothing finite can acquire for him substantial existence, that he can get no standard of measurement. This kind of dizziness consists rather in an excess of imagination, and, inasmuch as one might conceive of dizziness metaphorically with relation to the eye, one might perhaps call it *single-sighted dizziness*. The other kind of dizziness produced by an abstract dialectic, owing to the fact that it sees absolutely everything double, sees nothing at all. This kind of dizziness one might call *double-sighted dizziness*. Salvation from all dizziness, spiritually understood, is essentially to seek the ethical, which by qualitative dialectic disciplines and limits the individual and establishes his task.

It is especially from the first kind of dizziness that Adler suffers. As a dialectician he was first educated by Hegel, whose System has no ethic and whose dialectic, far from being an existential dialectic, is a sort of fantasy-intuition. From the dizzy height of the Hegelian metaphysic Adler plunges down headlong into the religious sphere, and now discovers, if one will, orthodoxy, but, be it noted, an orthodoxy without the ethical. When relationship to ethics is abandoned one may say that dizziness must come about by necessity.

As an example of A.'s dizziness I* will *first adduce* his teaching about *the instant*, which, it is true, he nowhere lectures upon, but every instant he alludes to it. His teaching is to the following effect: Grasp the instant, everything depends upon the instant, the next instant it is too late, so you have to go through life like the Wandering Jew. Throughout Adler's last works runs a paganish despairing joy at having himself grasped the instant, and a despairing dread at the mere thought – what if he had not grasped it?! For to Adler the instant means nothing more nor less than what luck meant in paganism – only he is man enough to combine this dialectically with the Christian conception, so that he also in a lucky instant was called by a revelation from the Saviour and got a doctrine entrusted to him. The play of luck disposes not only as it did aforetime over riches, honor, power, the most beautiful maiden etc., but a revelation is also a play of luck.

*What here and in the next following I must explain briefly belongs to the problems which the Pseudonyms have explained so clearly that I can refer to them – only not for Adler, that would certainly come too late.

Regarded as a problem, "the instant" is undeniably a very difficult one, since it must concern itself with the dialectic between the temporal and the eternal. The eternal is infinite in content, and yet it must be made commensurable with the temporal, and the contact is in the instant. Yet this instant is nothing. Thinking here comes to a stop with the most dreadful contradiction, with the most taxing of all thoughts, which, if it were to be held for long at the highest pitch of mental exertion, must bring the thinker to madness. To build card-houses on the table is not difficult, but that a huge edifice might be built upon what is smaller than the edge of a card, upon a foundation which is nothing (for the instant as such does not exist, it is merely the confine between time past and time future, it *is* when it *has been*) – that certainly is a dreadful contradiction. If fantasy is allowed to run wild, then from this comes about the pagan doctrine of luck and fate, or the *un*christian doctrine of election by grace, conceived in the despairing sense. To be saved by election in the despairing sense is dialectically entirely like fate, it is the unhappiest of all happiness. The despairing election by grace posits in mankind the most dreadful discord, and in another sense it makes all mankind unhappy. For it is unhappy to be shut out, rejected; and it is unhappy to be saved in that way. To be saved, to be happy – and to know that all others are not and cannot be saved, to know that one has not and in all eternity cannot acquire conditions in common with them, that one has no fundamental fellowship with them, to be saved and to know that one has no word to cry to others, no highest and last comfort which is common to all – yea, what human heart could endure such blessedness! If that word of the Scripture, "Call upon the Lord while He is near," were to be understood as though it said "the second," as though the Lord were a fleeting traveller who the next second would be far away, in case it were to be understood so enigmatically of "the second" that no one knew or could know when the second was – who could presume to preach about it? And how meaningless that once every year [*anno redeuente*] it is preached about! It must not be understood with a nervous dread, and it cannot be the understanding in what is written about the sick man who lay beside the Pool of Bethesda, that he who came first was saved. The Gospel recounts precisely that the sick man who for many years had come too late – nevertheless was healed. This is the Gospel, the glad tidings, that the cruelty of fate is abolished, that first and foremost the salvation of the soul is promised, whether a man be bodily sound or no. Who must not despair if it were necessary also for the salvation of the soul to come first – if such were Christianity? And who must not be in a desperately dizzy state in order as a Christian to bring back paganism again?

But what then can put a stop to this dizziness which comes about when a man stands still and will not seriously consider any life task for himself and therefore is like a galvanized frog which for an instant has a spasm? What can check this dizziness? What can master that desperate supertension of the instant? The ethical can. When in every moment of one's life there is a work to be done, a task, when often enough, alas, there is a serious concern for the fact that one has not attended to his work as one should – then there is no time to be fantastic or to give oneself to fantastic speculation about the instant and about the dialectic that it is all and nothing. The ethical, and the religious which has the ethical in it, resists with all its might the bringing over us again the hopelessness of paganism. And where does paganism show itself more hopeless than its theory of luck? The ethical knows nothing and will know nothing about luck, about one becoming a genius, about one having the lamp, about one coming first, about one winning the lottery. Ethics is weary of all the anecdotical twaddle, it shudders at the horror of those times when fantasy wrought havoc with the human race and played the unhappy game of luck. Ethics would only know how to speak of the universal human tasks – and therefore precisely it has power over the luck of the instant, which is a horror. Even to the most despairing, even to him who has lost most, the ethical cries: The instant *still* is there! The ethical does not let itself be fooled, any more than God lets Himself be mocked; by qualitative dialectic it knows well how to make the instant important as *decision*; but it will not alarm a man to the point of madness, nor madly make him happy with a game of hap or luck.

As an example of Adler's dizziness *may next be adduced his view of Abraham*, to whom he often returns in verse and prose. Here he warms up the old story about its being an evil spirit, the devil, who puts into Abraham's head the notion of sacrificing Isaac. Now by this explanation nothing is gained, for the difficulty recurs in another place, as was shown in *Fear and Trembling*. If such were the case, how can one explain that it could occur to the Church to make Abraham the father of faith and the friend of God? For he must himself after all have discovered at a later moment that it was a temptation he yielded to, hence he should not have been represented as the father of faith, but perhaps as the discoverer of repentance. Adler, however, is original. He assumes, as has been said, that it was the devil who suggested to Abraham the idea; but, lo and behold, God was so well pleased with this idea, "because it was brave and bold and great" (and suggested by the devil!) that, though He prevented it from being carried out, He made Abraham his friend – and in that way Abraham became the father of faith. The thing is carried so far that we men presumably might not be supposed to know exactly the difference between good and evil, that the evil may become so imposing that we mistake its greatness for its goodness, but that God Himself sits like a fool while He is given a course of treatment such as one administers to a little girl of sixteen who wishes only that she might have a lover who does something great and even falls in love with a robber chieftain. – That his dizziness might express itself thus is only to be expected. From Hegel he had no ethics, and when he plunged down into the land of orthodoxy hitherto unknown to him, he still was without ethics. Ethics lives and moves and has its being in the distinction between good and evil. The aesthetical, on the other hand, consists in the quantitative dizziness – the great, the astonishing – and metaphysics consists in disinterestedness.

As an example of Adler's dizziness may *finally be adduced the recklessness with which he counts that the great idea, the brave and bold idea of the individual, should be permitted to make itself heard, even though a little injustice is done thereby, even though some men thereby go to the dogs.* In defense of this view he appeals constantly to natural phenomena, to the fact that the sun remains just as glorious though it scorches several creatures, etc., quite à la Don Juan, who says to Leporello: "Thou seest me walk only in nature's tracks," and precisely about the sun, to which he appeals as a pattern, he says: "All round the course of the sun lovers are dying and being born, and he heeds not the sacrifice of their corpses." Well, naturally, for all that, Don Juan remains just as bold, and the sun remains just as glorious; for gloriousness, boldness, etc. are not exactly ethical terms. Everyone who has but a meager and commonplace conception of the ethical knows very well that nature is a very poor analogy of the ethical, and that to want to live à la nature is to want to live unethically, as well as that by way of such analogies one will come at last to the Neronic burning of Rome – but that was a proud and glorious sight! Nature is precisely indifferent to the distinction between good and evil, which to ethics is all in all.

Ethical sobriety, which is the opposite to Adler's dizziness, consists essentially in the fact that man's effort reduplicates itself in the dialectic of the means, so that the means we use, so that the way one fights for his idea, so that the least means one allows oneself for the sake of realizing them, are equally important, absolutely equally important, as the object for which one fights and labors. Think, for example, of the strictly orthodox Church teachers, of Augustine's strict teaching about truth, that no one may save even one's own chastity by an untruth. And why not? Because untruthfulness is more unchaste than the physical violation unaccompanied by concupiscence. Think of the scrupulousness of Pythagoras, who in ancient times was praised for his purity, who hardly dared to step upon the ground lest by his tread he might kill a living animal. But a Don Juan, a Napoleon, a Nero, in short, all headlong individuals, hail analogies from nature – and so does Adler, to whom a new doctrine was entrusted by a revelation from the Saviour. A new doctrine – but that is not the point, the important thing is that it was from the Saviour.

In his four last books then Adler is a deranged genius, and as *summa summarum* of his first and last positions it remains true that he is to be regarded as confused. So when one has made good this interpretation of him, as now has been done precisely by showing the astonishing incongruity between the first position (that of being called by a revelation and having received a new doctrine from the Saviour) and the last (that of being a genius of sorts), along with the fact that this incongruity has entirely escaped Adler's attention, then one can still further illustrate his confused condition by a glance at the external features of the books, which undoubtedly will suffice most readers for forming a judgment. It cannot be denied that it gives one a queer sensation to look into the books. In an extraordinary degree he has emancipated himself from every restraint as an author, from every requirement of order, from every regard for a reader. That this might be art, a maieutic tactic, cannot without great difficulty be assumed. Moreover, I have confirmed the denial of this notion by illuminating the total confusion in essential respects. – Not rarely A. treats the reader like a child to whom one is giving a lesson. Thus he prints the selfsame Scripture passage, which is six lines long, three times as a whole on two pages. Now one cannot well deny that every word of Scripture has the admirable quality that it always merits being read – wherefore one certainly ought to possess a Bible and read it again and again. But to fill a big book by having the same Scripture passage printed so often in so brief a space is something after all rather strange. Also in another way he sometimes treats the reader altogether like a child. It is well known that as a task for composition in the mother tongue one sometimes uses single disconnected words from which the pupils must form a connected sentence. So it is that Adler throws out quite abruptly brief clauses, sometimes meaningless, perhaps to give the reader an opportunity of practicing the composition of connected sentences. In other places he seemed to behave quite as if the reader did not exist, that is to say, as though what he wrote were not meant to be printed, but as though from time to time it had been written in a notebook and got printed through a misunderstanding.

Naturally, however, about all such matters I desire to speak as briefly as possible. I am very little concerned about dealing aesthetically with his works; his revelation and his relation to that is the only thing that concerns me. Nevertheless, I will make one remark which belongs here and which, as I believe, characterizes Adler essentially. Upon reading his last four books one gets the impression (and it is impossible to avoid it), one gets a suspicion and a notion that Adler is not really a thinker, but, on the contrary, that he must have the habit of putting himself into an exalted mood; he grasps at a solitary expression, a brief saying, detaches it without thinking, neither does he put it thinkingly together with something else, but continues to repeat it until the monotonous repetition stupefies him and puts him in a state of exaltation, so that it seems to him there must be something deep in it. But he is not much concerned about what this is, he is concerned only to reach the exalted state. One cannot help thinking of him as walking to and fro on the floor, constantly repeating the same particular phrase, supporting the particular phrase by altering his voice and gesticulating, till he has bewitched himself into a sort of intoxication so that he is aware of a wondrous and solemn buzzing in his ears – but this is not thinking. In case a person wanted to put himself into a solemn mood and therefore were to walk back and forth on the floor and say incessantly: 7–14–21; 7–14–21; 7–14–21 – then would this monotonous repetition have the effect of a magical formula or of a strong drink upon a neurasthenic, it would seem to him that he had got into touch with something extraordinary. In case another to whom he imparted his wisdom were to say, "But what then is there in this 7–14–21?" he likely would reply, "It depends upon what voice you say it with, and that you continue to say it for a whole hour, and moreover that you gesticulate – then you will surely discover that there is something in it." In case one were to write on small scraps of paper such short phrases as, "He went out of the castle," "He drew the knife," "I must have dislocated my hip" – in case one were to hide all these scraps in a drawer, and then sometime later were to go and open the drawer, take out a single slip of paper and repeat uninterruptedly what was written on it, he would in the end find himself in a fantastic state of mind and it would seem to him that there was something extraordinarily deep in it. For the abrupt, by reason of its accidental character and by reason of the play of accidental combinations it suggests, has something about it which is enticing to the imagination. Who has not experienced it? When one in rummaging among old papers finds such short phrases the whole connection of which has long been forgotten, there is some amusement in giving oneself over to the play of imagination. When one has done that he burns the papers. Not so Adler – he publishes them. And it is also certain that, if he can get a reader to indulge in this game, he too will be able for a moment to amuse himself with it. But in this way one becomes an author in a very improper sense of the word. Instead of desiring and requiring the reader to keep his mind in repose in order to reflect upon the thought communicated, as an author commonly does, Adler must rather recommend to the reader that he put himself into a state of ecstasy; for the more tense one is, the more droll the effect of the abrupt will be. In view of this it would be quite consistent of Adler if, after the analogy of sorcerers and wizards, he were to recommend and prescribe certain ceremonies, that one should arise at the stroke of midnight, then walk three times around the chamber, then take the book and open it (as simple people read their fortunes in the Bible), then read a single passage, first in a low voice, then raise it to its highest pitch, and then again backwards (like Peer Degn with his sol – mi – fa) till the voice becomes quite low, then walk the length of the room seven times – and at the eighth time see if there is not something in the passage! The abrupt and fantastic effect is enhanced essentially by mimicry and pantomime; on the other hand, it is disturbed by reflection and by connection of thought. And yet in the abrupt there lies hidden as it were a deep and unfathomable profundity of riches, whereas a clear, well-thought out discourse must be quite simply what it is. In the formulas of witches and conjurers the effect is due to the abrupt, to the enigmatical meaningless, and it is enhanced by mimic and pantomime: the witch comes riding on a broomstick, she dances around three times, etc. In case a man could make a multitude believe that he possesses a hidden wisdom, and thereupon he were to write abrupt phrases on small scraps of paper, in case he borrowed, moreover, the entire scenarium used in drawing the lottery, the big tent, the wheel of fortune, a company of soldiers, a minister of chancery before whom the soldiers would present arms, while one stepped out on the balcony, then to the accompaniment of soft festal music mingled with a swirl of notes in a higher pitch, let the wheel turn round and the boy in festal costume draw a ticket the content of which was read out – on that occasion several women at least would lose their senses.

What is said here about Adler's passion for raising himself into a state of exaltation contains absolutely no exaggeration, as I am very far from being tempted to exaggerate about Adler. It is not affirmed that his books contain such traits through and through, but there are plenty of passages which do. And inexcusable as it would be, according to my notion, were one to write something like this last and say nothing more about Adler; just as inexcusable would it be, to my thinking, if a veracious interpretation of his confusion found no place in a rather elaborate investigation of him.

As was said, his writings do not concern me directly; essentially my investigation deals only with that fact of his revelation, and with the question how he understands himself in such a thing as he has experienced, or with the suspicion that he has not understood himself in it. I use his works only with a definite aim. Had I to deal with them aesthetically and directly, it would give me pleasure to admit as officially as possible what my judgment is, that one really can learn something from them, or, to express myself quite explicitly, that I actually have learned one thing and another from them. A reviewer, it is true, is commonly accustomed to express his opinion with a superior air to the effect that, in spite of learning nothing himself, he can recommend the author's works to the public, for the public is not so loftily wise as he. But such is not the case here. People in general indubitably, nay, absolutely, can only be injured by reading A.'s works, for he confuses totally. But he who has what Adler lacks, dialectical clarity about the spheres and the totality, he and he alone, will in truth be able to learn something from the individual clever, lively, edifying, moving, sometimes profound sayings; and only he, secure against losing more than he gains, will find joy in what sometimes he succeeds in producing in a purely stylistic sense, though as a stylist he has no primitive merit. It is, strangely enough, a rather common opinion that it is easier to read epigrams than connected writings. And yet this is far from being the case, for to have any profit from epigrams one must be in full possession of a connected view in which one understands himself. This it is that Adler lacks, he does not understand himself, if the demands one makes upon him are according to a proper scale. And in this respect I cannot haggle. I do not believe that I will be taxed with clipping coins invidiously when as a reviewer I gladly pay the meed of praise to the distinguished author, but on the other hand, neither will I haggle, though I must admit with pleasure that, measured by another scale, a slipshod requirement, Adler appears to better effect, and that appraised by a reviewer who is just as good a dialectician as he (and no more), he naturally will be seen to stand like a victor with a palm branch in his hand.

SUPPLEMENT TO CHAPTER III

RECAPITULATION

The reader will remember that throughout this whole work the argument is only *e concessis*. Nowhere is it directly denied that A. has had a revelation: on the contrary, this is assumed, since he himself says so; and thus everything he says is assumed to be true, but thereby in turn the contradiction is made evident.

1. To illuminate the fact that confusion is present, Adler's reply to the ecclesiastical authority is employed. The dilemma may be expressed thus: *either* all the several answers are nonsense; *or* essentially they silently imply the revocation of his first claim (that he had a revelation and received from the Saviour a new doctrine). If we assume the latter (that revocation is implied in his answers), then the confusion is this: that he does not take seriously the matter of revocation, that he treats it as nothing, or does not himself notice anything, regards his answers as having meaning and reality, which they can only have in so far as they imply the revocation of his first claim.

Within the dilemma the argument is this: Adler so identifies himself with the first publications (the preface to the *Sermons*, the *Sermons* themselves, and the *Studies*) that in the ordinary and vulgar sense he must be regarded as the author of them; but then the doctrine was not revealed, then it was not written after Christ's dictation, he has not been merely an instrument. Adler admits authentically that he has nothing new, since like every Christian in general he holds to the Scripture, preaches Jesus, appeals to Scriptural passages as proof-texts in support of what he says – but with this he must essentially revoke all that first about the revelation, etc. – Adler hopes that later he will be able to state better the doctrine (revealed and dictated by the Saviour), he hopes in the perfectibility of the doctrine. But this hope is entirely meaningless, nay, blasphemous, if that doctrine is not Adler's own; and if it is his own, then he has had no revelation through which the doctrine was communicated to him by the Saviour.

2. In the next place, in order to illuminate the confusion, attention was directed to Adler's four last works. Instead of what one might be justified in expecting, in case a person did not remain in a confused condition, we find that now, occupied as he is in a literary way with all sorts of things, he has put himself to rest and settled down as an amateur lyrical genius. That he is a genius may well be conceded here where we have nothing whatever to do with such a thing. But so soon as his last four books are put side by side with the first claim in the interest of meaning and identity, then the dilemma appears: *either* the last four books, even though the occasional content were the most excellent, *regarded as books by A.*, that is to say *regarded as a part of his total production*, are to be regarded as nonsense; *or else* there is silently implied in them the revocation of all his first claims. If the latter is assumed, the confusion consists in the fact that he treats this as nothing, or notices nothing, and does not take the revocation seriously. The metamorphosis from an apostle to a genius is so decisive, so qualitative, and besides that so topsy-turvy, that least of all can it be ignored or treated as nothing. In civil situations, and generally in the world of finiteness, this may very well be done; there a person may more than once begin afresh and let the past be forgotten without more ado, there a person changes his situation in life, tries his fortune in a new career, and without more ado lets the past be bygone and forgotten. But in case a man thinks that also in the world of spirit this can be done, such an opinion is enough to prove that he is confused. In the world of finiteness it may be well enough to live haphazardly, it may be true, as the saying goes, *variatio delectat*; but in the world of spirit continuity is not only a joy but it is spirit itself, that is to say, continuity is spirit, not to respect continuity qualitatively is to lead one's life outside the sphere of spirit, either in worldliness or in confusion. Continuity is not monotony, in continuity too there is change, but continuity means that every change is made dialectic in relation to the foregoing. When the change is qualitative (as the change to

genius from apostle) the last expression of continuity is revocation of the first position, which again, inasmuch as one has communicated his first, ought to be made officially. In the world of spirit highflown romanticism is confusion, and just as much so is the distraction which does not notice that the change is a qualitative one. And to the same degree that one has ventured out, even to the point of saying that he has had a revelation, to that same degree is romanticism or distraction the more suspicious. – The confusion in the case of Adler becomes even greater by reason of the fact that he, in his position in life as an amateur lyrical genius, continues with a clever, paraphrastic exegesis, etc. to hold fast to that doctrine of his (communicated to him, according to his first claim, by a revelation from the Saviour). All the more clearly is his distraction and confusion manifested for the fact that he has entirely forgotten that this doctrine was communicated to him by the Saviour through a revelation.

He may revoke the first claim – then, as the author of the four last books, he confesses that he is in a confused genius. He may revoke the last and seek to array himself in the character of the first. But to let both stand is a proof that he is in a confused state of mind.

CHAPTER IV

Psychological interpretation of Adler as a phenomenon and as a satire upon the Hegelian philosophy and our age.

I

PSYCHOLOGICAL EXPOSITION

The aim of this section is to pave the way for an understanding of the catastrophe, to explain several presuppositions by which the catastrophe in Adler's life might have been psychologically motivated. Undoubtedly it would be a more interesting and a more grateful labor if one might venture to operate by the aid of possibilities alone, for even the most copious reality never has the pure ideality of possibility, but constantly has along with it something fortuitous. But to poetize in this way is not allowable since it is a contemporary whose life is in question.

Hence the psychological exposition is limited by reality and a respect for reality which always contains an element of the fortuitous. Even the understanding and explanation of his life which Magister Adler may possess internally will contain something fortuitous, because no actual man is pure ideality, so that any particular episode in his life will have a fortuitous *lack* or a fortuitous *redundance*. And the psychological exposition which can be furnished here is limited in another sense by reality. Thus it would be possible to think that one who knew Magister Adler thoroughly, one who was in possession of his confidence, might know of something (an impression of his life, an occurrence, an expression, etc.) which as a presupposition would in the highest degree be worthy of attention, but into which he as the knowledgeable person is in no wise justified in initiating others, let alone by publishing it in print. The investigation must therefore keep within more common terms, have a more universal character, making use at the most of single hints which Magister Adler himself may have given. The art consists in so putting together these qualifications that something results from it all the same. In this way the investigation can in no wise take too great liberties with Magister Adler, for the fact that essentially it makes use of only such general characteristics as universally explain the presuppositions of the age as a whole, whereas I completely renounce every private interpretation of Magister Adler for which I have no data at all.

We may imagine then a theological candidate who has passed with credit his professional examination, he is more than commonly gifted; it may be assumed that, aesthetically understood, he has lived so much that existence will one day be able in a decisive way to point him out. On the other hand, up to this moment he may not, either as a child or as a youth or as a theological candidate, have come into any decisive relationship with Christianity, still less with the serious question whether he himself is a Christian. In this respect it may be assumed that he has lived on, as so many do, according to the current definitions in everyday language of what it is to be a Christian: to have been baptized and confirmed as a Christian, to have legitimated his standing when he matriculated in arts, etc., to have acquired a *quantum satis* of theological learning, to have become a candidate.

So now he is a theological candidate, but as one who is eminently gifted he naturally cannot conclude his studies with the ordinary examination for a pastorate. On the contrary, he now begins for the first time to study properly, and with that begins the study of the Hegelian philosophy, a philosophy which, supported by almighty opinion, is supposed to stand at the very summit of all scientific knowledge, apart from which there is no salvation but only darkness and stupidity. With enthusiasm for the hero of philosophy, following gladly the slogan, "You lack everything, study Hegel and you will have everything," likely thanking the gods in the Greek style for the privilege of being contemporary with the highest development of the human race, he sets to work on his study. He is not in possession of one single presupposition which would make him inwardly aware of the fact that this philosophy totally confuses Christianity, there is in him no deeper religious life which might restrain him from going into this philosophy; in a religious respect he is without the heavy equipment of theology or the deeper impression of religion, he is a light-armed soldier to whom it comes only too natural and too easy to understand negligently what Hegel has negligently expounded, to the effect that his philosophy was the highest development of Christianity. Yea, in a religious respect he likely is so light-armed that it would hardly occur to him to question this. – So then he studies, and what many vain persons do carelessly and only to be in the fashion, he (though he too is carried away by the spirit of the age) does with zeal and interest; he even gives lectures in the university on this philosophy and publishes a popular exposition of Hegel's objective logic, but the question how the Hegelian philosophy comports with Christianity does not occur to him at all.

Magister Adler has now reached the age when one ordinarily feels an urge to conclude his student years and thereafter to teach others. This is the transition from *discere* to *docendo discere*. Also at that age, which is the critical time of maturity, there commonly develops an urge to reflect deeply upon one's own life. And again when making the transition and going farther in life one turns back to one's first recollections, to the first unforgettable impressions of one's upbringing, and tests how one now stands related to that which one then understood as a child and childishly appropriated, and tests whether one is in accord with oneself, whether and to what extent one understands oneself in understanding one's first impressions, and the concern is that one's life in a deeper sense might be a personal life essentially in agreement with oneself. One and another man surely stands at this parting of the ways, asking whether he shall let the first go, cutting down the bridge, and hold to what has been learned later, or whether he shall look back to childhood and learn conversely; for as a child he indeed learned from his elders, and now, being himself an elder, he should learn from a child, learn from his childhood. If now it had been Adler's case that he, turning back to himself, were to be struck by one or another essential Christian recollection, by one or another decisive impression of Christianity – then the case would have been different and at the same time rather more serious. Adler, on the contrary, may likely have found it all right as a result of his life's development to remain a Hegelian. The whole question about Christianity and Hegelian philosophy does not emerge at all.

Magister Adler seeks a place, not as professor of philosophy or of the Hegelian philosophy in particular, but as priest, as a teacher of the Christian religion, for which *also* he has fitted himself . . . by studying the Hegelian philosophy. And he was called. Relying upon having passed his examination for the priesthood creditably, relying upon his general culture, relying upon his talents, he hopes to be equal to the task; relying upon his exceptional knowledge of the Hegelian philosophy, he hopes to be an exceptionally able priest. This is by no means immodest on his part, not at all. If it is true that the Hegelian philosophy is the highest development of Christianity, then indeed it is an advantage for a priest to know this philosophy perfectly – not as generally happens, or at least sometimes, that a man, after having with the seriousness of reflection renewed himself by his childish impressions of Christianity, being in good understanding with a strict Christian upbringing, with the Bible in his hand, enters upon his work as a clergyman; no, in reliance upon his examination, with Hegel's eighteen volumes elegantly bound, almost regarding ordination and all that as an unwelcome interruption of his study of Hegel and writing about him – Magister Adler becomes a priest.

He does not become a pastor in the metropolis, where it would not be unthinkable that he might succeed in skulking through, yea, in going through life proudly as a priest, as a Christian priest . . . in Hegelian categories. Magister Adler becomes a priest in the country, and so is brought into contact and into responsible relation with simple and ordinary people who, lacking a knowledge of Hegel, have as perhaps men in the country still have, a serious though meager Christian instruction, so that, unacquainted with every volatilization of it, they simply believe in the Christian doctrine and have it before them as a present reality. For simple, believing men so deal with Christianity that they do not hold it historically at a distance of eighteen hundred years, still less fantastically at a mythical distance.

Magister Adler becomes a priest in the country and finds himself living in rural retirement. The conception he has of the Hegelian philosophy, perhaps also the conception this philosophy may give him about himself, makes it seem plausible that Magister Adler will hardly find among his clerical brethren or among his other acquaintances anyone with whom he can or really wishes to strike up an intimacy. So Magister A. finds himself living altogether isolated with his Hegelian philosophy, which after all is perhaps more appropriate for royal residences. So it must be if the relationships are to be tightened up to the point of a catastrophe; the individual in question must first and foremost be kept in isolation or keep himself in isolation. – On the other hand, that Magister A. might rusticate is entirely improbable, for that he is too highly gifted, and he is too much intellectually employed to become "a card-playing priest," or to reach the anti-apostolic climax, as sometimes happens – for the apostles were called from fishing to catch men: a man is appointed a priest to catch men and ends by fishing, hunting, etc.

The situation is now prepared: a man who is fully occupied with the Hegelian philosophy becomes a country parson in rural retirement, intellectually understood, in complete isolation. – The simple congregation represents quite simply the Christian position, and Magister A. as pastor and spiritual guide is *in duty bound* to deal with them. In capitals where a Hegelian has support in distinguished and cultured circles it may perhaps be possible to defend oneself against "simplicities" proudly and with aristocratic superciliousness; but Magister Adler as a Hegelian is like a wild, strange bird in the country, entirely without support and, intellectually understood, as thoroughly out of proportion with his environment as was Gulliver among the little bits of men or among the giants, whereas Gulliver had the advantage and the consolation that he was only a casual traveller. A., on the contrary, in spite of his disproportion and unrelatedness, is essentially in relation for the fact that he was appointed pastor, and besides that he is too good a head not to perceive that after all it would be foolish to be proud of his philosophy before the simple peasants.

One cannot deny that this is a desperate situation, and yet inwardly, in the direction of responsibility, it is still more desperate. To stand in the pulpit (and so before God's face) and preach what in consequence of his culture he presumably was through with long ago, to sit by a deathbed and comfort a dying man with what he himself was through with long ago, to sit by the deathbed and perhaps witness the fact that the dying man presses the hand of the priest and dies blessedly in the faith of that which the priest by the bedside was through with. To witness how a poor but God-fearing family prepares for the Holy Communion, with what solemnity they step up to the holy place (allow them in God's name to remain stupid!) – and then the priest who is through with all this, and then the priest, the teacher, who, if only he gets into the mood, actually steals this from these simple people at seeing their emotion and agitation! To be so developed that one, if he were really serious about the Hegelian philosophy, might rather feel himself obliged to pluck the simple people out of their errors – and then to be a priest, appointed to teach them the truth! And then the responsibility, that one is a priest! And then that one lacks any diversion, is without support and harmony with others; for in the metropolis one perhaps vaunts the Hegelian philosophy, but hardly in the country, and impossibly on the part of a priest.

It is well enough known that loneliness may drive a man to extremes; but Magister A.'s situation is worse than loneliness, for it is also contradiction and self-contradiction, and over all hovers the terror of responsibility. When then some time has gone by, when the contradiction and the terror hem him in closer and closer, the situation at last is this: that a Hegelian who has "gone farther" has now about reached the turning-point of decision, whether he will become a Christian – and this moment occurred in his life a *year after* he had been *well and happily installed as a Christian pastor*.

2

THE CATASTROPHE IN MAGISTER ADLER'S LIFE

Then there came to pass an occurrence, and Magister A.'s life was changed. How this occurrence is more precisely to be understood, I naturally am unable to elucidate. The only thing I might do is to explore poetically the possibilities, but in that way no factual elucidation is to be won. The one person from whom we might reasonably expect a precise and definite elucidation would be Magister Adler himself. But from him one seeks it in vain. After having in the first place furnished a detailed description of the occurrence, which was said to have taken place at night ("when an evil sound goes through the chamber and thereupon the Saviour bade him write down the words" – write down the words which are communicated in the preface to his *Sermons*), for this concrete statement he substitutes at the instance of the ecclesiastical authority the more vague and indefinite one that it was "an occurrence."

Every third party, including me and this investigation, when the desire for a more particular elucidation is checked by the confusion of Magister A. (the person directly concerned), may perfectly well rest satisfied with the statement that there came to pass an occurrence, and Magister A.'s life was changed, yea, even with the more meager notion that the occurrence consisted in the fact that Magister A.'s life was changed. *The principal point is* (and had not Magister A. originally undertaken to say more, all would have been well up to this point) that Magister A. *with a qualitative leap was transported from the medium of philosophy, and more particularly from the fantastic medium of the Hegelian philosophy* (pure thought and pure being), *into the sphere of religious inwardness. The principal point is that Magister A. from the objectivity of abstract thinking came to himself.* It is another question whether Magister A. within the religious definition of coming to oneself may be said to have as yet come to himself, inasmuch as, though now religiously determined, yet as a person in an exalted state he is still outside himself. But in contrast to the objectivity of abstract thought he may be said to have come to himself, inasmuch as he has reached the point of being concerned about himself. This is the new factor with which hitherto his whole life development has been unacquainted, this religious impression of himself in self-concern. – Nevertheless, as Magister A. himself says in the preface to the *Sermons* before he began to tell the story about the revelation, there arose before him a light, and it was not by thinking it arose but by the Spirit.

The catastrophe was accompanied by a symbolical action about the factual character of which there is no reason to doubt: Magister Adler burned his Hegelian manuscripts. When one has so decisively broken away from the Hegelian philosophy there is assurance that one will never more deal with it again diffusely, that by a single step one is assured against temptation from that side and from relapse into it again. Alas, the need of giving an inward resolution a striking outward expression is often an illusion. Perhaps it has not seldom happened that a young girl in the presence of the whole family has destroyed every reminder of the unfaithful lover, burnt all his poisonous letters, and then, without being conscious of it, longed to see the faithless man. Not rarely there is a suspicious incongruity between inward decision (the strength of resolution, salvation, healing) and the outward signs of decision. One can hardly draw conclusions from the latter to the former, one can rather conclude conversely that the stronger the need of striking decision in an outward sense, the less the security. That the outward expression is not always the inward is true not only of the ironists who intentionally deceive others by a false outward expression, but it is true also of immediate natures who unconsciously deceive themselves, yea sometimes feel a need of self-deception. Thus in case a man hardly takes time to sleep and eat, merely for the sake of being able to preach and spread abroad a view which would be a blessing to mankind, is intent early and late to prove its rightness – one might indeed believe that the man must have a firm and lively conviction. Alas, and yet it is not always so, sometimes he has no firm conviction, but feels the need that many might be in agreement with him, in order that his conviction might be convincing to himself. Strangely enough, he has a view, he has something to impart, it looks as if it were the others who had need of him and of his firm conviction – alas, it is he who has need of the other men, he wants to convince himself by convincing others. In case one were to put him, intellectually understood, in a vacuum, he would have no conviction; and, on the other hand, in the degree that many listen to him, in the same degree he is aware that he has a conviction, and in the degree that they agree with him, in the same degree – he is himself convinced. Every person of some seriousness who is accustomed to treat himself with precaution is inclined rather to avoid the striking outward exhibition of decision, or is on the watch lest it come too early. A man of some seriousness would rather hide the decision and test himself in silent inwardness in order to see whether it might not deceptively be true that he the *weak* one felt the need of a *strong* outward expression of resolution. If a man can hold out in silent inwardness, endure to be totally changed without being changed outwardly in the least, then likely he can take the striking step. The converse is not true. If I were to imagine two drinkers who both have resolved to drink no more: one has solemnly thrown bottles and glasses out of the window and gone in for total abstinence; the other has a bottle and a full glass in sight – but he does not drink. Which of these two may be regarded as surely saved? One so easily confounds the physical with the moral. No, to be able to be precisely as usual, to be able to live on with the daily and continuous reminders of the old, and yet to be changed in the deepest ground of his nature – that indeed is the art. But if the change has really come about, then it is permissible, then one always may change little by little the outward expression, if one has quite seriously been on the watch lest the change might be *before others in the outward*, not *before God in the inward*. I will imagine two men: at a decisive moment there comes about an essential change in both of them, but one of them at once expresses the change, the other only in the course of seven years expresses the change by outward signs which correspond with the inward change he underwent in that decisive moment; his change therefore is not conspicuous to others, because it is distributed through seven years – of these two changes, which may be regarded as the most secure? – It would therefore perhaps have been wiser and more prudent of Magister A. if, instead of burning the manuscripts, he had allotted an hour or two every day to occupation with Hegel, in order to assure himself that he really was changed, for one can so easily confound the moral with the physical: the abandoning of Hegel with the burning of his manuscripts. If my memory does not deceive me, it was the celebrated Johann Arnold Kanne, whose life was acquainted with considerable spiritual alterations, when one time he was gripped by Christian truth, he also burnt up all his mythological manuscripts – and yet relapsed once again. Goethe also burnt his manuscripts containing his poetical works – and when he had done that he became in a full sense a poet.

As it was with Goethe, so was it not with Adler – that after having burnt his Hegelian manuscripts he became for the first time a thoroughgoing Hegelian. But on the other hand, deceived by this striking outward sign of decision, he managed to hide from himself in self-deception that he continued to be a Hegelian. Lyrically, subjectively, fully and firmly convinced that once for all and forever he had broken with the Hegelian philosophy, by burning his Hegelian manuscripts, that by a revelation he was saved forever from the prolixity of the Hegelian philosophy. But, lo, when he then had occasion to explain what he understood by the revelation and how he understood himself in what had happened to him, he recurs to the old Hegelian volatilization. If one were to call his attention to this, it would not be unthinkable that A. would reply: "How can you come with such an absurd objection, that at bottom I might be a Hegelian? I assure you by all that is holy I burnt my Hegelian manuscripts that night. Now believe me!" In that way Magister A. puts the Hegelian philosophy in an extremely comical situation, for the fact that one who is fully and firmly convinced that he has had a revelation uses that philosophy to volatilize this same conception. But thereby A. has the merit of making evident indirectly-satirically the contradiction in the Hegelian philosophy. For when one takes away the eighteen hundred years, the roguish trick, and puts the Hegelian philosophy in the situation of contemporaneousness, then its method of procedure becomes clear, that it fraudulently *explains away* a revelation instead of *denying* it openly. And the extraordinary merit of the comical is reserved for Magister Adler, to be in every way man enough for the whole thing: man enough to have a revelation, and man enough to explain it away.

3
MAGISTER ADLER'S ADVANTAGE

The good, the admirable quality in Magister Adler is that he is moved, is profoundly affected, that thereby his life has acquired a very different rhythm from that of the cab-horse with which most men, religiously understood, go sluggishly through life. Whether it be a panting press of business or a worldly interest, or whatever the distraction may be, it is certain that most men, religiously understood, go through life in a sort of abstraction and absent-mindedness, that never are they sensible of their own ego, of their pulse, of their own heart-beat, in self-concern; they live too objectively to be sensible of any such thing, and on hearing anything said about it they quiet themselves with the explanation that all such things are hysteria, hypochondria, etc. Most men live in relation to their own self as if they were constantly out, never at home; the occurrences and undertakings of their life flutter indefinitely about this self; they sometimes perhaps shut their door . . . in order to be at home, but they do not shut out the distracting thought, and so are themselves "out." The admirable quality in Magister A. consists in the fact that in a serious and strict sense one may say that he was fetched home by a higher power; for before that he was certainly in a great sense "out" or in a foreign land, at the time when he was a Hegelian and objective. In a worldly sense, the misfortune of the Prodigal Son consists not exactly in the fact that he journeyed into a foreign land, but that he wasted his substance there: spiritually and religiously understood, perdition consists in journeying into a foreign land, in being "out," in being objective, so that one gets no impression of oneself by remaining at home with the inward self-concern of conscience.

All religiousness consists in inwardness, in enthusiasm, in strong emotion, in the qualitative tension by the springs of subjectivity. When one beholds people as they are for the most part, one cannot deny that they have some religiousness, some concern to be enlightened and instructed about religious things, but without allowing these things to affect them too closely. For, observing more nearly, one easily discovers that in their religiousness they relate themselves to their self at a certain distance; they make good resolutions *for the future*, but not for the *present*, not for the present instant, to begin right away; contemporaneously with the resolution they do not carry it out, contemporaneously with the resolution they have rather the notion that there is still some time, if it were only half an hour, before they need to begin. They make sacred promises, they resolve . . . tomorrow, etc., but what is really the decisive point, *to be entirely present to themselves in self-concern*, is something with which they are totally unacquainted. Therefore they well may have religious notions, sometimes also may find edification, yet I find no better comparison for their religiousness than the exercises in the field of maneuvers. As these exercises are related to battle or to being in battle (where there is danger, which in the field of maneuvers is absent), so is distance-religiousness related to inward religiousness.

Most men in their religiousness are present at the most *in a bygone time or in a time to come*, but not *in a present time*. They think about the religious, hear it talked about, deal with it in the medium of fantasy, have it with them in the form of the wish, of longing, of presentiment, in the form of the illusory resolution and purpose, but the impression of the religious, that it is to be used now, now at once, now at the very instant, they do not get. They think about the immortality of the soul. In this consciousness they repose at a distance, but for this thought they have no use in concern and self-concern; they think about it in this wise: It is always well to know that you are immortal, for the sake of the chance that you may die; but that, however, may be many years off. So they do not think the thought of death at the same instant with the thought of immortality, they do not reflect that every instant when one has not this consciousness of immortality one is not really immortal. They are like the man full-fed who labors for the food for the coming day, not like the famished man who at once has use for what he can scrape together. At bottom their lives are lived in other categories which give them a deceptive sense of security. While they are busied about or occupied with the religious they do not comprehend that the religious is *the one thing needful*, they regard it as *also needful*, for the sake especially of hard times; they understand very well that a man may die of hunger if he doesn't get anything to live off, but they do not comprehend that man lives by every word which proceeds out of the mouth of God. When men who live thus religiously at a distance talk about religion (and priests of that quality are of course not altogether rare, indeed they are even of a better sort than card-playing parsons or horsy and newspaper parsons) one notices at once by their talk that they are not in it, just as though while existing they are not really existing, are not present to themselves. Therefore, though the hearers do not sleep through the sermon, which nowadays is rather rare, yet they are *distrait*, for in the discourse itself there is an interval, a space, between the need and the satisfaction of the need, between the means of salvation and the instantaneous use of them, which is the interval of illusion, of time lost, of delay. One notices in the discourse that there is not that fresh outpouring of an experienced religion which now at the moment of the discourse arises to a present life; one notices that it is not as though the speaker needed to defend himself against the wealth of past experience; against the overwhelming power of present experience; one notices rather that it is as if every time he wiped the sweat from his brow he went home and fetched a new factor, as if when he had to say anything he must go away and fetch it. He on the contrary who is present to himself in religious experience has what he is to say at hand, in his mouth and in his heart – indeed, just as nowadays one has in well-equipped buildings water on every floor and never needs to go down and fetch it from the courtyard but only to turn on the spigot, so has such a religious man always the essentials with him in the present.

To be entirely present to oneself is the highest thing and the highest task for the personal life, it is the power on account of which the Romans called the gods *presentes*. But this thing of being entirely present to oneself in self-concern is the highest in religion, for only thus can it absolutely be comprehended that one absolutely is in need of God every instant, so that everything belonging to time past or to time to come or generally to indefinite time, such as evasions, excuses, digressions, etc., grows pale and vanishes, as the other sort of jugglery, which also belongs to the indefinite time of the gloaming and the twilight, retreats and vanishes before the bright light of day. When one is not present to oneself, then one is absent in the past or in the future time, then one's religiousness is recollection of an abstract purpose, then one dwells perhaps piously in the piety of an ancient and vanished age, or builds, religiously understood, the objective religiousness like the Tower of Babel – but this night shall thy soul be required of thee.

So it is with most men – but it is different with Magister Adler. He truly is shaken, he is in mortal danger, he lies (to employ an expression used by another author)* over 70,000 fathoms of water; what he discovers must be used at once, the help he cries

*How scrupulous it is of S.K. to dissociate himself thus from his pseudonym!

for must at once be employed – or the same instant he sinks. He is absolutely subjective, inwardly wounded, and must therefore remain present to himself in his need. Indeed, Magister A. is so far from the sure ground of indolence and illusion that rather he is so tossed out into the extremity of mortal danger that the words, "today," "tonight," "this very instant," are about to destroy him, so inwardly is he fighting in the instantaneous situation of mortal danger between the intense struggle of self-preservation and the surrender of inwardness.

But Magister A. possesses an advantage in being thus shaken, a qualitative advantage, and verily I shall not in envy depreciate the value of this advantage. As it is an advantage to be truly in love, to be truly enthusiastic, so also it is an advantage, religiously understood, to be shaken and therewith to have found the place of which it is said, *Hic Rhodus, hic saltus*. For where is that place, religiously understood? It is neither at Gerizim nor at Jerusalem, neither in thinking nor in learning, but at the most tender and subjective point of inwardness. When one is deeply affected there, then is one rightly situated at that place. And this deep experience is in turn the trading capital and the true riches. With envy I shall certainly not talk of this advantage of Magister A., but neither with curiosity. There is such a thing as cowardly, effeminate religiosity which will not itself venture out for decision upon the deep, but rather with curiosity likes to feel the shudder with which one who is himself secure sees another struggling out upon the deep. A cowardly and effeminate religiosity which itself writhes at seeing the dreadful experiences which prove what a prodigious power the religious is, but prefers to see the proof adduced by another. As the shades in the underworld sucked the blood of the living in order to live a while longer, so the cowardly and effeminate religious people, conscious that at bottom their religiosity is a hypocritical and rouged-up thing, would therefore like to try occasionally to work up some strong impressions ... at second hand. Such religious people are not better by a hair's breadth than the idle people who long to see an execution, or a great conflagration, etc., in order to see without danger to themselves the death struggles of men. But precisely because such religious people exist, and only too many of them, especially in our effeminate, shrewd, refined Christendom, it is necessary that the man deeply moved does not abandon himself to them in his inwardness, that in holy wrath he may know how to get behind these cowardly effeminates in order to push them out into the current, instead of abandoning himself to be a diversion and a spectacle. But for this Magister A. lacks reflection and coolness and schooling and holy upbringing, and hence one cannot deny that, even if everything were all right with him in other respects, he nevertheless does harm, for the fact that, instead of helping others out into decision, he presents a diversion to the cowardly and effeminate who love voluptuous shudders. But his advantage over most men is and remains none the less something qualitative, and something to be highly regarded especially in our age. The more that culture, training, and discretion get the upper hand, and the more that men come to live comparatively, all the more common becomes a certain lawyer-like dexterity in handling spiritual determinants. For every situation one knows evasions and exceptions and limitations and excuses; now audaciously, now dispiritedly, one pleads the example of others, so that one constantly avoids a decisive impression of spirit. Culture and training and discretion and life in the flock work precisely to the end of making men, religiously understood, *distrait*, absent-minded.

The advantage of Magister A. is recognizable also in his writings, and the good that is in them must be attributed to this advantage. And the good which is in them is precisely that there is something stirring about them. He is sometimes moving by a noble childlikeness, he alarms by a harrowing description, he sometimes aims and hits with such precision that this is identical. What he has to say is not said by an indifferent man and not fetched from afar; no, he himself is *in* the hasty movement, *in* the danger, *in* the effort, or *in* the repose of comfort, *in* the hope; and what he says he has ready to hand, it is outburst, quite genuinely an outburst of feeling and emotion, and one may say that not rarely has he overwhelmed the reader with his outbursts. – In his style therefore there is sometimes a lyrical seething which, though aesthetically appraised it is sometimes foolish, is nevertheless religiously worthy. There is in it an impatience which outbids itself in expression – and then breaks off abruptly, and thereby precisely makes the impatience still more evident. At the head of a cavalry troop of predicates, each one braver than the other, he hurls himself upon the reader. Aesthetically appraised his style has no merit, and I cannot find a single expression in all his books which I can venture to recommend as correct, there is always something accidental (which lies in the fact that he is *himself* only in the instant of reality and that he comes, in an anguishing sense, too close to reality), either sometimes too much or sometimes too little, either an abundance in which he remains so to speak defeated in the sortie, or a scantiness which indicates that imagination will not stretch so far and which has the effect that one sees him struggling for breath; but religiously his presentation makes its impression. What Frater Taciturnus presumably must know very well how to do, since he, though he used a style of a very different sort, lets Quidam of the experiment express himself in this style, examples of which one finds in wild forms in Adler. Building rhetorically upon the antecedent clauses, he lets the consequent clauses be nothing, an abyss from which the reader (if he reads aloud) will shrink away and fall back as it were upon the antecedents; rushing forward on a run as though the wealth would never be exhausted, and precisely in the same second breaking off, which is like the trick of stopping a horse in full career. Most riders fall off on that occasion, whereas ordinarily one makes a transition to a full stop, a shift in the modulation, a veering of the concepts, in one word, the unexpected stopping, etc. Like all southern nations (the Jews, of instance) and like the vocal organs of passionate nations, so does every passionate person speak in such a way that his voice continually breaks – so also it is possible to produce this effect stylistically.

However, this would carry me too far. And how many men are there who even have merely a notion how prose can be used lyrically, and that I engage to do, namely to produce a lyrical effect in prose better than it can be done in verse – in prose where people first learn to read and to require thought in every word, whereas verse contains always a little filling of lime. I break off, for what I have to say concerns only authors. In this respect all the Pseudonyms have a linguistic value for the fact that they have cultivated lyrical prose. Adler has also learned something from them, as is easily seen; for it is not true as the flattering reviewer in the *Church Times* relates, that he began contemporaneously with the Pseudonyms, but he began after them, and the style in his four latest books is notably different from that in his *Sermons*, when he was not yet strongly under their influence. On the other hand, it is true, as this reviewer says, that one sometimes finds passages in A. (in the last four books) which strongly remind one of the Pseudonyms; but I see no merit in this, whether in copying another, or in forgetting that one by having had a revelation has entirely different things to think about than linguistic exercises.

4

THE FUNDAMENTAL FAULT IN MAGISTER ADLER WHICH OCCASIONS THE INCONGRUITY

The fundamental fault consists in the fact that Magister Adler's theological, Christian-theological culture and schooling, is defective and confused and stands in no relation to his lyrical enthusiasm, whereas, presumably led astray by his conception of what it is to be a theological candidate, a priest and a philosopher, he believes he is in a position to be able to explain something and therefore precipitates himself into literary production, instead of seeking an education and self-discipline.

If it is true that even to be beautiful is an excuse for many things, that to be in love may be urged as an excuse for much imprudence, to be enthusiastic as an excuse for much impetuosity, to have made a great discovery as an excuse for running through the streets of Syracuse naked – well then, so the fact of being deeply moved and shaken, religiously understood, ought to be an excuse for many imperfections, and in relation to Magister A. a critic ought to beware of being peevish and Philistine. However, imprudence, offense, in short, whatever has to be excused, or the fact that there is something to be excused, must not be taken to imply that there is something wrong with respect to the good, with respect to the excellence which serves as an excuse; no, the offense must consist in something accidental which is different from this. Running naked through the streets of Syracuse has thus nothing whatever to do with the discovery, which therefore remains absolutely just as good as before. Hence it is quite right that the discovery serves as an excuse for the offense, that because of that one quite forgets that Archimedes was naked, as he himself did. Only prudery could dwell long on the offensiveness of the act, and only a crazy Philistinism triumphant in a small town could turn everything round about and reach the conclusion: It is certain that Archimedes ran naked through the streets – *ergo* he has made no great discovery. On the other hand, it would be something different if there had been doubt about Archimedes' discovery; for a misunderstanding, a mistake (instead of a great discovery), affords no excuse for an offense. This too is really the Philistine's train of reasoning; for Philistinism has no conception of the great, the sublime, and therefore no notion of the excuse afforded by the great. Philistinism in interpreting the distinguished man would say as did the merchant Bearend, according to a well-known story, when a bird dropped something on the table: "If I had done that," said he, "you would have heard a great row." So it is that the Philistine, too, leaves out the point: he says, "If I had done that" – yes, quite right, but the Philistine is no Archimedes. However, as was said, if there are any irregularities with respect to the discovery, then has Archimedes no excuse.

Now, as we have seen, it was Magister Adler's advantage that he was deeply moved, shaken in his inmost being, that hence his inwardness came into being, or he came into being in accordance with his inwardness. But to be thus profoundly moved is a very indefinite expression for something so concrete as Christian awakening or conversion, and yet one dare say nothing more of Magister A. To be shaken (pretty much in the sense that one speaks of shaking a person to make him wake up) is the more universal foundation for all religiousness; the experience of being shaken, of being deeply moved, the coming into being of subjectivity in the inwardness of emotion, the pious pagan and the pious Jew have in common with the Christian. Upon this common basis of more universal emotion the qualitative difference must be erected and make itself felt, for the more universal emotion has reference only to something abstract: to be moved by something higher, something eternal, by an idea. And one does not become a Christian by being moved by something indefinitely higher, and not every outpouring of religious emotion is a Christian outpouring. That is to say: emotion which is Christian is checked by the definition of concepts, and when emotion is transposed or expressed in words in order to be communicated, this transposition must occur constantly within the definition of the concepts.

With regard to all inwardness which reflects upon the purely human, the merely human (*so with regard to all inwardness within the sphere of immanence*), the fact of being deeply moved, of being shaken, is to be taken in the sense of shaking a man till he awakes. If this emotion expresses itself, breaks out in words, the transposition occurs in feeling and imagination within such concepts and definitions of concepts which every man may be said to discover in using the words; the transposition is not limited by specific, qualitative concepts which have an historical validity outside the individual and higher than every human individual and paradoxically higher than every human individual, a paradoxical historical validity. – Let us take, for example, falling in love, understood purely in an erotic sense. With regard to the purely erotic experience of being in love there is no specific, qualitative difference between the experience of a Greek, a Jew, or a Christian. The lyrical outburst of love is within the merely human qualification and not within the distinction of the specific, qualitative concepts. The lyrical is appraised with regard to its ability to express the purely human, though with delicate distinctions of feeling in individuation according to race and personality, which differences nevertheless are a vanishing quantity in the immanent, eternally conceived, human equality.

It is different with the definition of a Christian awakening to a religious interest *which lies in the sphere of transcendence*. The emotional seizure of the individual by something higher is far from defining a Christian adequately, for by emotion may be expressed a pagan view, pagan conceptions of God. In order to express oneself Christianly there is required, besides the more universal language of the heart, also skill and schooling in the definition of Christian concepts, while at the same time it is of course assumed that the emotion is of a specific, qualitative sort, the Christian emotion. – But since Christian thought through the centuries has gradually absorbed in a more universal way the whole world-development, its conceptual language having passed over into a volatilized traditional use (which lies on a line with being a Christian of sorts by virtue of living in geographical Christendom), it may come about that one who only in a more universal way is emotionally gripped by something higher expresses himself in the language of the Christian concepts – of course, this is a result which might well be expected. The fault or irregularity is then a double one: that a person thus moved begins to talk in a language which stands in no relation to his emotion, since the language is specifically, qualitatively concrete, and his emotion is more universal; and that he naturally speaks this language in a confusing way. For when one is not in a stricter sense seized by a Christian emotion, and on the other hand is not familiar with, is not strictly disciplined in the language of the concepts in which he expresses his emotion – then he is like one who talks too fast and does not articulate clearly ... it is twaddle. And in the field of the Christian religion this is not only unfortunate but it is dreadful; for the danger indeed is not merely that of saying something unclear, something foolish, but unconsciously it may be blasphemous. – For a Christian awakening what is required, on the one hand, is being grasped in a Christian sense and, on the other hand, conceptual and terminological firmness and definiteness.

If then Magister A. is regarded as an awakened man in the sense of the Christian religion, his misfortune is just this, that he is not sufficiently and thoroughly acquainted with the language of Christian concepts, that he does not have them under his control. For what chiefly seems to have secured his character as a Christian, the fact that he had had a revelation from the Saviour, seems to be something in which he is not secure, not being in agreement with himself about what is to be understood by a revelation. Since Christianity has been volatilized in the same degree that it has been spread abroad, and since the qualitative emphasis has been lost by the fact that we all of us are Christians, it occurs not so seldom that one without more ado assumes that every religious emotion in the case of an individual who lives in geographical Christendom is *eo ipso* a Christian awakening, and from the fact that he so promptly uses the whole language of the Christian concepts which he was accustomed to use as a conversational language. Before he was religiously moved (in a more general sense) he had been a Christian after a sort, and precisely this is his misfortune, he is therefore not capable of testing himself rightly as to whether his emotion is really a Christian emotion, and after being gripped by emotion he uses again the Christian language of concepts as a careless conversational language. If it is factual that the language of Christian concepts has become in a volatilized sense the conversational language of the whole of Europe, it follows quite simply that the holiest and most decisive definitions are used again and again without being united with the decisive thought. One hears indeed often enough Christian predicates used by Christian priests where the names of God and of Christ constantly appear and passages of Scripture, etc., in discourses which nevertheless as a whole contain pagan views of life without either the priest or the hearers being aware of it.

Hence in case Magister A. had been a layman (lawyer, physician, military officer, etc.), things would perhaps have gone better with him. After being moved by a mighty religious impression, in consideration that he was not a theologian, he would have sought repose in order to become himself thoroughly conscious of what had occurred, sought schooling on the part of teachers of Christian orthodoxy, and perhaps in this way he would have succeeded in attaining the necessary sense of proportion before he began to express himself. But Magister A. was a theological candidate, he was even a priest, he was a philosopher – must he not then long ago have been preeminently in possession of the schooling in concepts which is necessary for ability to express his emotion with assurance? So it might appear perhaps; but, alas, the knowledge acquired for the theological examination – if one does not bring along to the university what purely religiously must be held in infinite esteem, a deep veneration for the Christian faith instilled in childhood and by upbringing, so that in later moments of decision he will resolutely and frank-heartedly stand up for the choice he had made, rather forgo everything else than to alter the least tittle of the Christian faith – alas, the knowledge acquired for the theological examination, though it might be worth ever so much regarded as knowledge, avails but little for standing fast in time of battle. As a priest he had very little opportunity for a schooling since he was so fully occupied with Hegel – and as a Hegelian he was initiated, initiated with complete devotion and conviction, into the total confusion of the Christian faith. But to be *ex animi sententia* a votary of a particular philosopher and his philosophical view, to have with that and in that experienced the culmination of his life and of his life's development – that for a man is pretty much the same as love towards a woman. And certain it is that, if there has been reality in this love, it helps but little to burn all the letters "he wrote to her." He must labor methodically and slowly. If there had been reality in being a Hegelian, it was of no avail to burn the Hegelian manuscripts. And that this was a reality for Magister A. I do not doubt. It would have been the saddest thing of all if even his study of Hegel had been idle talk.

I shall now show briefly how the incongruity between his subjective emotion and his imperfect education in Christian concepts expresses itself in the decisive points of Magister A.'s appearance as an author. The incongruity naturally consists again in the fact that it is dialectical how far his awakening may be called Christian. For of this one can judge only by attending to his utterances, but these precisely are confusing for the fact that they are in the language of the Christian concepts which he has not mastered.

(a) *Here we are* at Magister Adler's *first claim, the preface to his Sermons, or rather the content of it.*

Magister A. is gripped by something higher, but now when he would express his condition in words, would communicate it, *he confounds the subjective with the objective, his subjectively altered condition with an external event*, the experience that there rose up a light before him with the notion that outside of him there came about something new, *the fact that the veil fell from his eyes with the notion that he had a revelation.* Subjectively his emotion reached the highest pitch, he chose the highest expression to indicate it, and by a mental deception he used the objective determinant that he had had a revelation.

To illustrate his confusion in the use of the concept revelation

I shall take an example which reflects pure humanity, an example from the sphere of immanence. He who is truly in love can say also that he discovers love, and this from Harold's time [from of yore] every lover can say. Falling in love is a determinant of pure, downright inwardness, it has no other dialectic than that which belongs to inwardness itself, it has no dialectic determinant outside itself, it is the simple identity of subject-object. Love is falling in love, the primitivity of falling in love is the genesis of love. Love does not exist as something objective but comes into being every time a man loves, and it exists only in the lover; not only does it exist only *for* the lover but it exists only *in* the lover.

It is otherwise with every relation within the sphere of transcendence, and then again otherwise with the Christian concept of revelation. Christianity exists before any Christian exists, it must exist in order that one may become a Christian, it contains the determinant by which one may test whether one has become a Christian, it maintains its objective subsistence apart from all believers, while at the same time it is in the inwardness of the believer. In short, here there is no identity between the subjective and the objective. Though Christianity comes into the heart of never so many believers, every believer is conscious that it has not arisen in his heart, is conscious that the objective determinant of Christianity is not a reminiscence, as love is of the fact of falling in love, is not an apparently objective something which nevertheless is subjective, like love which as an objective something is an illusion and loving is the reality. No, even if no one had perceived that God had revealed Himself in a human form in Christ, He nevertheless has revealed Himself. Hence it is that every contemporary (simply understood) has a responsibility if he does not perceive it.

So Magister A. is deeply affected. That in the first moment of emotion one is easily exposed to the confusion of confounding the change within oneself with a change outside oneself, of confounding the fact that one sees everything changed with the notion that something new must have come into being, this is a thing well enough known, I do not need to dwell upon it. Though Magister A. had for a long time been ensnared in this confusion it would be foolish to blame him – partly because it is nobody's business, partly because it is human. The question is only whether in this condition he expresses himself. If once one is ensnared in this confusion, it is only too easy to support this confusion with a plausible poetical invention and get dramatically an occurrence, a scene, explaining how it came about. Not only every religiously awakened individual, but everyone who in a marked degree possesses inwardness, has also an inclination and dexterity for turning his monologue into a dialogue, that is, for talking to himself in such a way that this self becomes like another self which has reality apart from himself, that is so say, duplicating himself. Instead of being content with the experience that a light suddenly rose up before him, it comes easy to say that it was as though the Saviour appeared to him and bade him, etc. The confusion is undeniably very suspicious, but the principal thing is to hold back the expression until one has come to one's senses.

If from an earlier time Magister A. had had a strict and serious schooling in the concepts, had had a veneration for the dogmatic, qualitative concept of "a revelation," he would have had something to resist with, something to hold on to, something that might prevent the precipitate utterance. But, unfortunately, Magister A. is a Hegelian. So there can be no hope that something might save him from the confusion, since the whole of his philosophic learning must precisely confirm him in the notion that altogether correctly and with philosophical precision he expresses his subjective change by the invention that he had had a revelation. By confounding the subjective with the objective Magister Adler is ensnared in the notion that he has had a revelation, by having had a revelation he likely thinks that he has broken entirely with the Hegelian philosophy which has in its system no room for a qualitative revelation. But, on the other hand, how has the Hegelian philosophy treated the concept of a revelation? It has not bluntly denied it, but it has volatilized it so far that at last it becomes a determinant of subjectivity, the simple identity of subject-object. It is precisely in this confusion Magister A. is, but then he has the support of the Hegelian philosophy in saying of himself that he has had a revelation. The confusion is not brought to a stop, for A. has not been schooled earlier in the definition of Christian concepts, and now he gives himself no time for it. He is subjectively ensnared, and in this condition he thinks that he breaks with the Hegelian philosophy, but he has no other education in the concepts more essential than he finds in Hegel's philosophy, and the topsy-turvy, the double confusion, appears in its second power in the fact that he breaks with this philosophy – and it is precisely that which triumphs.

However, Adler spoke out the word, he proclaimed solemnly that he had had a revelation, that at night *the Saviour* had bade him get etc. – *et semel emissum volat irrevocabile verbum*, at least a greater self-conquest is required to retract what has been spoken than to refrain from speaking it.

(b) *Magister Adler's answer to the ecclesiastical authority*. The word spoken meets, however, with the serious opposition of the authority. Magister A. is required to explain himself more particularly, and now we have the same situation raised to the second power.

This confusion of Adler's in the situation raised to a higher power was already shown in Chapter III, §1, together with the exposition that the incongruity consists precisely in the fact that he lacks schooling in the Christian concepts, and therefore explains and explains, substituting the qualitatively most diverse determinants in place one of another, and yet thinks that he is in identity with himself.

(c) *Magister Adler's four last books*. Time and repose was what Magister A. then needed, a strict, fundamental schooling in the language of Christian concepts, in order to get the proper sense of proportion. Magister A. himself gives expression to this need: "that with a longer time to revise the ideas quietly he will in the future find himself in a position to give them a more appropriate form" – and thereupon he begins a new, voluminous literary productivity, in which, however, he does not seem to have got any farther along, so far as qualitative education is concerned. The fact that he himself seems to perceive that he stands in need of a pause, the fact that instead of acting in virtue of this perception he continues his productivity, is thoroughly characteristic psychologically, and unfortunately is an indication that it will be hard enough for him to give himself time for serious reflection. The fact that a man who puts the opposite course of action into effect uses the adage that for the future he hopes to change – rather indicates that there will not likely be much of a change. The urge he might feel for a change gets no power over him, precisely because it is constantly proclaimed, so that, at last, all that remains is the urge to say it once in a while or very often – whereas he does the contrary. It is strange that Holberg has not made use of this characteristic trait in depicting "the bustling man"; it would have been thoroughly characteristic of the bustling man to have had an adage: "It cannot be endured, the press of business; but beginning from New Year's Day I shall retire completely from business life." It is quite certain that this line, when the spectator by the aid of the situation must also be dramatically aware that it was an adage, would precisely characterize the incessant movement of the bustling man and prove that he was incorrigible. When a student has for a long time been reading for his professional examination it becomes with every year less probable that he will ever take it, only when it becomes an adage, "Next time I will" – it is clear enough that he will not take any examination. Trop (the hero of the play) is precisely for this reason hopeless and given up because he possesses his hope in the form of an adage.

Magister A. hopes indeed in the future, but if one were to ask him where the last four books have a place in a sustained literary effort or in the development of a personal life, where A. now is, intellectually understood (which is something different from asking him about a particular utterance, the particular explanation of a Biblical passage, the particular study, etc.), then one may say that he has been productive at the wrong place, his productivity sails before a false wind. *For instead of giving himself time, gaining repose, coming to his senses*, going to school; instead of acquiring respect for what after all it means to have had a revelation, and coming to an understanding with himself and to a qualitative decision, *in short, instead of keeping silent and acting and laboring, he becomes so productive in a literary way about all this*, *that he has not yet attained repose*, that "he is fatigued, that he is shaken, pale, that he is on the point of making the leap, that with a longer time for working quietly to revise the ideas he hopes, etc." First and last the task is to get out of the tension, to understand himself in the fact of revelation, instead of which he becomes productive literarily about his condition, and *moreover deceives himself with a dreadfully grandiose means of diversion*: a voluminous literary activity about detached particulars, individual texts from Scripture, individual thoughts, prolix productivity on detached sheets of paper.

Here we have it again: Magister A. lacks education in the definition of Christian concepts, his lyrical emotion bears no proportion to this, as is shown from the fact that he has so little respect for the concept "revelation" that he can let his declaration that he has had a revelation remain dubious, indeed it would seem that he has quite forgotten the whole story and has become literarily productive about everything else one can possibly conceive. And furthermore the incongruity is another, that he lacks ethical firmness to procure for himself repose, in order "by having a longer time to revise quietly the ideas, etc."

Everyone who knows something about the dangers of reflection, and about the dangerous course followed in the course of reflection, knows also that it is a suspicious circumstance when a man, instead of getting out of a tension by resolution and action, becomes literarily productive about his situation in the tension. Then no work is done to get out of the situation, but the reflection fixes the situation before the eyes of reflection, and thereby fixes (in a different sense of the word) the man [in the German slang sense of reckoning on his fall]. The more abundantly thoughts and expressions proffer themselves to a writer, the more quickly the productivity advances – in the wrong direction – all the more dangerous it is, and all the more is it hidden from the person concerned that his labor, his most exacting labor, perhaps also, for a third person who has the total view, his very interesting labor – is a labor to get himself deeper and deeper involved. For he does not work himself loose, he works himself fast, and makes himself interesting by reflecting about the tension. And one notes clearly enough that Magister A. is unacquainted with, and with the use of, the innumerable prudential methods which he who is experienced upon the ocean of reflection knows very well and practices constantly, to test the direction of the productivity, to regulate the speed, to determine the place where one is, by stopping an instant, by devising quite arbitrary, trivial, and mechanical measures for determining the powers of the mind, by forcing reflection into an entirely opposite direction in order to see whether any illusion is in play, etc. No, Magister A. goes on producing at *one* speed, which quite consistently increases the productivity with every step in advance; and so in production he is as it were far out upon the ocean of reflection, where no one can directly call out to him, where all sea-marks are dialectical, he steers at a considerable speed – in the wrong direction.

If then Magister A. had had from an earlier time an impression of a strict ethical view, had had a serious schooling in ethics, this surely would be of advantage to him now. But Magister A.'s life-development was such that it must quite naturally culminate in Hegel's philosophy, which, as is well known, has no ethic. It may happen to the most serious ethicist when he is far out upon the sea of reflection that once for an instant he makes a mistake, but he will quickly discover it, for he tests his life to see where he is. It may happen even to the most serious ethicist that for an instant he is ensnared in an illusion, but he will soon discover it. When a serious man says to himself, "You must give yourself time, collect yourself for reflection, in order that for the future you may be able to present the ideas in a more appropriate form," and he notices that he remains nevertheless in the same old path, then he discovers that his reflection was humbug, he takes the thing up seriously, instantly he defines the limit, that the indeterminateness of time may not deceive him, he starves himself with trivial labors in order that he may not deceive himself and waste his time upon literary productivity, which is interesting to him really because he has an apprehension that there is something else he should be doing. It is so true what Paul Moler once said as the fruit of experience: "In almost absolute idleness one may yet escape boredom so long as a practical duty is neglected through idleness, for one is in a way preoccupied by the constant strife in which one is involved with oneself; but so soon as the duty ceases, or one has not the least remembrance of it, boredom ensues." The teacher who prescribes a lesson from hour to hour is amused so long as he is on the alert to look after his pupils, but when he has resolved to neglect the lesson hour his amusement ceases. In this instance the reminder of his conscience is something unpleasant which serves to give relish to something unpleasant. A poet who is writing a tragedy when it is part of his life-plan to study for an examination does it with greater enthusiasm than he would later when he has relinquished that plan. And so also perhaps it is the obscure consciousness he has that now instead of being literarily productive he ought to be doing something else which makes Magister A. so productive and makes his productivity interesting, while he, instead of becoming clear to himself by his productivity, rather defends himself against what ethical simplicity would bid him do.

So then Magister A. has no decisive ethical presuppositions, the Hegelian philosophy has taught him to dispense with ethics; so that there is nothing to bring him to a halt and let him see that his latest productivity, be it never so clever, is a mistake which does not lead him to understand himself more clearly in respect to what is the decisive event in his life, to have had a revelation, but rather leads him farther from it. The Hegelian philosophy, far from being able to explain this to him, must simply confirm him in the notion that the direction of his productivity is the right one.

The Hegelian philosophy has no ethics, it has therefore never dealt with the future, which is essentially the element or medium of ethics. The Hegelian philosophy contemplates the past, the six thousand years of world-history, and then is busy in pointing out every particular development as a transitory factor in the world-historical process. *Charmant!* But the late Professor Hegel of blessed memory had when he lived, as every man has or at least ought to have, an ethical relation to the future. Of this the Hegelian philosophy knows nothing. Hence it comes about quite simply that every living person who by the help of the Hegelian philosophy would understand himself in his own personal life falls into the most foolish confusion. As a Hegelian he will be able to understand his life only when it is too late, when it is past, when he is dead – but unfortunately he now is alive. With what then must he properly fill his life while he is living? With nothing; for really he must wait for the moment of death to understand with the averted glance of this moment the meaning of his past life. But when the past life was filled with nothing, what is there really left for him to understand? But suppose a man lives nevertheless, lives forward in the direction of life's course, and thus does after all fill a section of his life with something, then as a Hegelian he must as quickly as possible construe his past as a factor in his life, and then, so long as his glance is turned backward, he ceases for a moment to be an existing individual with an ethical direction towards the future. If he is entirely absorbed in desiring to understand his own life as a factor, then he regards himself essentially as dead.

Let us now think of Magister A. He has gone astray in reflection, he is absorbed in reflection about his situation in a tension, instead of working out of it. Thus indeed an ethicist will view his productivity. But a Hegelian must confirm him in the notion that his procedure is the right one, since he is in fact engaged in construing this situation of his as a factor in the development of his life. But to construe it as a factor is not to get out of it, and on the other hand he must be well out of it before there can be any question of construing it as a factor. In general the ethical at once inverts everything: the main thing is to act, to strive, to get out of the wrong situation – at the most there may be conceded incidentally a little half-hour to construe individual experiences of the past as a factor in one's life. Adler is ensnared in self-reflection, but then too he is so far from having anything to help him out of it that he also has within him Hegelian reminiscences which must confirm him in the notion that this after all is the profound thing and the highest wisdom.

It is perfectly unbelievable what confusion the Hegelian philosophy has wrought as a sorry consequence of the fact that as a philosopher a man is such a hero, and in a purely personal aspect a Philistine. Among philosophers subsequent to Hegel who have appropriated the Hegelian method there are to be found astonishing examples. One such philosopher writes a new book and becomes conscious of himself as a factor within the endeavor which began with his first book; but this is not enough, for his whole endeavor (which as a whole is not yet in existence) he becomes conscious of as a factor in the whole endeavor of philosophy, and then again as a factor in Hegel, and of Hegel as a factor in the world-historical process from ancient times, through China, Persia, Greece, Judaism, Christianity, the Middle Ages. This to my notion is the most inhuman whim any philosopher can have, also it is a story à la Münchhausen, that a poor individual man wants to make us believe he can do such things.

But this baleful inclination to construe has become a fixed idea by which philosophers become self-important, sometimes even adding to the confusion by indicating future factors. The ethical view of being in the future, and the metaphysical view of construing everything as a factor, contend with one another for life and death. Every living man, if he is not thoughtless and *distrait*, chooses decisively; but if he chooses the metaphysical view, he commits, spiritually understood, suicide.

As in general, so here, A. has indirectly a merit in satirizing Hegel unconsciously. A tame, domesticated professor, leading a still life, can skulk through better with the illusion of living backwards. He himself is No. 0, and therefore presumably is busy only with the past and with construing it as a factor. But an itinerant scholastic (the word itinerant being used almost in the sense of confused), a lyrically exalted dithyrambic poet – well, up to this point he may be right in saying that he has broken with Hegel, but when he goes on and gets himself stuck in reflection, and then moreover wants to be thought-conscious that his present condition is a factor in his life-development – then he produces in the Hegelian philosophy, quite literally, a state of flatulence, which is not at all to its advantage.

5

MAGISTER ADLER AS AN EPIGRAM UPON CHRISTENDOM OF OUR DAY

How Magister A. satirized the Hegelian philosophy indirectly by breaking with it conspicuously but nevertheless conniving with it unconsciously and then by the confusion of his life bringing the Hegelian philosophy into a situation where it must show itself to be as self-contradictory as it is, has often been demonstrated. The fact too that he is an epigram upon the Christendom of our day will also be pointed out and utilized.

Magister A. was in fact born and confirmed in geographical Christendom and belonged to it . . . so he was a Christian (as we all of us are Christians), he was a candidate in theology . . . so he was a Christian (as we all of us are Christians); he became a Christian priest – and then for the first time he had a curious experience: owing to a deep impression upon his life he came more seriously into contact with the decision ... to become a Christian. Just then when he had come nearer to being a Christian than ever before during all the time he was a Christian, just then he was deposed. And his deposition was quite proper, for then for the first time the State-Church had an opportunity to become aware how it stood with his Christianity. But the epigram remains nevertheless that as a pagan he became a Christian priest, and that when he had undeniably come somewhat nearer to being a Christian he was deposed.

By a single occurrence of this sort one has undeniably an opportunity of acquiring an insight into what after all must be understood by the notion that we are all Christians of a sort; one gets a suspicion whether after all it is not an illusion about the many Christians in geographical Christendom. This certainly is not said by way of judgment – far be from me all preoccupation with externals. It is a different matter whether the individual by himself might not be able to learn something for himself from the whole business about Magister A. This certainly is my opinion; and, though I am doubtful how far one really can say that Magister A. has had a Christian awakening, it seems to me that the catastrophe of his life must be able to exert some awakening effect upon every one, whatever be the result for Magister A. At all events, it is undeniable that, while at one time in the world to become a Christian was a decision from which most men shrank, now the thing of becoming a Christian of sorts is an enchanting delight in which one is confirmed in so many ways that there well may be needed a special sort of awakening which will be able to pluck one out of the illusion, if one is ensnared in it after the example of a man who can even become a Christian priest though he is ensnared in the delusion that he is a Christian and essentially is only a pagan.

Perhaps this is not so – I know nothing about it and want to know nothing. But let us imagine it, that many live on in a way as Christians and really are pagans, owing to the fact that existence, the world around them, has transformed itself into a great illusion which again and again and in every way confirms them in the notion that they are Christians. Let us imagine that these many in a more advanced age constitute each of them a family. These fictitious Christians bring up in turn their children – what will the next generation of Christians become?

In general it is certainly characteristic of our time that the concept of *upbringing*, at least in the sense of former times, is vanishing more and more from man's speech and from his life. In former times men set a high value upon the significance of bringing up, understanding by this a harmonious development of that which was to support the various gifts and talents and peculiarities of personality ethically in the direction of character. In our times one seems to want to do away impatiently with this upbringing and therewith emphasizes *instruction*. One wants the young to learn quickly and as early as possible much and all sorts of things, to learn what one almost palpably can ascertain is knowledge and is something. Formal culture, the ethical culture of character, is not such a something, and yet it requires much time and much diligence. In our time one seems to think that if only one takes pains in all ways to see that the child learns something, learns languages, mathematics, religion, etc., then for the rest the child can pretty much bring up himself. In every age and in every land this is certainly a great misunderstanding, but it is especially dreadful in Christendom. For if a person is not to be simply disappointed in Christianity, one of two things must be done: *either* one must keep the child from his earliest childhood, so long as he is under tutelage, far from every relationship with Christianity, one must allow him to grow up without any Christian knowledge whatsoever, in order that at a mature age he may get a decisive impression of Christianity and choose for himself; *or* the parents must assume responsibility for giving him from his earliest childhood by a strict Christian upbringing a decisive impression of the Christian faith. But let him grow up from childhood with the view of his environment of what it is to be a Christian of sorts as a matter of course, and with that one has done everything a man can possibly do to deceive him with regard to the absolutely qualitative decision in human life. He then is a Christian in about the same sense that he is a man, and as little as it could occur to him in later life to reflect seriously whether after all he really is a man, just so little will it ordinarily occur to him to make an accounting of himself as to whether after all he is now really a Christian.

I will now imagine – for it is abhorrent to my soul to meddle in the God-relationship of any man, even so far as to know that there actually lives such a man as I describe – I will imagine the father of a family. He is capable in his business, not without cleverness, rather a little of everything, hospitable and sociable in his home, he is no reviler of religion (which, though it is dangerous, might perhaps be still better for the children, for it provides elasticity), neither is he in the strictest sense indifferent, he is in a way a Christian, he would think it strange, far-fetched and remarkable to make any further fuss about the matter, either inwardly or outwardly; he is in a way a Christian, through the reading of one or another recent work he is in agreement with the view that Christianity represents the highest culture of the soul, together with the opinion that every cultured man is a Christian. In his home life, whether there be company or no, he never has occasion to express himself religiously about religious matters. If it happens occasionally that one or another religious individual calls attention to himself and becomes the subject of the day and the subject also of conversation in the home of that *paterfamilias*, the judgment upon such a man and upon his conduct is not a religious judgment but an aesthetic one, it stigmatizes such form and substance as bad form, as something that cannot be tolerated in cultured circles. – This man's wife is a lovable woman, free from all modern womanish whims, good-hearted as a mother and wife. She has also at a single instant in her life felt a need for deeper religious reflection. But since such matters and such concerns had never been broached between her and her husband, and since she has perhaps an exaggerated respect for the requirements of a husband so superior to her with respect to culture, she feels that it might betray a lack of culture or be offensive were she to talk about religious subjects. Therefore she keeps silent and with womanly devotion submits herself entirely to her husband, gracefully appropriating an attitude which is so becoming to her husband as a man; and these two harmonize as rarely a couple in Christendom do.

Under the eyes of these parents the children grow up. Nothing is spared to enrich them with knowledge, and while the children grow up in knowledge and information they pick up naturally the cultured manners of their parents, so that this family is really an exceedingly pleasant home to come into. It follows as a matter of course that the children are Christians, they were born in fact of Christian parents, so this is just as natural as that a person is a Jew who is born of Jewish parents* – where in all the world could the children get any other notion? That there are Jews, pagans, Mohammedans, fetish worshipers, they know well enough from history and from their scientific religious instruction, but they know it also as something with which they are entirely unconcerned.

Let us take the oldest child. He has now reached the age when he is to be confirmed. It is a matter of course that the boy answers "Yes" to the question put to him. How in the world could anything else occur to this boy? Has anybody ever heard tell that somebody answered "No," or has the boy ever been told that he might answer "No"? On the other hand, one may perhaps have heard his father say not to answer too loudly nor too softly, but to do it in a becoming and polite way; he remembers perhaps to have heard his father say that the whispered yes was something rather affected in church. To that extent it is a matter of course that he must answer "Yes" – to the extent that, instead of having his attention called to the significance of the answer, it was called to the purely aesthetic side of the formality. So then he answers "Yes" – neither too loudly nor too softly, but with the frank and modest decorum which is so becoming to a boy. His father is somewhat more serious than

*The notion of being a Christian because one is born of Christian parents is the fundamental delusion from which a multitude of others stem. One is a Jew by being born of Jewish parents; quite right, because Judaism is essentially connected with and founded upon a natural determinant. But Christianity is a determinant of spirit, so that in it there is neither Jew nor pagan nor a *born* Christian, for the determinant of spirit is higher than the natural determinant. On the other hand, one cannot well *become* a Jew, for one must be born a Jew. One cannot be a Christian and yet not a Christian; on the other hand, one can be a Jew and yet not be a Jew, because the natural determinant is preponderant; for though one is not a believing Jew, he is just as fully a Jew; but a Christian who is not a believing Christian is not a Christian at all. The determinant "Christian" is precisely that of which it must be said in the most absolute terms, one is not born to this determinant – exactly the contrary, it is precisely what one must *become*.

usual on the day of confirmation, yet his seriousness has rather a festal than a religious character and therefore harmonizes with the cheerfulness which makes its appearance when they have come home from the church, where the father is not only as agreeable as ever but employs his talents to make that day a festival. The mother is moved, she even wept in church. But motherly tenderness and worldly concern for the child's future fate is not restricted to Christianity. The boy therefore on the day of his confirmation got a more solemn impression of his father and a more touching impression of his mother; he will remember that day with gratitude and gladness as a beautiful recollection; but he gets no decisive Christian impression. The boy gets the impression that this day must be rather a significant day in life – but not so significant as the day he becomes, for example, a university student and matriculates.

The youth is confirmed, and now little by little begins for him the busy time, since he has to get ready for his examination as an officer – we may assume that he will follow that course. So he passes his examination with distinction; he goes to the university, distinguishes himself further, the parents are delighted with their son, whom now, however, they see more rarely, since he has moved away from home and is always busy. He is fortunate, at the age of twenty-six he is already captain. – Our young captain falls in love. She is a lovable and charming girl, corresponding entirely to the parents' wish, and the family, already so agreeable, acquires a new enchantment by receiving her into their circle, and by the comfortable feeling which was diffused over the home life when it was implied that the older generation is now about to be rejuvenated in the new one. The captain is really in love. But to be really in love is after all no specific determinant of Christianity; surely lovers have lived just as well in Greece as in Christendom, indeed the erotic determinant is not properly Christian. The wedding day is appointed. One finds that a church wedding is the most solemn. The captain's father holds the opinion that a church wedding, with the impression of the lofty vaulting of the church, with the tones of the organ, with the whole environment, and with having the priest in his proper environment, attunes the soul quite otherwise than to sneak off to the priest in a carriage to be married upon a silver salver. To this was added the opinion expressed by the captain's father, that over all mysteriousness there hangs a nemesis, that every unforeseen fatality acquires an almost ridiculous power over one. Thus in case the carriage goes wrong or overturns and there is a disorderly mob – if the affair were publicly known and official, if the unfortunates were on the way to a church wedding, well, that would always be an unpleasant delay; but if it were secret, it ought to be secret, if it was a quiet wedding it ought to occur in perfect quietness. – So then the captain stood before the altar with his young bride – a charming couple. And the priest asks, "Hast thou taken counsel with God and with thine own conscience, etc." What shall the captain answer? Well, after all, it goes without saying that the captain, who, erotically understood, is really in love, doesn't wait to be asked twice whether he wants to have the girl. So he answers "Yes" – not too loudly and not too softly, but precisely with the noble, self-confident yet modest tone which is so becoming to a young man. Whether this indeed might be just entirely a precise answer to the priest's question does not occur to the captain; he is fortunate in his love, he is happy, confident and honestly convinced that he will make the girl as happy as he can. – So the marriage couple are united. The notes of the organ roar a worldly farewell, the crowd looks wonderingly, almost enviously, at the charming couple, and everyone who can see more closely sees love shining from the captain's eyes. Indeed, there is reason to be envious of him, reason for the family to be proud of him: he is young, happily developed, beautiful in a manly way, honest enough to be truly in love, happy in his love, faithful to a sincere resolution.

Suppose now that this had taken place in geographical Christendom – who then has been more deceived in respect to Christianity than precisely our captain! For one who has never heard anything about Christianity is not deceived, but one who without having the least decisive impression of Christian truth has from the first been confirmed in the notion that he is a Christian – he is deceived. Where in all the world might it occur to him to be concerned about how far he is a Christian, or even to be concerned about becoming that which from his earliest recollection he was in a way assured that he is? And in this assurance everything has confirmed him; his parents have said nothing about the Christian faith, they thought, "That the priest must do," and the priest thought, "To instruct the young about religion, that I can do for sure; but to give them a decisive impression, that must be the parents' affair." So he has grown up, been confirmed, become lieutenant, captain – and now a Christian husband.

In case one who was not a priest should ask our captain whether he were a Christian, the captain undoubtedly would smile. There would be nothing rude or offensive in this smile, as though by the smile he would give the questioner to understand what a stupid person he was; no, for this the captain is too cultured, for he really is a cultured young man. But he would smile involuntarily, because the question would seem to him just as strange as though somebody were to ask him whether he were a man. In case that evening at the tea-table in our captain's house the story was told about Socrates, that he is reported to have said that he did not know definitely whether he was a man, our captain would perhaps say, "That undoubtedly is very ironical, and one cannot help smiling at it; but on the other hand there is something whimsical in expressing such a doubt which concerns the very first and simplest and most necessary presuppositions in life; thus today there was a man who asked me seriously whether I were a Christian."

Let us imagine the opposite: that one by a strict Christian upbringing has already received as a child a decisive impression of Christianity. If this is to come about, the parents themselves must be essentially Christians, so that the child gets the constant impression of how his parents for daily use lead a religious life, concerning themselves with Christianity both for their own edification and in order to express it by their conduct. So then the child grows up, and during the age which is most receptive and in which memory is most faithful the decisive impressions of Christianity are imprinted indelibly upon his soul and *κατά δύναμιν* modify his character. For, as was said, might not the observation that one nowadays so rarely meets a man of strong character have some connection with the fact that people have no conception what upbringing is, that they confound it with learning [*discere*], confound learning with learning to obey, to bow before the mighty and daily impression of ethics and religion?

And now that such a child, because he had had a serious Christian upbringing, must be a Christian, would again be an illusion; and next to the notion of being a Christian because one is born of Christian parents, comes the erroneous inference: his parents were pious Christians, *ergo* he is a Christian. No, the unforgettable and profound impression due to upbringing is only a presupposition.

Then this child too goes out into the world. Undeniably he has presuppositions with respect to becoming a Christian; humanly speaking, everything has been done for him that was humanly possible. But there is not yet a decision; for even though his "Yes" on the day of confirmation was the result of upbringing, it still is not the decisive act.

Now in the course of years entirely different sides of life, entirely different factors of the soul, will presumably advance their claims; the young man will be sensible of impressions which are quite unknown to him. For the strict Christian upbringing is a presupposition, and such a one as he must grow up in order properly to accept it. As parents at an age when the children are growing most rapidly have their clothes made a little larger, made to grow up to, so one may say seriously of one who has received a strict Christian upbringing that his parents have given him a garment which is made to grow up to, but also a garment which no one can outgrow. He will now make acquaintance with the world, and then perhaps for a time it will seem to him as though his parents had deceived him; for what he gets to see now that he makes his appearance youthfully upon the dancing-floor of youth, all the joy of life, this lightheartedness – this his parents had as it were hidden from him. He will stand wondering and confused: with the grave conception due to a strict Christian upbringing of what it means to be a man, he stands now in the midst of this worldliness – and in the main it seems good to him. Yes, he will undoubtedly feel as one who has been deceived. As for the captain, he presumably will never discover that he was deceived; he precisely was initiated and educated into that medium in which he permanently belongs. But the other, he as a child has heard nothing about the glory the world has to offer, or he has heard of it only as a strict admonition against it; with the presuppositions of his strict Christian upbringing he stands as a stranger, indeed, as one deceived, in all this worldliness, which now when he must examine it himself seems quite different from the description given him as a child.

Yet, humanly speaking, for this young man was done everything that could be done: his life must so lie before him that he cannot avoid a catastrophe, he must come to a decision whether he will become a Christian, or actually give up Christianity. And if it is true as Socrates says that the most frightful thing of all is to live in error, then must that young man be accounted fortunate. In every Christian land where Christianity has so permeated all relationships that everyone as a matter of course (i.e. without the decision of inwardness) is in a way a Christian, it is important first and last to pose the problem ... of becoming a Christian, and that the problem be not confused by theological debates. However, on this subject I can refer to *The Concluding Postscript* by Johannes Climacus.

Whether it is a pure illusion for a man to imagine he is a Christian, or whether it may rather be that by a strict Christian upbringing he has got a decisive impression of Christianity, he faces exactly the same problem: to become a Christian. To this intent cautions and admonitions may well be needed in a Christian land. But such an admonition is contained precisely in Magister A.'s life. What difficulties lie in the way of becoming a Christian; in what sense a Christian upbringing is after all only a presupposition; how precarious such an upbringing may be; what responsibility the parents assume in undertaking it, but also conversely by not undertaking it – about all such things one finds of course no illumination in Magister A.'s life or in the catastrophe involved in it. He quite gives the impression of a pagan who has suddenly come into touch with Christianity. But precisely for this reason his life is an admonition for many, or may be; for in fact he was a Christian of a sort, as all men are Christians, he was confirmed, became a theological candidate, a Christian priest in geographical Christendom – and yet the catastrophe revealed how his being a Christian is to be understood. Here it is an occurrence which is the admonition, and also the admonition is indirect, it depends upon the individual whether he for himself will allow himself to be admonished; it is not as when a religiously exalted person thunders and condemns, which so easily may exasperate men instead of profiting them.

No, Magister A. exerts an effect by his life, and he exerts also an indirect effect. His significance for our time will surely not consist so much in what he became through the catastrophe, or in the literary productivity which derives from it, as in the fact that by the catastrophe he indirectly reveals how in geographical Christendom one may in a way become a Christian, and even a Christian priest, without having the least impression of Christianity in the way of . . . becoming a Christian.

POSTSCRIPT

This treatise was written before the events which have now altered the shape of Europe. If in reference to a time long gone by one might say justly that as a whole it lacked action, it may seem that now on the contrary we have got only too much action. But this only seems so. Everyone who has a well-developed notion of what it is to act will on closer inspection easily see that in all of Europe almost nothing at all is done that can be called action, that everything that comes to pass resolves itself into a mere occurrence, or that something comes about, something prodigious, but without there being any active personality who knows definitely beforehand what he wills, so that afterwards he can say definitely whether what came about was what he would or no. So in France – a republic of that sort does not properly belong to history, nor does it come absolutely under the rubric action; it finds its place more properly in a newspaper under the heading: *Advertisement.* In the greater part of Europe it is just the same. Everywhere and altogether what comes to pass is an occurrence, in many places an imitation, which not even regarded as imitation is action, for there is no individual who imitates a foreign institution and then in the situation of his country is after all active. No, imitation consists precisely in the fact that there comes about, God knows how, a sort of commotion – and so nothing really comes about. But there is nobody that rules, nobody that acts, nobody that could say with truth, It is this and this I willed, and now there has come about what I willed, or it has not come about. Hence the introduction of a change or a novelty must, at the moment when it is introduced, begin with an untruth, it must take several days for people to imagine and make others imagine that what had come about was what one willed. Since for the single individual there is something insipid in finding that "one fair morning," God knows how, he has become something or another – therefore one must try to help oneself out with divers untruths, that what he has now become he willed to be from his earliest childhood, etc.,

etc. As in the case of a man who in an exalted moment at a ball falls in love with a girl he is not acquainted with and knows hardly who she is – he feels the need or the temptation for shame's sake to begin with a little untruth about having loved her from his earliest childhood, about already having once before made love to her, etc., etc. So the race also falls into the embarrassment of having to help itself out with a little untruth, in order to get the story started again. Yet one still has a little recollection of what it must be to be a free rational being. To secure this conception one must poetize that what has come about is what one willed – unless one assumes with Hegel that it came about by necessity. But that a revolution of affairs came about in such a way (i.e. by necessity) is again the same old evil tendency to shove off from oneself the responsibility – in this case indeed it is raised to so high a degree, carried out on such a scale, that in the end existence must acknowledge the paternity of what comes to pass in the world of free rational beings, pretty much as in nature, so that these meaningless and inhuman revolutions are to be regarded as natural phenomena, so that revolutions simply *are* and republics come into existence in the same sense that there is cholera.*

If one were to say that then the *extraordinarius* begins with an untruth, indeed makes God a party to the untruth, it may be replied that all true communication of truth must always begin with an untruth. In part, this has its ground in the fact that it is indeed impossible to tell the whole truth in one minute or even a shorter time; on the contrary a long, long time may perhaps be needed for it. In part, this first untruth is merely reduplication, that the true communication of truth is cautious and aware of the fact that it might indeed be possible that the recipient of the communication was in the untruth, in which case the direct communication of the truth would be untruth. This is "reflection," the critical moment in the communication of truth. Thus the ignorance of Socrates was in fact untruth; but it was only for the sake of truth, i.e. it is precisely reduplication's expression for the fact that he truly would communicate truth, that he was

*The following paragraph (which is to be found in *Papirer* IX B/ 3 b) was written at the same time as the *Postscript*, evidently with the intention of adding it to the text. The translator can find no place for it more appropriate than this.

profoundly aware that those who were to receive the communication were possibly in the untruth of delusions of all sorts, so that it would not do to communicate truth quite directly, expectorating it cheerfully or declaiming it or lecturing it. To mention the highest instance, Christ's own life shows this; for when one is God it is indeed an untruth (in the sense that truth is merely direct) to come in the form of a lowly servant; and, viewed from the other side (since he had come for the sake of suffering and dying), it would have been an untruth to accept for one sole instant the favor of the people and occasion this misunderstanding. However, I shall carry this out no farther. But in the case of the *extraordinarius* precisely this must be a part of his dreadful responsibility, that in a stricter sense he has to begin with an untruth. And an untruth to begin with is in the case of the *extraordinarius* not to be avoided. Dialectically this lies in the nature of the case. If this untruth is not present, then the *extraordinarius* is not the *extraordinarius*, this title is then taken in vain, it is a direct superlative in contrast to the ordinary. But this is an altogether undialectical definition of the extraordinary.

As for the present treatise, the reader, I hope, will constantly get from reading it the impression that it is ethico-religious and has nothing to do with politics, that it investigates ethico-religiously how it comes about that a new point of departure is created in relation to the established order; that it comes about by the fact that *the point of departure is* FROM ABOVE, *from God*, and *the formula is this paradox that an individual is employed.* Humanly understood, an individual, according to all reason, is infinitely nothing in comparison with the established order (the universal), so it is a paradox that the individual is the stronger. This can be explained only by the fact that it is God who makes use of him, God who stands behind him; but just for this reason one sees God again, just because the situation is a paradox. When there are hundreds of men, what comes to pass is explained simply by the activity of the hundreds of men, but the paradox compels us (in so far as freedom can be compelled) to take notice of God, that He is taking part in it.

Politically the whole thing, even when it comes to decision, goes far more easily: the less paradox, the simpler it is. Politically one has nothing to do with God, suffers no inconvenience from the thought that He takes part: *the starting-point is* FROM BELOW, *from that which is lower* than the established order; for even the most mediocre "establishment" is preferable to and higher than the vaguest of all vague conceptions, "the multitude," which, if you please, accounts for the fact that nowadays this absurdity finds a place in the State, that there exists a monster of fairyland with many heads, or, more correctly and truly, with a thousand legs, or, according to circumstances, with a hundred thousand: "the multitude," an absurd monster or a monstrous absurdity, which nevertheless is physically in possession of power, of outcries and of noise, and besides that has an extraordinary virtuosity in making everything commensurable for the decision of the hands upraised to vote or the fists upraised to fight. This abstraction is an inhuman something, the power of which is, to be sure, prodigious, but it is a prodigious power which cannot be defined in human terms, but more properly as one defines the power of a machine, calling it so and so many horsepower: the power of the multitude is always horsepower.

This abstraction, whether you will call it the public or the multitude or the majority or the senseless people – this abstraction is used politically to bring about movement. Just as in whist or other social games there is some stake for which men play, so is this abstraction the stake for which men play politically. Truth and such like things, God in heaven, etc., death, judgment and more of this sort, the politician regards in about the same way as when one finds it tiresome to play cards for nothing. No, cards must be played for money, and politically the game must be played for the multitude, as to whether one can *à tout prix* get the most on his side, or the most who go over to his side with their many legs. So when one of the players sees that he has got the most he hurries to put himself at the head to lead this monster – or rather there is not even any player, this is rather too much a characterization of personality; the whole thing is like a game where there is no player, or like a speech where yet there is no speaker, as in ventriloquism. But certain it is that in an evening hour, or possibly for several evenings in succession, there is a monstrous multitude on its legs, which for the organism of the State is certainly a very suspicious situation which can only be likened to wind. This human mass becomes at last enraged by friction, and now demands – or rather it demands nothing, it does not itself know what it wills, it takes the threatening attitude only in the hope that something after all will come to pass, in the hope that the weaker side (the established government, the ruler) will perhaps become so much alarmed that it will go ahead and do something which neither the multitude nor those at the head of it, the stronger ones, the courageous ones (if there be any such), have the courage to speak out in definite words. The fact of being the stronger therefore does not mean to act, but by an abstract possibility, by a sound of nature (such as is heard in Ceylon), to frighten the weaker into doing something – as Louis Philippe went off in alarm and by running away gave France a republic, or brought France into a situation out of which (who ever would have thought of it!) a republic came about. In alarm the king goes off and does something – and what the king does, that the human multitude then adores, maintaining that *it* had done it.

While the individual who truly connects himself with a religious movement must watch out and be ready to fight lest the dreadful thing should come to pass that this monstrous abstraction should wish to help him by going over with its legs to his side (for to conquer by the help of this is, religiously, to help untruth to conquer); while the religious individual must suffer indescribably under the weight of his responsibility and of doubly reflected contention in loneliness (for he contends alone – but at the same time contends for life and death to be permitted to be alone), it goes far easier for the political hero, and easiest of all for one who is not so much as a political hero. But if there be such a hero, he only takes care to assure himself of these thousands before venturing anything, and when he is assured of them he ventures – that is, he does not in fact venture anything, for physically he is by far the stronger, and he contends physically.

But for this reason also almost every political movement, instead of being an advance to the rational, is a retrogression to the irrational. Even a poor government which yet is organic is better than the senseless situation when such an abstraction rules the State. The existence of this abstraction in the State (like an unwholesome fluid in the blood) puts finally an end to the rational State. Wherever this abstraction is set upon the throne there really is no government. One is obedient only to the man whom he himself has boosted up, pretty much as the idolater worships and serves the god he himself has made, i.e. one obeys himself. With the discontinuance of the rational State the art of statesmanship will become a game. Everything will turn upon getting the multitude pollinated, and after that getting them to vote on his side, with noise, with torches and with weapons, indifferent, absolutely indifferent, as to whether they understand anything or no.

Since such is the case and since everything in these times is politics, I do not wonder that many may find that the present treatise deals with nothing, is concerned with difficulties which absolutely do not exist. Well – be it so then, it deals in fact with God and with the God-relationship in the individual.

APPENDIX

TRANSLATOR'S NOTES TO "FEAR AND TREMBLING"

(I am indebted for most of these notes to the editors of the Danish edition of S.K.'s Complete Works.)

1 The motto recalls the well-known story of old Rome, which relates that when the son of Tarquinius Superbus had craftily gained the confidence of the people of Gabii he secretly sent a message to his father in Rome, asking what he should do next. The father, not willing to trust the messenger, took him into the field where as he walked he struck off with his cane the heads of the tallest poppies. The son understood that he was to bring about the death of the most eminent men in the city and proceeded to do so.

2 The Preface is aimed especially at Martensen's review of J. L. Heiberg's "Introductory Lectures to Speculative Logic," *Danske Maanedskrift*, No. 16 for 1836, pp. 515ff.

3 Descartes is mentioned here because Martensen made appeal to him in the article mentioned in the preceding note.

4 Remembering, however, as I have already said, that the natural light is to be trusted only in so far as nothing to the contrary is revealed by God Himself. ... Moreover, it must be fixed in one's memory as the highest rule, that what has been revealed to us by God is to be believed as the most certain of all things; and even though the light of reason should seem most clearly to suggest something else, we must nevertheless give credence to the divine authority only, rather than to our own judgment. (*Principia philosophiae, pars prima* 28 and 76.)

5 Let no one think that I am here about to propound a method which everyone ought to follow in order to govern his reason aright; for I have merely the intention of expounding the method I myself have followed. ... But no sooner had I finished the course of study at the conclusion of which one is ordinarily adopted into the ranks of the learned, than I began to think of something very different from that. For I became aware that I was involved in so many doubts, so many errors, that all efforts to learn were, as I saw it, of no

other help to me than that I might more and more discover my ignorance (*Dissertatio de methodo*, pp. 2 and 3).

6 Martensen gave such "promises" in the article referred to in notes 2 and 3.

7 S.K.'s contemptuous way of referring to the *Berlingske Tidende*, a newspaper owned and edited by his *bête noire*, the wholesale merchant Nathanson. This advertisement attracted particular attention because the enterprising young gardener accompanied it with a sketch of himself in the ingratiating attitude here described.

8 In J. L. Heiberg's *The Reviewer and the Beast*, Trop tears his own tragedy, *The Destruction of the Human Race*, into two equal pieces, remarking, "Since it doesn't cost more to preserve good taste, why shouldn't we do it?"

9 Only three years before this the first omnibus was seen in Copenhagen.

10 One might blamelessly be in doubt how to translate this title (as the four translators into German, French and English have been) had not S.K. himself indicated (IV B 81) that he here uses the word *Stemning* in the sense of *προοιμιον*, the Greek word which gives us proem. I have preferred to use the word prelude because it will be more commonly understood. Cf. IV A 93.

11 Genesis, Chapter 22.

12 Judith 10:11. S.K. quotes this passage in the *Postscript*. Cf. III A 197.

13 Alluding to various passages in Homer (e.g. *Iliad* III 381) where a divinity saves a hero by enveloping him in a cloud and carrying him away. We discover additional pathos in this picture of the "lover" when we remember that at the end of *The Point of View* (pp. 62f and 100ff.) S.K. looks for the coming of his poet, his lover.

14 It is evident from the sequel that Jeremiah is meant.

15 Here we have a glimpse of "repetition."

16 Cf. Plato's *Phaedrus*, 22 and 37.

17 In Oelenschläger's play *Aladdin* the hero is contrasted with Noureddin the representative of darkness.

18 Isaiah 26:18.

19 Themistocles, as related in Plutarch's *Themistocles*, 3, 3.

20 Eleven months later (with only one pseudonymous work intervening) S.K. published *The Concept of Dread*, and this remained one of his most distinctive categories. Although all have agreed to use the word "dread," no one can think it adequate as a translation of *Angst*. For though it denotes the presentiment of evil it does not sufficiently emphasize the anguish of the experience.

21 The connection requires a masculine pronoun, but Regine is meant, and she must have known it, for such were her words when she refused to give Kierkegaard back his freedom.

22 As Professor Martensen had claimed to do (*Danske Maanedskrift*, No. 16 referred to in note 2 above. Cf. I A 328, p. 130). But Sibbern too claimed for Heiberg that he "goes beyond Hegel" (the same review, No. 10, year 1838, p. 292).

23 Quoted from Horace's *Letters*, I. 18, 84: "It's your affair when the neighbor's house is afire."

24 The reader may need to be apprised that Johannes *de silentio* is in that religious stage which by Johannes Climacus in the *Postscript* is called "religiousness A," the basis of all religiousness, but therefore not the distinctively Christian position, which here is called "religiousness B," or the paradoxical religiousness which is characterized by faith in the strictest sense.

25 This is decidedly autobiographical.

26 S.K. attributed his spinal curvature to a fall from a tree when he was a child.

27 The reader who has not heard or has not heeded S.K.'s warning not to attribute to him personally a single word the Pseudonyms say may need here to be reminded that it is not S.K. who reiterates so insistently that he cannot understand Abraham. It is Johannes *de silentio* who says this, and the purpose of it is to emphasize the fact that the paradoxical religiousness (religiousness B) is and remains a paradox to everyone who stands on a lower plane, even to one who has got so high as to be able to make the movement of infinite resignation, so long as his religion is in the sphere of immanence.

28 Introduced about 1840 in Copenhagen.

29 The "princess" is of course the most obvious analogue to Regine, and one which she could not fail to discover; but

every other reader may need the hint that in this whole paragraph S.K. describes his own act of resignation.

30 At the time of his engagement S.K. registered in his *Journal* the observation that certain insects die the instant they fertilize their mate, and he repeated this in the sixth Diapsalm of *Either/Or*.

31 "A blissful leap into eternity."

32 Cf. what is said in *Repetition* about the young man who "recollects" his love as soon as he is engaged. It is quoted in my *Kierkegaard*, p. 212.

33 It seems clear enough that this passage was written after S.K. learned of Regine's engagement, and the tone of it suggests that he had had time to repent of the very different language he used when he rewrote *Repetition*. It is therefore an additional argument for the view that this book was written later than the other.

34 "The pre-established harmony" was a fundamental concept of Leibniz's philosophy.

35 See *Magyarische Sagen* by Johan Graf Mailáth (Stuttgart u. Tübingen 1838), Vol. II, p. 18. Cf. *Journal* II A 449.

36 An entry in the *Journal* (IV A 107) dated May 17 [1843], at the time, that is, when he was composing these two works in Berlin. S.K. says: "If I had had faith, I would have remained with Regine." He was then only a knight of infinite resignation, but he was in the way of becoming a knight of faith.

37 It would have been well had I remarked earlier that the Danish words *resignere* and *Resignation* have a more active sense than we attach to the word "resignation," that they imply an act rather than a passive endurance of a situation, and therefore could be translated by "renounce," "renunciation" – yet it would not do to dub our knight the knight of renunciation.

38 See Rosenkranz, *Erinnerungen an Karl Daub* (Berlin 1837), p. 2. Cf. *Journal* IV A 92.

39 S.K. liked to be called "Master of Irony" in view of the big book on *The Concept of Irony* by which he won his degree of Master of Arts.

40 A Greek word meaning end or goal – which S.K. writes with Greek letters but I transliterate because it is of such common

occurrence, and also because it is in the way of becoming an English word.

41 This is the conception of the ethical which is stressed in the Second Part of *Either/Or*. Perhaps Schrempf is right in affirming that what caused S.K. unnecessary agony was his acceptance of the Hegelian notion of the relation between the universal and the particular.

42 Cf. *Philosophie des Rechts*, 2nd ed. (1840) §§129–141 and Table of Contents p. xix.

43 The Trojan war. When the Greek fleet was unable to set sail from Aulis because of an adverse wind the seer Calchas announced that King Agamemnon had offended Artemis and that the goddess demanded his daughter Iphigenia as a sacrifice of expiation.

44 See Euripides, *Iphigenia in Aulis*, v. 448 in Wilster's translation. Agamemnon says, "How lucky to be born in lowly station where one may be allowed to weep." The confidants mentioned below are Menelaus, Calchas and Ulysses. Cf. v. 107.

45 Jephtha. Judges 11:30–40.

46 The sons of Brutus, while their father was Consul, took part in a conspiracy to restore the king Rome had expelled, and Brutus ordered them to be put to death.

47 This is temptation in the sense we ordinarily attach to the word. For temptation in a higher sense [*Anfaegtelse*] I have in the translation of other books used the phrase "trial of temptation." Professor Swenson, in an important passage in the *Postscript*, preferred to use the German word *Anfechtung*. In this work I have used "temptation" and added the German word in brackets. The distinction between the two sorts of temptation is plainly indicated by S.K. in this paragraph.

48 This is the Scriptural word which we translate by "offense" or "stumbling block." Only Mr. Dru has preferred to use the identical word "scandal."

49 *Docents* and *Privatdocents* (both of them German titles for subordinate teachers in the universities) were very frequently the objects of S.K.'s satire. He spoke more frequently of "the professor" after Martensen had attained that title.

50 It would be interesting and edifying to make an anthology of the passages in which S.K. speaks of the Blessed Virgin; for surely no Protestant was ever so much engrossed in this theme, and perhaps no Catholic has appreciated more profoundly the unique position of Mary.

51 In *Auszüge aus den Literatur-Briefen*, 81st letter, in Maltzahn's ed. Vol. VI, pp. 205ff.

52 E.g. Hegel's *Logik*, ii, Book 2, Sect. 3, Cap. C (*Werke* IV, pp. 177ff.; *Encyclopedie* I §140 (*Werke* VI, pp. 275ff.).

53 It appears from the *Journal* (I A 273) that S.K. had in mind Schleiermacher's "Theology of Feeling," and also (with not so obvious a justification) the dogmatists of the Hegelian school. The Danish editors refer to Marheineke, *Dogmatik*, 2nd ed. §§70, 71, 86.

54 Unexpected.

55 In this particular instance S.K. could define precisely what he understood by Isaac, that is, Regine; and the formlessness of this sentence was intentional – it is a smoke-screen.

56 The Danish editors refer to Bretschneider's *Lexicon*; but no language lacks "exegetical aids" which serve the purpose of emasculating the New Testament. In this instance the absolute word "hate" is weakened successively by each term used to define it: "feel dislike," "love less," "put in a subordinate place," "show no reverence," "regard as naught."

57 The Hebrew consonants *yodh* and *vav* originally indicated vowel sounds, and when the vowel sounds came to be written below the consonants these letters became superfluous in this respect and were said to repose [*hvile*] in the vowel. So S.K. understood the situation in his *Journal* II A 406, but here he has inverted it.

58 Fabius Maximus, who in 217 B.C. conducted the war against Hannibal and received the appellation of Cunctator for his successful strategy of delay or procrastination.

59 Public property.

60 A play by Olussen, which in Act II, Scene 10 and elsewhere speaks of "two witnesses" but not of beadles [*Stokkemændene*] i.e. four men appointed to attend legal proceedings as witnesses.

61 The corresponding passages are Deut. 13:6f. and 33:9; Matt.

10:37; 19:29. In the manuscript 1 Cor. 7:11 is spoken of as a "similar" passage, but not with good reason.

62 Two parts of the myth, viz. change and recognition, have to do with this [about which he has been talking].

63 The word is literally "carrom." The Danish editors explain that it means here to coincide at the same instant. Thus Oedipus by "recognizing" who he is brings about a "change" in his fortune.

64 Oedipus in Sophocles' tragedy of that name.

65 Iphigenia in Euripides' *Iphigenia in Tauris*.

66 In his *Natural History*, V, 4, 7. Cf. *Journal* IV A 36.

67 Book viii (5), Cap. 3, 3.

68 Title of a Roman priesthood, which S.K. (I know not for what reason) applies here to the Greek soothsayers.

69 Vol. I, §§1 and 2 – p. 10 in Maltzahn's ed.

70 Theology of pilgrims – contrasted with *theologia beatorum*, an ancient division no longer in vogue.

71 It is to be remembered that S.K. believed his marriage was prohibited by a "divine veto." Hence the prospective bridegroom of Delphi presents the closest analogy to his situation. In fact, the *Journal* shows that every line of conduct contemplated in this passage was seriously considered by S.K. – even the possibility of a "romantic union" without marriage. But it was the second line of conduct he chose.

72 Axel and Valborg are the pair of unhappy lovers most celebrated in Danish literature. Because of their close consanguinity the Church forbade their marriage.

73 This in fact was S.K.'s position.

74 Cf. Lessing, *Hamburgische Dramaturgie*, Vol. I, art. 22 (in Maltzahn's ed. VII, p. 96).

75 Nowhere, not even in the *Journal*, has S.K. so perfectly described the modest confidence with which Regine committed herself to him.

76 It is found in the fairy tale of "Beauty and the Beast" (Molbeck, No. 7), but not in the legend of "Agnes and the Merman."

77 Cf. the *Stages*, pp. 193ff.

78 S.K. uses here the word "emotion," but it is clear that he has in mind what a modern psychology has called *libido*.

79 Letter of credit on happiness. See Schiller's "Resignation," 3rd strophe (*Gedichte, 2te Periode*).

80 For no one ever has escaped from love or ever will so long as there be beauty and eyes to see with. Longus, *Daphnis and Chloë*. Introduction, §4. Cf. *Journal* IV A 30.

81 Unfortunately the Danish word *bedrage* means to defraud as well as to deceive. I seek to straddle both meanings (imperfectly) by using the word "cheat."

82 So it was S.K. was accustomed to think of himself. How ingenious of him to make this story fit his case by the device of "supposing" Sarah was a man!

83 *The Jew*, a play by Cumberland which was many times presented at the Royal Theater in Copenhagen between 1795 and 1834 and was published in a Danish translation in 1796. Scheva the Jew every one regarded as a miser and a usurer, but in secret he did great works of beneficence.

84 In *Kirkegaarden in Sobradise* (Danske Værker, I, p. 282).

85 There never was great genius without some madness. As quoted by Seneca (*de tranquilitate animi*, 17, 10) from Aristotle the phrase is: *sine mixtura dementiae*. S.K. quoted it in his *Journal* (IV A 148) at a time when he was anxiously inquiring whether his state of mind might not be close to madness.

86 If before the beginning of this century S.K. had been widely known in Europe, we would trace to him rather than to Dostoevski or any other the modern preoccupation with such topics.

87 It is to be remembered that in his university days S.K. was absorbingly interested in the legends of Faust, Don Juan, and Ahsverus (the Wandering Jew), which he took to be typical of doubt, sensuality and despair. The following footnote deals with other themes which interested him at the same time. He wrote a big book (his dissertation for the master's degree) on *The Concept of Irony*, and he made preparation for a work on satire.

88 In one financial crisis S.K.'s father increased his fortune by investing in bonds issued by the Crown (i.e. on the credit of the absolute sovereign), and in a later crisis S.K. lost much of his by investing in the same security.

89 The honor of destroying. Herostratus, to make his name

immortal, burnt the temple of Artemis at Ephesus in the year 356 B.C.

90 Executioner of infants. This name was given to this Augustinian monk (who was Professor in the University of Paris and died in 1358) because he maintained the view that unbaptized infants went to hell – instead of the limbo to which the common Catholic view consigned them. *Tortor heroum* means torturer (executioner) of heroes.

91 Holberg's *Erasmus Montanus*, Act i, Scene 3: Peter Deacon says (about bargaining for the price of a grave), "I can say to a peasant, 'Will you have fine sand or simple earth?' "

92 *Werke* (2nd ed.), VIII, pp. 195ff; X, 1, pp. 84ff.; XIV. pp. 53ff.; XVI, pp. 486ff.

93 Adherents of Grundtvig who advocated his doctrine of the Church.

94 This is S.K.'s word, and here it means, leaping from one point to another so as to illuminate the subject from all sides, or in order that the unintelligibility might be broken down into its several parts.

95 Shakespeare's *King Richard III*, Act II, Scene 1.

96 Plato's *Apology*, Cap. 25. The best texts now read "thirty votes," but in the older editions "three" was commonly read.

97 "The Tailor in Heaven," one of the brothers Grimm's *Fairy Tales*. But according to the Grimms the tailor was really dead (2nd German ed., I, p. 177).

98 Cf. the *Journal*, IV A 58.

S. K.'S PREFACES TO "THE BOOK ON ADLER"

1

S.K.'S PREFACE AS AUTHOR OF "THE BOOK ON ADLER"

Essentially this book can be read only by theologians, and among these again it essentially can interest only the individual in so far as he, instead perhaps of becoming self-important and setting himself up as my judge (with the objection, How could it ever occur to me to write so big a book about Magister Adler!), undertakes the labor of reading and then perceives in what sense A. is the subject of this book, and in what sense he is used to throw light upon the age and to defend dogmatic concepts, in what sense there is just as much attention paid to the age as to Adler.

January 1847. S. Kierkegaard.

2

S.K.'S PREFACE AS EDITOR OF "THE CONFUSION OF THE PRESENT AGE"

I myself perceive only too well how obvious is the objection and how much there is in it, against writing such a big book dealing in a certain sense with Magister Adler. But truly it is only in a certain sense it deals with him, and I simply beg the reader not to let himself be disturbed by the plausibility of the first impression. If he will read the book as I have read it, and if at the same time he is a theologian, I venture to vouch that from it he will get a clarity about certain dogmatic concepts and an ability to use them which otherwise is not easily to be had. Furthermore I am confident that, if the reader will read attentively and at the same time possesses the theological equipment which enables him to pass judgment, he will agree with me that what the author accomplishes, and what perhaps it was important for our age that he should accomplish, could be accomplished in no other way. For much as I deplore the confusion of Magister Adler, and what at least for the time being we have lost in him, however seriously and slowly I have pondered over publishing this book, which for a year and a day has lain before me completely finished, I count that the author of it may be jealous of his good fortune, for Magister Adler was just what he needed – without him he could not have given his presentation the liveliness and the ironical tension it now has, nor the satirical background which now is to be had gratis. No physician can be better pleased with the normal development of a sickness than the author is with Magister Adler and his abnormal development; and perhaps never has a man by going astray come so opportunely into the hands of Petrus Minor.

The whole book is essentially an ethical investigation of the concept of revelation; about what it means to be called by a revelation; about how he who has had a revelation is related to the race, the universal, and we others to him; about the confusion from which the concept of revelation suffers in our confused age. Or, what comes to the same thing, the whole book is an investigation of the concept of authority, about the confusion involved in the fact that the concept of authority has been entirely forgotten in our confused age. Now the author might have dealt with the subject thus: he might have shown that this concept (revelation) lent itself to confusion (the possibilities), describing also how it has been confused, and he might seek to describe the whole age and its confusion. But upon the reader this perhaps would make the impression that the confusion described was after all only a possibility which did not actually exist, something the author had hit upon just to find something to do, so that after all he was only fighting the air. How very differently he proceeded, if not by Adler's aid, at least by the fact that Adler exhibits almost all possible confusions with respect to this concept, and at the same time declares that he has had a revelation.

Thus it is that by careful reading and rereading I have understood the author, and I wish that the reader would understand him in the same way. It can hardly be supposed that the author has found any special pleasure in reading Magister Adler's many books. Yet he had done that, presumably, because he had assured himself that it might serve his purpose; and likely in the course of his work he became more and more clearly conscious of his purpose, and so of the expediency of his plan. He has used Magister Adler as a foundation or made him a transparent medium for seeing the confusion of our age. Even where the treatise seems to concern itself merely with Adler's writings like a literary review, he has perhaps succeeded in adverting to some little trait which is characteristic of our age, or to a little quirk in the confusion which, even though it is misleading, serves to illuminate the concept more thoroughly. By this plan he has made it possible for the whole monograph to gain liveliness by having constantly the appearance of being a clinic, and besides that to gain an ironic duplication for the fact that Magister Adler, who admirably satirizes the whole age, is precisely one who has broken with the whole modern age, so that he satirizes himself without knowing it; and finally to gain the advantage of a contemporary instance. And as a good dish can be spoiled entirely by being served cold when it should be served hot, so it is in the spiritual sphere. A confusion always has the most interest *in presenti* – and here everything is *in flagranti*.

In case one should wish to affirm that Magister Adler, inasmuch as he has claimed a revelation, stands entirely outside this present age or is entirely isolated in it, I would reply: By no means. Precisely this confusion lies closer to our age than one might be disposed to believe, and Magister Adler, so understood, is, I could almost say, just as much in rapport with our age as Strauss, Feuerbach, etc., were with theirs. Without religion no generation can endure. But when the first rank, the levies which would abolish Christianity (by no means the most dangerous enemies), are through with their attack, there comes another rank of the missionaries of confusion, those which either will have a new religion or be themselves apostles. These are the most dangerous, precisely because they are under religious influence and are religiously confused, but also because they stand in relation to the deeper things in man, while the first enemies were irreligiously possessed. For the misfortune of our age – in the political as well as in the religious sphere, and in all things – is disobedience, unwillingness to obey. And one deceives oneself and others by wishing to make us imagine that it is doubt. No, it is insubordination: it is not doubt of religious truth but insubordination against religious authority which is the fault in our misfortune and the cause of it. But, dialectically, insubordination has two forms: either wishing to cast down the ruler or wishing to be the ruler – and so religiously: either wishing to be a Feuerbach or wishing willfully to be an apostle. Disobedience is the secret of the religious confusion of our age. This same spirit of disobedience is also, as the *πρότον ψεῦδος* (but rather hidden and unconsciously), at the basis of that which is the fundamental evil of modern Speculation, the fact that men have confused the spheres, confounded profundity of mind with authority, the intellectual and the ethical, the notion of being a genius and the notion of being an apostle. This book, though to many this affirmation will appear strange, is really an edifying book . . . for one who has the predisposition to let himself be edified by a reading which is in other respects laborious.

And herewith I would recommend this book, begging the reader to read slowly, in consideration of the fact that the author has often been obliged to take a step backward to get the point of view. I could wish that for once I might experience the good fortune of getting a good book well read. As editor it would have been easy enough to separate the whole into smaller parts, into little treatises at 4 farthings apiece; but against this the author has protested as though his life depended upon it – and that is reasonable enough. For my part too I have reflected that a regular plan is made impossible by a dismemberment, and that our little land is not well served by letting the rubric literature vanish entirely, so that Denmark would have only pamphlets and newspapers.

"My reader," may I simply beg you to read this book, for it is important for my main effort, wherefore I am minded to recommend it.

Of this I have assured myself in a peculiar way. For various reasons I have let this manuscript lie on my table. Then after having in the meanwhile written "discourses," I wanted to write a more dogmatic work. But precisely then I perceived that I was constantly obliged to presuppose this book. Therefore I resolved to publish it.

So now I part with this book. It is, what to many will seem

strange, an edifying book – for him who understands it. And, what to many may seem stranger still, I could desire nothing better, for the sake of the small renown I have as an author, than to have written this book. For in relation to it there is an element of good luck which is rarely presented to one, for perhaps rarely has a man by going astray come so opportunely to hand as has Magister Adler to me.

1847. S. Kierkegaard.

3

S.K.'S PREFACE AS AUTHOR OF "A CYCLE OF ETHICO-RELIGIOUS TREATISES"

This whole work was written before, in part a long while before, the European war, the world-historical catastrophe of the present year, which shows and confirms catastrophically the yawning difference between a negative and positive reckoning of time. Yet by the catastrophe this work is not antiquated but is brought within the present age, not put negatively outside but positively inside the time-reckoning, it has not lost but gained by the help of the catastrophe, which makes its publication still more evidently a duty. In its time it was afraid lest by publication it might come too early, now on the contrary it fears that it may come too late.

In order that for once I may signalize a bit with regard to what he who has been able and willing to see doubtless must have seen lying at the basis of my activity as an author totally understood, in regard, *ut ita dicam*, to my program as an author (which, it is true, comes not first as usual, but last) – this was and is my unaltered reckoning and aim; the catastrophe has only helped me to understand it better, while it also will help me to be better understood, or at least to be more passionately misunderstood. The question is not about one or two chambers, nor about the seating of committees or the unseating of ministers. For sure enough there is question about these subjects, again and again these questions are raised by thousands, there is really no question about anything else; but, behold, all this is what the age requires, not in the deepest sense what the age needs; it is simply unfortunate that the age requires what it doesn't need, what therefore is foolishness and a waste of time: in part, at least in certain instances, it is a lust for pleasure. No, ideally and essentially viewed, there is a question, or *the question* about Christianity; about Christianity, as to whether that is what men need; about Christianity, whether that is what men have abolished, whether a so-called Christendom, or rather a fallen Christendom, openly or more hiddenly, now by attack, now by defense, has abolished Christianity. Divine governance has lost patience, will not put up with it any longer, but will, as thoroughgoing as is its teaching, thoroughly make it evident how self-contradictory all this is, that men in general assembly or by casting their votes, or by handshaking, shall be, if you please, a surrogate for religiousness.

And therefore even the catastrophe, as hitherto it has manifested itself, is only an introduction, it belongs among rough drafts, not finished books; for only when one has got so far that he knows what the question is about, only then begins a new time reckoning. Throughout Europe people have in a worldly way, with ever-increasing velocity of passion, lost themselves in problems which can be solved only in a godly way, which only Christianity can solve, and *has* solved long ago. With amendments to the Constitution, with the fourth estate, with all men wishing to solve the problem of likeness and equality between man and man in the medium of worldliness, i.e. in the medium the nature of which is difference and inequality. Though all travel in Europe must stop because one must wade in blood, and though all ministers were to remain sleepless for ruminating, and though every day ten ministers were to lose their reason, and every next day ten new ministers were to begin where the others left off, only to lose their reason in turn – with all this not one step forward is made, an obstacle to it is sternly fixed, and the bounds set by eternity deride all human efforts, deride all presumption against its exalted and lordly privilege, with the pretense that the temporal will explain in time what in time must remain a riddle, which only Christianity can or will explain. The problem is a religious, a Christian problem, and, as

I have said, it has already been solved. For give us eternity, a prospect of eternity every instant, its seriousness and its blessedness, its relief; give eternity again to every individual – then no more blood-shedding will be needed, and the ministers may be allowed to retain their respective reasons. Ah, but to get the conflagration quenched, the spontaneous combustion brought about by the friction of worldliness, i.e. to get eternity again – bloodshed may be needed and bombardments, *item* that many ministers shall lose their reason.

How long a time the merely convulsive period may last no man indeed can know. But one need not be a great psychologist to know how difficult it is to get the better of the situation with man's worldly and earthly understanding when, as now is the case with the whole generation, one has a superstitious belief in the saving and beatifying power of the understanding, how difficult it is therefore, and how long drawn out the transition may be before one lets the understanding go and makes a leap into the religious. The worldly understanding is established all too firmly in the worldly man, or he in it. It is like a wisdom tooth – it may take many efforts and violent ones to rock it loose and to take the life out of a thing so tenacious of life. Neither does it require a man of great dialectic power to discover that for worldly passion the notion may seem very deceptive and alluring that after all it must be possible finally, if one keeps on calculating and calculating, to bring about likeness and equality between man and man in worldliness. In any case the finite dialectic will be able to construct an incredible multitude of combinations. The oft-repeated refrain will be: Treachery, treachery; no, when one does it in another way, when one takes a little more from here and puts a little more there, and then distributes that more evenly, without forgetting the difference in the harmony with the here and there, and here and here and yonder and up and down – then one must necessarily succeed in finding the likeness, the common divisor, the stencil, for man's likeness and equality in worldliness (i.e. in difference), likeness for the *worldly* human likeness and equality – i.e. likeness for the different. The System [i.e. Hegel's system] sought the "pure" man, and now this age must seek the "equal" (or straight) man, for in worldliness we are crooked, or crookedness, i.e. relativities.

Worldliness is a prodigiously variegated complex of more and less, a little more and a little less, much, something, little, etc.; that is, worldliness is differentiation. But the understanding in the service of worldly passion will constantly imagine that it can reckon this out and get likeness and equality in worldliness. Every new construction becomes then – yes, in the now antiquated style it becomes a paragraph with the appropriate sign – it now has become, *stili novi*, a new ministry. And then when the new ministry goes out, or is convulsively thrust out, has one then reached the conclusion that the misfortune did not lie in the accidental mistakes or defects of the combination but in the fact that what was needed was something entirely different, namely, religiousness? No, this conclusion one will not draw. There will immediately be a new combination and a new ministry in the offing, which having shaken the relativities kaleidoscopically in a somewhat different way imagines that it has found what it sought. And one will say almost quite systematically, "Well, no, in the way the former ministry wanted to do it it cannot be done, but if only one reckons rightly it must come out all right" – and there comes the new ministry which does less for the beer-sellers, more for the candle-makers, and then you take more from landowners and bring the proletariat more to the fore, equalize priests and deacons, and above all make a humpback watchman and a bowlegged blacksmith's apprentice into straight and equal men. The age would recall in many ways the age of Socrates (only that it is far more passionate and violent, for it is the sophistic of violence and of palpability), but it would be nothing that might recall Socrates.

With all this curriculum of §§ or the curriculum of ministers the human race has become more and more confused, like a drunken man, who, the more he rushes about, the more drunken he becomes, even if he gets no more to drink. And then when this provisional convulsive phase has been passed through, and the *political* ministers are gone, the race will be so tired out with sufferings and loss of blood that this thing of eternity might get permission at least to be taken into consideration, as to whether it might not, from the very first, heat passion anew and give it new powers. The reaction (conversely to that of the Reformation) will transfigure what seemed to be, and imagined itself to be, politics into a religious movement. To get eternity again requires blood, but blood of a different sort, not the blood of thousands of warriors, no, the precious blood of martyrs, of the individuals – the blood of martyrs, those mighty dead who are able to do what no living man can do who lets men be cut down by thousands, what these mighty dead themselves could not do while they lived but are able to do only as dead men: to constrain to obedience a furious mob, just because this furious mob in disobedience took the liberty of slaying the martyrs. For the proverb says, "He laughs best who laughs last"; but truly he conquers best who conquers last – so not he who conquers by slaughter – oh, dubious conquest! – but he who conquers by being put to death – an eternally certain conquest! And this sacrifice is the sacrifice of obedience, wherefore God looks with delight upon him, the obedient man, who offers himself as a sacrifice, whereas he gathers his wrath against disobedience which slays the sacrifice – this sacrifice, the victor, is the martyr; for not every one who is put to death is a martyr.

For tyrants (in the form of emperors, kings, popes, Jesuits, generals, diplomats) have hitherto in a decisive moment been able to rule and direct the world; but from the time the fourth estate has come into the picture – when it has had time to settle itself in such a way that it is rightly understood – it will be seen that in the decisive moment only martyrs are able to rule the world. That is, no man will be able to rule the human race in such a moment, only the Deity can do it with the help of absolutely obedient men who at the same time are willing to suffer – but such a man is the martyr. And when in an elder formation the decisive moment was overcome, then the ordinary worldly government took over; but from the moment the fourth estate came into the picture it will be seen that even when the crisis has been overcome it is not possible to govern in a *worldly* way. To rule in a worldly way, to be a ruler in the worldly sense, however much labor and responsibility is involved in it, is a *pleasure*, and therefore is posited upon the possibility that by far the greater number of men are not aware that they have no part in the life of the state or else are godfearing enough not to bother about it. So soon as the fourth estate comes into the picture it is possible to rule only in a godly way, religiously. But to rule religiously, to be religiously the ruler, is to be the sufferer, ruling religiously is suffering. These sufferers (the rulers), in case they are allowed to follow their own counsel, will naturally wish many a time that they were far away and could say good-bye to the human race, either to lead their own lives in the solitude of contemplation or to enjoy life. But they do not venture to do so when in fear and trembling they bethink themselves of their responsibility before God. To be selected to be the ruler in a worldly sense is regarded as good fortune, but to be selected to serve as a ruler in a religious sense is, humanly speaking, rather like a punishment, in any case, humanly speaking, it is suffering, humanly speaking, it is the opposite of an advantage.

Discontented, unsatisfied, with the State, with the Church and with everything related to them (art, learning, etc., etc.), the human race, if allowed to follow its own devices, would resolve itself into a world of atoms – whereby nevertheless this progress will be made that now God will Himself come directly into relation with the single individuals, not through abstractions, neither through representative persons, but God will Himself, so to speak, undertake to educate the countless individuals of the generation, to become Himself the schoolmaster who looks after all, everyone in particular. Here thought comes to a stop. The form of the world would be like – well, I know not with what I should liken it. It would resemble an enormous version of the town of Christenfeld [an example of Christian Communism], and so there would be present the two greatest possible contrasts, striving with one another about the interpretation of this phenomenon. On the one hand *communism*, which would say, This is the correct worldly way, there must not be the slightest difference between man and man; riches, art, learning, rule, etc., etc., are of the evil one, all men ought to be equal like laborers in a factory, like cattle in a barnyard, partake of the same food, be washed in one common tub at the same stroke of the clock, be of the same dimensions, etc., etc. On the other hand *pietism*, which would say, This is the right Christian way, that one make no difference between man and man, we ought to be brothers and sisters, have all in common; riches, art, learning, etc., etc., are of the evil one; all men should be equal as it was once in little Christenfeld, all dressed alike, all pray at fixed times, marry by casting lots, go to bed at the stroke of the clock, partake of the same food, out of one dish, at the same time, etc., etc.

Ideally and essentially viewed, everyone who knows with God that he in truth believes in Christ, has "more than conquered," in spite of all the confusion and uproar of the world. He recognizes only one superior power, that of him who is able to pray more inwardly, with more fear and trembling, than he does; but such a superior is not his enemy but his mighty ally. Every opposition – that of power, talents, numbers – ideally viewed, is already overcome, even though *accidentally* he has experienced or may experience suffering for it. Accidentally, for in a *worldly* sense one makes a fuss over sufferings, one suffers in order to conquer – and then perhaps he doesn't conquer after all. In a *Christian* sense he has already more than conquered in advance, so that he does not suffer in order to conquer, but rather because he has conquered, which simply gives him pleasure in putting up with everything and exalts him above sufferings, for since one has conquered he can surely put up with a bit of suffering. In a worldly sense one must wait in the tension of uncertainty to see what follows after suffering, whether victory follows. In a Christian sense there is nothing to wait for, victory was long ago placed in one's hands by faith. This one learns from the Pattern. His last word in His suffering was not, Only wait a little and you will surely see that my cause triumphs. No, He said, "It is finished." What was finished? Suffering. But then He didn't talk at all about conquering? No, how could that occur to Him – He knew indeed from eternity that He had conquered.

This is my interpretation of our age, the reflection of a lowly man who has in his nature something of a poet, who moreover is a thinker, but – ah, how often have I repeated this which for me is so important and decisive, my first utterance about myself – "without authority."

October 7, 1848. S. Kierkegaard.

ABOUT THE INTRODUCER

GEORGE STEINER became in 1995 the first Lord Weidenfeld Visiting Professor of Comparative Literature at Oxford University. He was Professor of Comparative Literature at the University of Geneva (1974–94), and is a pensioner Fellow of Churchill College, Cambridge. His many books include *After Babel*, *The Death of Tragedy*, *Tolstoy or Dostoyevsky* and *No Passion Spent. Essays 1978–1996*.

This book is set in BASKERVILLE. John
Baskerville of Birmingham formed his
ideas of letter-design during his
early career as a writing-master
and engraver of inscriptions.
He retired in middle age,
set up a press of his
own and produced
his first book
in 1757.

E L